For Kevin and my students, and for Eva Spar-
rowgrove, my seventh- and eighth-grade English teacher who still instructs me

iv

1982

THE RELIGIOUS DIMENSION OF TWENTIETH-CENTURY BRITISH AND AMERICAN LITERATURE

A Textbook in the Analysis of Types

James L. Lucas

UNIVERSITY
PRESS OF
AMERICA

Copyright © 1982 by

University Press of America, Inc.

P.O. Box 19101, Washington, D.C. 20036

ISBN (Perfect): 0-8191-2109-6
ISBN   (Cloth): 0-8191-2108-8

Library of Congress Catalog Card Number: **81-40605**

ii

ACKNOWLEDGMENT

I wish to express my appreciation for all those who through the years have been a pointer and a guide, from Clarence C. Stoughton, the late President of Wittenberg University, Springfield, Ohio, who first appointed me to teach, and provided the means to begin advanced study, to Dr. Arra M. Garab at Northern Illinois University, who shepherded this book through its original stages as a doctoral dissertation. In between are those distinguished scholars and professors who provided seminal instruction, including the late Paul Tillich whose genius lay in making disparate thought, study, and experience coherent.

I am immensely grateful to Ernest V. Clements, President of Wright College, Chicago, whose support was indispensable during the years of preparation and full-time teaching at Wright College; to Dr. James J. Zigerell, former Dean of TV College of the Chicago City Colleges, who for a number of years provided me an enormous invisible television classroom, with students tuning in from their kitchens to cells in the Illinois Correctional Institutions; and to Sonja T. Mast and Nancy B. Robinson of the Chicago North Shore academy, Greenerfields, where my theories were given a gracious hearing by classes of avid lay students of literature.

And there are my colleagues at Harper College, Palatine, Illinois, who simply placed the teaching mat at my feet, permitting my generously responsive students to be both my audience and feedback.

Without such sustained interest and encouragement I could not have completed this work.

CONTENTS

THE ORTHODOX

PREFACE

The character and development of this study are prompted by the need demonstrated in senior undergraduate and beginning graduate classrooms for an approach to modern literature which attempts to bridge two disciplines integrally woven into the modern literary ethos: literature as an art and craft expressing the writer's vision and experience, and religion as the manifestation of ultimate concern out of which the writer makes meaning, or finds none, in the life, the world, and the spiritual circumstances enmeshing him.

The effort is further impelled by the compulsive religious concern of almost every major writer of the twentieth century, a legacy of the final destruction of nineteenth-century optimism remaining at the beginning of the twentieth century. While we have restricted our study to British and American writers--almost artificially--the phenomenon is era-wide. However, the pitfalls are many. We have taken care to show respect for the most dangerous--that of the theologian who seeks little literature, and that of the literary critic who eschews the religious, when both systems of value are inextricable at the deepest, most enduring level of the artistic conscious.

No attempt, therefore, has been made to provide an exhaustive account of any writer's corpus, a task which would be both Quixotic and impossible. Instead, we have selected specific works paradigmatically illumining the religious vision of the writer being examined, and offering optimal examples for teaching, whether a poem, or several poems, a novel or certain aspects of several novels, a play or the motif of a number of plays. We have also freely adverted to essays, letters, biography and autobiography when they illumine a theme under consideration.

The fundamental idea holding the parts of our investigation together is the observation that the most significant British and American literature of the twentieth century began in repudiation of Christian orthodoxy, and with the exception of reaffirmation by several major writers, descended into nihilism from which the most discernible trend is an ascent into secular humanism which calculates the religious experience in terms of existence as confronted by modern man.

Thus, humanism, the central element in modern literature, should be understood in its decisive influence upon the writer's approach to religion. To this extent, Chapter I is a lengthy and carefully detailed tracing of the humanistic concept as it evolved out of theocentrism, into which the literary schools have been fitted. To aid the student unfamiliar with this indispensable development the notes to Chapter I have been elaborated much beyond those necessary for the chapters to follow. Whenever possible, references are cited which are readily available, particularly where some essential, but highly abstruse source has been broken down into much more readable basics by a welcome student-minded teacher-scholar.

We have drawn a sharp distinction between theological and religious, with literary value uppermost on the principle that art and religion are complementary and do not clash.

The writers selected reflect both our limits and our purpose. Through 1965 they can be said to be surpassed by few in significance, though certainly others may be added.

We have further found it necessary to refer frequently to critics and commentators, those by whom most classroom discussions are guided. Often enough, the critic or commentator is afield; in some instances he is dead wrong. With writers whose work so resiliently defies penetration that received or definitive reading has not yet been established--as with Dylan Thomas, for example--we have presented the student with the most current interpretations, making appropriate observations and permitting him to choose among them upon a methodological basis which respects the work itself above all else.

The organization of the study follows the classifications by which orthodoxy knows the writer. The labels, therefore, seek only to make the literary distinctions more sharply discernible and more apprehensible in religious significance.

Chicago
Summer 1981

J.L.L.

x

CHAPTER I

SOME PRELIMINARY CONSIDERATIONS

Among questions which arise in dealing with twentieth-century Anglo-American literature of religious
significance are the following: literarily, when does
the twentieth-century begin; how is the period classi-
fiable; what and whom does "Anglo-American" include;
what indeed is "religious"; and what is "significant?"

The most common term used interchangeably with
"twentieth-century" is "modern." However, "modern"
has both a technical and ordinary meaning. For example,
Charles I. Glicksberg construes "modern" literature as
concerned with "the death of God."[1] On the other hand,
Frederick J. Hoffman defines "modern" as descriptive of
the "history of the twentieth-century novel in terms of
two primary issues" [to 1950]: the Jamesian "critical
aesthetic" and the naturalistic concern for "social
relevance."[2] Helen Weinberg publishes a study entitled
The New Novel in America: The Kafkan Mode in Contemporary Fiction.[3] Alfred Kazin begins "modern American
prose literature" with the realism of the 1890's and
carries it through to the "literature of crisis (1930-
1940)."[4]

In poetry Cleanth Brooks distinguishes the "modern"
from the "traditional," discerning how in technique,
aims, devices, and prosodic invention "twentieth-century" poets radically depart from the romantics and other contemporaries.[5] The "modern" in drama is traced by
Eric Bentley to the late nineteenth century beginnings
of two antithetical traditions, the realist-naturalist
and the anti-realist,[6] while S. Marion Tucker and Alan
S. Downer date "modern" drama from Henrik Ibsen's revolt against the banalities of the well-made play.[7]

At the same time, we discover that "modern" in its
ordinary chronological sense includes considerable literature which is quite "traditional," expressing religious values which are the very opposite of a technically defined modernity. Instead of finding God "dead,"
contemporary commentators such as Edmund Fuller,[8] William R. Mueller,[9] William F. Lynch,[10] and William T.
Noon,[11] to suggest a few, find Him quite alive and in
abundant evidence, though often negatively among "modern" writers.[12]

1

It seems clear, in any event, that Anglo-American literature is in no sense unique. Many of its most significant developments are reflected in Western literature generally, especially in the early realist-naturalist roots of much later French nihilistic existentialism.[13] Many of the sources of technical modernity lay, therefore, in those latter nineteenth-century developments in religion, philosophy, science, and socio-economics which shattered the ancient cosmic synthesis, what was left, particularly in England, of the plenitude, continuity, and gradations described by Arthur Lovejoy in The Great Chain of Being.[14] Having reached apical expression in Alexander Pope's Essay on Man, that chain was now showing numerous broken links.[15]

Beyond these considerations are the political and military. Based upon them four overlapping, perhaps ambiguous, literary periods are distinguishable: the pre-World War I era whose fundamental scientific optimism had not been decisively affected by the rise of naturalism; the post-World War I period of disenchantment during which naturalism reigned supreme; the World War II time of shock which brought about various forms of existentialism; and the presently ensuing period of struggle among writers to affirm or reaffirm something.

What is "Anglo-American" in a narrow sense can apply only to England and the United States, or it can be expanded to include writers from any country in which English is a principal language, and whose culture derives principally from that of England. Thus, Australian, New Zealand, Irish, Scotch, South African, and Canadian writers could be included. However, we shall restrict our study to representative writers of unquestioned stature. For example, William Butler Yeats and James Joyce, both Irishmen, are among our choices. Paul Horgan, on the other hand, a Roman Catholic novelist of the American Southwest, is not. Samuel Beckett wrote most of his plays and stories in French, although he was an Irishman. His significance for us, nevertheless, is too great to omit him. But in no sense is there an implication of unworthiness in a writer excluded. Our purpose is to provide a distinct profile of religiously significant twentieth-century literature without attempting to be encyclopaedic.

When we confront the questions of what is "religious" and what is "significant" we encounter once more the highly individualistic. If it were possible to ask each twentieth-century author what religious significance he ascribed to his work, the results would not be

any more definitive than those obtained from the critics. From the artist's standpoint, of course, no other
result can really obtain. The realities with which he
grapples are forged in the furnace of his private experience and vision. It is that uniqueness of intensely unique revelation which identifies his artistry. His
religious experience, therefore, becomes significant to
the extent that it catches or illumines the moods of an
era, the essence of experiential reality, or in some way
performs a prophetic function.

A quite different situation obtains when theological critics assume to determine religious significance
in an author. Many apply theological canons or parochi-
al dogmatisms to the literary work, with an aim to ap-
praise it more as theology than as literature or art.
Nathan A. Scott, Jr., a cardinal example of early modern
theological theorizing upon literature, insists that the
literary work qua literary work be respected,[16] while
demanding that his student be first and foremost a *theologian*[17](italics his). From a literary standpoint these
requirements appear not only contradictory but a bit absurd.

What is "religious" in literature to other commentators varies according to theology. Vernon Ruland
cites Gordon Allport, an amenable psychologist, who

> describes the religious drive as a person's mas-
> ter sentiment, giving comprehensive shape to his
> experiencing, whereas the poetic drive would be
> a further concrete specification of the same ba-
> sic dynamism. Thus, the governing entelechy in
> a poet's and his public experiencing, in the
> form of the literary work itself, is the reli-
> gious drive, given definite poetic specification.[18]

According to Charles Moeller

> literature is religious and Christian when it is
> not just "words," but the circumstances of the
> Word, which summons us, like that work of Var-
> ouna which follows the chain of destiny and fi-
> nally gives the key to the "eternel retour" of
> death and suffering by fastening them to the
> Cross that makes time unfold and the past give
> occasion for hope.[19]

Thomas L. Hanna declares that

> The most likely approach . . . would be to con-

sider a work of literature to be religious when
and if it exhibits the visible or invisible presence or potency of the divine. This would seem a
sine qua non of the religious, for, without it,
we would not in a presumed religious work appear
to have something clearly religious but, at best,
we would have perhaps a literary work concerning
moral behavior conditioned by social mores and
expectations.[20]

Father William F. Lynch has this to say about "The
Theological Imagination":

1.   Over against every naive and romantic assumption to the contrary, there is no such thing
as a purely spontaneous and autonomous literary
image, absolutely "creative" and free of metaphysics or theology; 2. Theology itself is not
transcendental in the pejorative sense. For it,
the "short way" and the "long way," the absolute
specificity of human experience and the "meaning"
of it all, are not two different things. Theology gets into the interior of our images and
is not an exploiting appendage.[21]

He is further convinced in his idea of "The Christian
Imagination":

In our terms of analogy the act of existence has
descended and keeps descending into every created
form and possibility, adapting itself to every
shape and form of difference. Is it true or not
that the natural order of things has been subvert-
ed and that there has been a new creation, within
which the one, single, narrow form of Christ of
Nazareth is in the process of giving its shape to
everything? To think and imagine according to
this form is to think and imagine according to a
Christic dimension. It would also make every dimension Christic. However, like analogy itself,
this would not destroy difference but would make
it emerge even more sharply.[22]

Unlike most of his theological colleagues, the
late Paul Tillich was an incisively influential thinker.
He defined the religious as whatever is of "ultimate
concern." In sharp contrast to Lynch he is crystal
clear in his relevance to today:

The religious concern is ultimate; it excludes all
other concerns from ultimate significance; it makes

4

them preliminary. The ultimate concern is unconditional, independent of any conditions of
character, desire, or circumstance. The unconditional concern is total; no part of ourselves
or of our world is excluded from it; there is
no "place" to flee from it. The total concern
is infinite: no moment of relaxation and rest is
possible in the face of a religious concern
which is ultimate, unconditional, total, and infinite.[23]

Thus, under the canopy of Tillich's Theology of
Culture[24] all literature, whatever its theological implications for whatever theology, has an inherently religious dimension. Glicksberg categorically affirms
Tillich's statement that even the writer who is convinced that "God is dead" cannot abandon the heritage of
Christianity which has shaped the past and made a decisive contribution to human culture.[25]

In specifically defining religious poetry Helen
Gardner reviews the work of T.S. Eliot, Lord David Cecil,
and Dr. Samuel Johnson, and concludes similarly: religious poetry is "poetry that treats of revelation and
man's response to revelation."[26] Although the great majority of religious poems are Christian, she notes, such
poetry does not have to be Christian. Equally religious
are poems which specifically reject Christian propositions, or which mock or scorn.[27]

But just how profitable it is delving into the esoteric labyrinth of competing theological theories can be
debated endlessly without definitive results. Notwithstanding, the religious crisis is at the very center of
twentieth-century literature. The impasse of theological intrusion invites a happy alternative--turning to
the writer himself, in his own medium, his own art, his
own reality. The results promised, however, require a
methodology and vocabulary which try to grasp the writer's own religious dimension, the ultimate concern peculiar to him. Such a method and critical language
must meet several criteria:

1. They must define the religious in such a way
   that it is phenomenologically recognizable in
   whatever literary guise in may appear.

2. They must distinguish among the various "heretical" forms of humanism, existentialism, and nihilism, but without sectarian bias, denomination-
   al variance, and theological dogmatism.

3. They must respect, indeed, be critically sensitive to the requirements of art: structure, form, convention, and genre, inclusive of the aesthetic, without which <u>no</u> writing can qualify as <u>literature</u>.

4. Finally, method and language must convey a sense of <u>artistic</u> experience, that sometimes mystical process by which the artist performs a unique and unduplicable service to his fellow man, both intensifying and illumining the common lot, as experienced, for example, by Andre Malraux as <u>La Condition humaine</u>.[28]

There is no system of thought, no epistemology which will satisfy everyone, nor, in any sense, completely account for literary genius. Any effort is piecemeal at best. We shall, in full awareness, proceed on the following proposition: we are students of literature, not theology, however much we are compelled by religious considerations. Upon definition "theology" is the study of <u>God</u> in some systematic, intellectually representative way; it is not the content of literature, bearing if at all only peripherally. A treatise on the Book of Job is not the same thing as Archibald MacLeish's play <u>JB</u>, a modern non-believing adaptation.[29] Applying theological dictates to the play to determine its value is as gross and obscene as purporting to judge the merits of a Shakespearean sonnet by the theological content of a Psalm of David.[30] Here, of course, "gross and obscene" directly imply the aesthetic factor which bears an equally direct relationship to the literary value of the play. Similarly, the theological is fundamentally opposed to the artistic which is grounded in a recognition and exploitation of the senses primarily, and often independent of the implications of any spiritual demand to deny the senses. This is not to say that the sensuous and the spiritual must ever be at war, however much the whole history of Christianity has tried to put them at loggerheads.[31] It is to say, simply, that the nature of man's sensuous apprehensions are at the very basis of everything he has created out of his human state, both good and bad, both transcendent and earthbound., and that they should not be circumscribed by attitudes, theoretical propositions pronounced as fiat, and theological presumptions which, in effect deny the validity of their creations. Literature is the product of the senses; otherwise, it is not literature. Theology is not literature because it is concerned with transcendence of the senses; its values and concepts are intellectually and spiritually opposed to those of

art gratia artis. The attempt to use either as the
measure of the other, without recognizing their co-
equal function in the economy of human reality. is a
distortion of the whole, certainly of the artist who, if
he cannot involve himself with his creatureliness in
all of its crises, ceases to be an artist and becomes
an effete vessel drained of its content, a form deprived
of its shape, a man prevented from creating out of his
pain, sweat, and struggle what we know as art. The religious aspect lies in the substance of the struggle,
in the creature himself said by dogmatic assertion to be
"made in the image of God," but who has, somehow, along
the way lost the blueprint of his Creator. His artistic efforts to re-discover it, to substitute for it, or
to reject it outrightly are what we seek to discern and
measure when we speak of literature which is "religiously significant."

THE PHENOMENOLOGY OF THE RELIGIOUS

We are primarily indebted to Edmund Husserl's phenomenological researches in philosophy, as specifically
applied to the religious by G. Van der Leeuw, which
makes it possible to discern and isolate the internal
elements of the religious experience, as opposed to the
external descriptions of a variety of human sciences
and arts which often force it to reflect the theories
advanced, rather than its own nature.[32] Husserl's
work is no mean achievement when seen also against historical Christian epistemological dualism.[33]

Distinguishing his approach from that of the "de-
ductive" sciences, of which mathematics is named as
chief, Husserl describes the phenomenological method as
an "eidetic," or a priori science based on the presup-
position that

> in the transcendental sphere we have an infinitude
> of knowledge previous to all deduction, knowledge
> whose mediated connexions (those of intentional im-
> plication) have nothing to do with deduction, and
> being entirely intuitive prove refractory to every
> methodically devised scheme of constructive symbo-
> lism.[34]

From this basic idea Husserl arrives at a "trans-
cendental-phenomenological reduction," a typical Ger-
manic word train whose meaning is not as formidable as
it sounds. That "reduction" is simply the fundamental
element of the conscious experience of the "I" (Ego--

7

the non-Freudian concept), as free as possible of theories of causal explanation, uninvestigated preconceptions, and as close as possible to "absolute data grasped in pure, immanent intuition."35

Van der Leeuw became intrigued with the possibilities of a religious phenomenological reduction, after reading Rudolph Otto's Das Heilage (The Idea of the Holy: An Inquiry into the Non-Rational Factor in the Idea of the Divine and Its Relation to the Rational) in which God is characterized as ganz andere (wholly other), who is experienced as mysterium tremendum, majestas, and mysterium fascinans.36 Noting that if God be "wholly other," Van der Leeuw concluded that He could not be "reduced" to the language of the descriptive sciences:

> That which those sciences concerned with Religion regard as the Object of Religion is, for Religion itself, the active and primary Agent in the situation or, in this sense of the term, the Subject. In other words, the religious man perceives that with which his religion deals as primal, as originative or causal; and only to reflective thought does this become the Object of the experience that is contemplated. For Religion, then, God is the active Agent in relation to man, while the sciences in question can concern themselves only with the activity of man in his relation to God; of the acts of God Himself, they can give no account whatever.37

The validity of the religious experience, therefore, would depend far more on the nature of the phenomenon itself than on predetermined, super-imposed concepts of God, concepts which Van der Leeuw insists are merely "figurative." God is chiefly recognizable, therefore, by the power He generates:

> We must in this respect accustom ourselves to interpret the supernatural element in the conception of God by the simple notion of an "Other," of something foreign and highly unusual, and at the same time the consciousness of absolute dependence so well known to ourselves, by an indefinite and generalized feeling of remoteness.38

Thus, the writer who is caught up in the ferment of ultimate concern, the concrete manifestation of religious experience,39 may express it in terms wholly at

8

variance with some received doctrine, system of belief, or infallibly decreed dogma. Indeed, his experience may be such as to deny established canons wholly. In this instance, the jingle "God is dead" loses all substantive significance. It frequently is, however, a writer's cry of profound religious experience, anguished and doubting, to be sure, but nonetheless as real as consciousness itself.

Thus, what the phenomenological approach would avoid is graphically illustrated by the theological criticism of William R. Mueller and William Lynch.

Mueller seeks "certain thematic relationships between the Bible and six novels which proceed with high seriousness, passionate intensity, and literary skill in their search for answers to our dilemmas."[40] --vocation, fall, judgment, suffering, love, and remnant. Aware of the charge of bare didacticism to which he exposes himself, Mueller tries to deny the implications: he has only desired, he states

> to let the Bible and modern fiction speak freely from their own inner beings, and not to make an assault on either. To do otherwise would be to fall to the most cardinal of literary sins, the dishonest manipulation of a literary work through forcing it to say what the critic might like to hear rather than allowing it to speak from the springs of its heart.[41]

How well he heeds his own caveat is illustrated by his handling of James Joyce's novel, A Portrait of the Artist as a Young Man, as his choice for illustrating the theme of "vocation." Stephen Dedalus, Mueller declares, is a "lost soul" because he has chosen a vocation outside the community of believers.[42] Therefore, Mueller concludes,

> It would, of course, be foolish to argue that Stephen is a Christian, since he neither accepts his place gratefully as a member of Christ's Body nor points to Christ as the way of salvation.[43]

And there is further lesson: Stephen serves to chide the lethargy and decay of the priestly function.[44]

Consequently, Joyce, a repudiator of everything for which Mueller stands, is in the peculiar position of instructing "Bible believers" that to be a Stephen

9

is to be Biblically damned.[45]

Father William F. Lynch approaches the matter more abstrusely. If we do not go beyond his essay on "Theology and the Imagination," appearing in the Fordham University quarterly, Thought in 1954, we shall be spared the Herculean task of making sense of his expanded book version of 1960. In the second installment of the essay Lynch seeks to lay down a Christic analogy for the creative act. Consistent with Thomistic rationale, he asserts that

> The act of Christ, His assumption and pene-
> tration of all the full and complicated actu-
> ality and stages of the human finite, must
> be taken as the fundamental model for the
> literary imagination, for aesthetics in gener-
> al, and for the act that is involved in any
> total human culture.[46]

When applied to Stephen Dedalus the dramatic limitations of this theory become manifest. Chapter III of the novel pristinely reflects Lynch's Christic analogue. But in Chapter IV Stephen completely reverses himself, throwing the Christic perspective into hopeless distortion. What has happened in Stephen; what has become of Lynch's spiritual "athleticism,"[47] between Stephen's abject confession of sin and the sensuous exaltation at the stream, between his epiphany of Virgin beauty and the bathing girl's "thighs, fuller and soft-hued as ivory . . . bared almost to the hips where the white fringes of her drawers were like feathering of soft white down?"[48] Obviously, what has occurred is the collision of theological concept and artistic criteria where they ought conjoin. Where Mueller violates the critical injunction against addressing the present in terms of the past, Lynch clamps down smothering medieval sanctions upon the artist. Neither Lynch nor Mueller seems to understand the inner demands of artistic autonomy, the ferocious struggle for freedom from the centuries old dichotomy of sense-flesh and soul.

Certainly, this approach draws the relentless fire of secular critics. Northrop Frye and F.R. Leavis are among them. They "tell us insistently," Lynch complains, "that the literary imagination is altogether professional and autonomous and is not science and politics or metaphysics or theology."[49] But again, neither Lynch nor Mueller seems concerned about genre, the elements of art by which literature is recognizable--form, language, individuality, aesthetics. Therefore, literary worth rises or falls upon its surrogation to the proselytizing mission of theology. Were it possible to impose such terms imaginative writing would not long endure.

As any work of art, Joyce's <u>Portrait</u> with its direct theological implications is a thing-in-being, whose power and significance lie in its pointing beyond itself to a world of experience in which the rules are not set by the skirted minions of a priestly tradition, nor by the Bible-thumping zealots of a frontier heritage. It points to the existential depths of entrapped men, excited within the innermost precincts of the self by the image, or lack of the image, of man and God estranged, united, or in a state of search for each other; to the awareness of the artist of the depth of his own soul reaching out of its abyss toward self-affirmation. Here, the artist encounters reality at a level below systematic proposition, struggling as he must struggle, yet not losing the ineluctable sense of the drawing power of ultimate reality, but surely, deliberately shedding the deadweight of worn-out religious shibboleth, dead symbol, meaningless ritual, and churchly effeteness. The difference between a novel and a tract, between a poem and a hymn is the difference between the sensuous, aesthetic imperative and the sepulchral command of the ancient forced cleavage between it and the "spiritual," a concept somehow stripped of its sensuous dimension. Phenomenologically we need no longer fear this obsolete, though persistently obstructive dualistic approach to great literature.

THE LITERARY HERESIES

Humanism

Humanism initially became literarily significant as a variation of Christian emphasis. Its route to classification as a heresy begins with Renaissance man's rediscovery of himself as existentially exciting. The Renaissance Christian exalted his senses and proclaimed his essence through them. In spite of his woes Hamlet could exclaim

> What a piece of work is man! how noble in reason! how infinite in faculty! in form and moving how express and admirable! in action how like an angel! in apprehension how like a god! the beauty of the world! the paragon of animals![50]

The term Renaissance itself, long associated popularly with emergence from darkness and primitivism, is descriptive of changes long short of a rebirth. E.W.M. Tillyard notes, for example, that the Renaissance remained as theocentric as the Middle Ages--Western men did not reject their Christian identity.[51] What it did mean was a relaxation of Augustinian Neo-Platonic asceticism, an aesthetic modification to include existence (flesh, nature) a _rightful_ place in the divine economy. It could not be done, however, without reaffirmation of pagan values, particularly those of Plato purified of the misconceptions of Plotinus and the Neo-Platonists. Sir Philip Sidney echoed the common Renaissance view that Plato was in essence a poet: "And truly even Plato whosoever well considereth, shall find that in the body of his work, though the inside and strength were philosophy, the skin, as it were, and beauty depended most of poetry."[52] Sidney's observation, of course, is a welcome reminding correction of the notorious misunderstanding of Plato's views on poets, which resulted from the never quite resolved early Christian conflict over an anthropomorphic God. Sidney's perhaps inadvertent correction of the Neo-Platonists, however, came a little over a century after Marsilio Ficino, a reverent disciple of Augustine, worked to unite his Neo-Platonic ideas with Christian thought.[53] But Francesco Petrarca (Petrarch), the most important figure of them all, preceded Ficino by more than a century. He revived classical studies in reaction to Dante's concern with theological rectitude and meaningless artful niceties, and is given credit for turning Europeans to human values, but yet within an emphasis on superior divine essence. Although he placed man at the center of the world, he never quite resolved the conflict between his exalted love for Laura and his affirmation of Augustinian piety. Chaste and idealized, that love nevertheless competed with his commitment to divine love which, in no Petrarchan sense, was of the same substance.[54] Even though he ultimately rejected his love of Laura, the Renaissance would not have been possible without him.[55]

Thus within Christian humanism from the outset were the seeds of ultimate alienation from, and rejection of, the Christian faith. The church-dominated order would begin to tie itself to the Aristotelian universe of Thomas Aquinas in reaction to the revival of Greek scientism, culture, and rationalism. What today may seem the sterile debates and picayune disquisitions of the Schoolmen were their rationalization of the world as a mechanism permanently and unchangeably set by its causal agency, God. What the new emphasis implied is superbly represented in Erasmus. While leaving the centrality of the church untouched, he sought to purge it of superstition, to apply intelligence to the translation of doctrine into practice, to be rid of monks, and the aburdities of the Schoolmen. He saw the ethical life as the supreme Christian testimony.[56]

Inevitably, once man began to emphasize himself, whole commitment to theocentrism would suffer. Martin Luther demanded a new soteriological focus on an individualistic and intensely personal relation between God and man. He recognized only two sacraments: baptism and the Lord's Supper. The churchly superstructure, for all of its purported efficacy, became residual, useful only to funnel men to free grace. It is clear, then, why the Reformation in northern Europe coalesced with Erasmian humanism, although the great reformer himself did not join the Reformation.[57]

Vacillating, therefore, between the arch-architects of Western epistemology--Plato and Aristotle--Western men relentlessly chipped away at Christian theological absurdities. Yet generally optimistic, they were unwilling to give up belief in a rationally organized universe presided over by Divine Intelligence. With the inanities of Scholastic Platonism having been superseded by Aquinean Aristotelianism, the emphasis of the Renaissance upon a more pristine Platonic humanism gave way once more to the reassertion of Aristotelianism now in neo-classical form. Its chief representative in England was Alexander Pope. At the same time, Deism confronted soteriology, the fundamental idea that having made the world aright and given man reason, God did not wish to be annoyed by petitions to re-do his handiwork. To guide men God gave them Nature and her rules, the universe and its rational structure. All men needed to do was to apply to the clearly revealed universal charter. In the meantime, God would sit back with a weather eye cocked on man's actions, and smoke a heavenly cigar while reading the <u>Paradise Gazette</u>.[58]

This Deistic neo-classical humanism has inspired much that modern humanism builds upon, including the philosophical base of the American founding documents, the Declaration of Independence and the United States Constitution. Many patriots, particularly the Fundamentalist variety, are shocked to discover that both documents are non--as opposed to anti--Christian testaments to the march of humanism away from Christian orthodoxy. Between their lines can be read the dramatic

13

climb from the puerility of Scholasticism to the Neo-Platonism of Ficino, from the Christian humanism of Petrarch to the Deism of Pope (however much he misunderstood and misapplied both Aristotle and Leibnitz).[59] They do not see the humanistic chain leading to Montesquieu's political theory of the separation of governmental powers enshrined in the United States Constitution, and to Rousseau's cry of human dignity. Nor are they disposed to the further ascent from damnation by the Hebrew God--whom the Christians borrowed but buffered themselves from by the all-forgiving Son--to Hamlet's exclamation of the beauty of man, and to the Popish dictum that "The proper study of mankind is man."[60] Thus, humanism began the repudiation of the severest of all Christian doctrines, that of the innate depravity of man, partial in most variations of the faith, and total in the Calvinist branch. The English and American variety would become popularly known as Puritanism.[61] While remaining technically within the Divine periphery, Western men began to claim a centrality in the cosmic scheme undreamed of by a Petrarch, Erasmus, or Luther. No longer fearing the caprice of an inscrutably vengeful God, men themselves would become the measure of all things. Humanism, then, would become the bedrock of secularism. This, the unreconstructed Christian does see, indeed, and it is this result that he excises from its considerable roots and hurls back at the literary artist whose job is to deal with it as it fulminates in his soul.

Practically any discipline can claim significant input. However, for our literary purpose three areas of nineteenth-century development are focal: the romantic-realist-naturalist progression, scientific optimism, and Biblical scholarship as complemented by Nietzsche's declaration that "God is dead."

Romanticism. What Wordsworth and Coleridge wanted to do with their new ballads, as Wordsworth tried to explain in his celebrated "Preface," was to restore the mystical element to an already well established humanism carried over from Neo-classicism. Where Pope had tried to remain poetically within the great chain of being, Wordsworth moved quite beyond to a natural religion[62] and an intuitive grasp of the transcendental. Close examination of Wordsworth's poetry indicates a distinctly secularistic outlook. In no sense is it orthodox.

On the other hand, Coleridge became enamored of German idealism, and tried to make of the Church of

14

England an overlord of the Commonwealth, both temporal and spiritual. In a syncretism uniquely his own, he combined Platonic ideality with seventeenth-century English Neo-Platonism, and engrafted both onto Trinitarian concepts to which he converted after a season with Unitarianism. While Wordsworth never quite overcame his disillusion with the French Revolution, he maintained an essentially naive attitude toward nature and its unspeakable power to destroy. In contrast, the tenor of the Coleridgian dynamic is optimistic, though hardly systematic.[63]

William Blake provides an excellent nineteenth-century example of what is repeatedly encountered in the twentieth-century--the religious writer without a religion. Blake dispenses with the false dualism of orthodoxy, and envisions God as an exalted man-like creature. In the process he deifies man himself.[64] He is the paradox of the mystical coalescing with the secular to produce a religiosity which, phenomenologically, is as authentic as any experience validated by the established churches.[65]

In the American colonies the Puritan character had effectively stifled imaginative literature with few exceptions. Ann Bradstreet managed now and then to reveal a poetic soul peeping out of a rigid Calvinist prison.[66] Over a century later James Fenimore Cooper reached an entirely secular humanism which would elevate and idealize. He was viciously libelled by his contemporaries, and calumniated by Mark Twain nearly fifty years after his death.[67] Nevertheless, he left a theologically unfettered legacy of human dignity which is yet the model for much preoccupation with romantic heroes, women in distress, the good and the bad guys, and the ultimate triumph of pedestrian morality in fiction.[68]

On the other hand, Nathaniel Hawthorne produced in The Scarlet Letter perhaps the greatest American novel of the nineteenth century depicting the conflict between orthodox religion and humanism. The dilemma of Hester Prynne and her ill-fated clergyman lover was inescapable; her crime: she loved the right man in the wrong place: his crime: he had the right calling under the wrong banner. So utterly polarized were the demands of the creature and the non-human laws of the theocracy that disaster was inevitable. No tragedy, a concept which we shall examine in the contexts of Saul Bellow's novel, Herzog, and Eugene O'Neill's drama, the chronicle of Hester and her Arthur Dimmesdale is that of their struggle against total destruction by those whom Hawthorne charged with "being of the most intolerant breed that ever lived."[69] Below the colony's hypocrisy, malice, and simple frailty lies the central problem confronting the writer today: the irreconcilable nature of epistemological dualism, the challenge of the human imperative to the hostile theological command.

Herman Melville carried his humanistic emphasis to enigmatic extremes, doubting orthodoxy and contemning many of its manifestations. At the same time, he declared in an anti-intellectual sally that "I stand for the heart, to the dogs with the head!"[70] The clash between Captain Ahab and the white whale in Moby Dick is symbolic of the creature seeking to impose his will upon that of invisible, hostile cosmic forces. Neither secular nor orthodox, Melville created such literary dilemmas as The Confidence Man in which cupidity, foolishness, and deceit are exposed, while the deeper yearnings of the spirit are implicitly acknowledged. His humanism, then, cannot be readily classified. It is, however, essentially pessimistic, as discernible clearly in the double suicides of Pierre. Nor did he ever quite outgrow his strong early immersion in Calvinist depravity. But that at least mystical, if not divine, significance inheres in the universe is suggested when the sainted Billy Budd of Melville's last work becomes the martyred patron of sailors.[71]

Realism. Reaction to romanticism was certain to come both in the United States and England, but for distinctly different reasons. In England the Victorian era was beset with religious crises both among orthodox Protestants and Roman Catholics. The scientific impetus of the seventeenth century and the rationalism of the eighteenth had combined to produce deep skepticism of the claims of Christianity, particularly among the educated. Liberal Protestant and Anglo-Catholic forms of the religion rose to the challenge. Methodism, appealing mainly to the lower classes forgotten by the Church of England, and Evangelicalism forming a "Low Church" within Anglicanism, directly challenged cool rationalism with heated emotionalism. The battle of the "isms" especially enervated the artist. The fervid Methodist and Evangelical insistence upon the horrors of sin, combining with the romantic's equal passion for individual intuitive self-validation, created doubt and skepticism, and ultimately atheism.[72] Despair and profound frustration replaced optimism and self-hope. Becoming the most influential incarnation of of the malaise of his age, Thomas Carlyle emerged with

16

a philsophy to which the realist writers would repair for a literary theory upon which to build their profoundly serious novels, the literary form which was replacing poetry as the dominant genre.

The humanistic goals of English realism varied little from those of romanticism. Nor were they critically at variance with the rationalist humanism of Henry Fielding and Samuel Richardson. The distinguishing characteristic of realist fiction is concern for external material aspects, the observable laws of life, the conditions of living, and their measurable effect upon the individual. Concern only for these elements, however, would suggest the rawest kind of naturalism always so abhorrent to English artistic sensitivity in the nineteenth century. Carlyle added to the external descriptions the idea of the _ideal_ taken directly from the romantic poets and the transcendentalism of Kant, Fichte, and Goethe. Whatever the state of the man described, it should be so presented that the ideal of man is nonetheless discernible.[73]

Here, humanism becomes a do-it-yourself athleticism, the very opposite of Father Lynch's, where man the creature no longer relies upon supernatural intervention, but takes the experiential bull by the horns and wrestles it into control. The motivating principle is faith in mankind, the moral order, and ultimate intelligibility in the universe.

The two great Victorian realist novelists immensely influenced by Carlyle were Charles Dickens and George Eliot. In _Dombey and Son_ Dickens achieves what Ioan Williams claims as "the first English novel in which an organic view of life is given organic form,"[74] or a synthesis of Carlylean idealism infusing the externally real. Human love is pitted against graspingly cruel wealth, and social concern against the greed of raw capitalism. Dombey, the rich, cold, insensitive London merchant, callously excludes from his affections his daughter and soon-to-die wife, while lavishing his attentions upon his young son, Paul, whom he loves above all else. He intensely grooms Paul to take over his business. The pace is too much. The boy dies. Dombey neglects his business. It fails. His second marriage collapses. On the day he decides to commit suicide his daughter, Florence, returns, bringing with her, her year-old son named after Paul. Discovering the love he had scorned, Dombey becomes a changed man. In true Dickensian manner, all live happily thereafter.[75]

17

Dickens shared Carlyle's disdain for Philistinism and for what Michael Goldberg calls Christian "mammonism."[76] Dickens found so few human values in orthodoxy that he did not concern himself with its postures. Thus, his humanism, fused with sentimentality and idealism, was distinctly of a secular variety. This is manifestly heretical to the orthodox. Indeed, much in recent scholarship finds Dickens a forerunner of twentieth-century revolters against bureaucracy and totalitarianism.[77]

George Eliot, like Carlyle, wrestled deeply with religious conflict. However, she was first moved to question orthodoxy after reading the novels of Sir Walter Scott. Finally, she rejected orthodoxy completely, and turned to the spiritual and religious values of human experience itself.[78] She maintained, however, a recognizable Carlylean base for her theory of literature, where the real comprised the external and the internal in direct relationship regardless of how much they appeared to be contradictory. She believed in moral evolution, in the capacity of mankind for continuous growth. It would not be long, though, before her new faith in "The great conception of universal regular sequence without partiality and without caprice"[79] would become outmoded in the surge toward naturalist theories. Yet, it can hardly be denied that she was the greatest novelist of her day, pursuing a secularized humanism with such clarity of intent and purpose as to make her novels veritable paradigms of a realism which held man to a moral law, while giving him freedom to determine his way. This is humanism at its synthesized best.

By these terms her greatest novel is <u>Adam Bede</u>, a story of causal patterns in human relations comparable to those in nature. Hetty Sorrel's terrible disaster in the novel--accused of murdering her child, imprisoned, and finally deported--thus can be traced to the lack of application in human experience of "that invariability of sequence which is acknowledged to be the basis of physical science, but which is still perversely ignored in our social organization, our ethics, and our religion."[80] Chastened by all of the human grief and misery around him, Adam Bede, himself, is morally rectified and spiritually nurtured enough to seek the woman who, by George Eliot's vision of the universal principle, will make him happy.

In the United States realism was distinctly minus a Carlylean factor. Idealism was associated too much with romantic embroidery, with pleasant gloss of harsher reality, of the kind Mark Twain camplained about in Cooper's handling of Indians. The American realist rejected the whole notion that underneath the rough exterior, the rude circumstances, and the ugly social structure lies a reflection of the best that is in humanity. He derided the Victorian notion of the virtuous poor.[81] In fact, William Dean Howells scathingly observed that the young writer "is instructed to idealize his personages, that is, to take the life-likeness out of them, and put the book-likeness into them."[82] He then gives his famous example of the real grasshopper to be described, rather than the one made up of wire and cardboard to look better than the real one, and held up as an ideal preferable to the insect in the grass.[83]

This realism, it should be noted, is not without its comparable humanist emphasis. But George Eliot's universal law to which the quest for human happiness must be tied does not obtain. Howells concentrates on "the common average man" who always "has the standard of the arts in his power."[84]

Howells' moral aspect is substantially more Puritan than one would expect of a realist. Indeed, he would not have written, as every freshman "lit" student knows, what would offend young girls.[85] He insisted on separating American "freshness" and "purity" from European "decadence," noting that few Americans, like Dostoyevsky, are ever sent to the mines:

> Our novelists, therefore, concern themselves
> with the more smiling aspects of life, which
> are the more American, and seek the universal
> in the individual rather than the social in-
> terests.[86]

In spite of a prudishness that even the most strait-laced Victorians might have found somewhat more than necessary, Howells wanted to free the American novelist from false traditions and effete conventions, to urge him to depict--in spite of Howells' disdain for the term--the American "ideal," and to bolster democracy which he believed realism really implied.

Few of Howells' thirty-six novels sustain the interest of modern readers; yet, some impelling human crises can be found in some. His short novel, An Imperative Duty, is an admirable example. In 1891, five years before the United States Supreme Court's fateful decision codifying racial segregation in the artful

19

phrase, "separate but equal,"[87] Howells investigated the effect of color on a young woman named Rhoda Algate. She has remote black ancestry all but invisible in her "rich complexion of olive."[88] Dr. Edward Olney, a tolerant man sympathetic to the plight of blacks, initially recoils at learning of Rhoda's "taint." He quickly regains his composure and rejects his instinctive racism. Rhoda's aunt, Mrs. Meredith, is ultimately unable to cope and escapes through an overdose of sleeping tablets. Upon her own discovery, Rhoda feels that her place is among the blacks. She resolves to spend her life educating them. Olney dissuades her, marries her, and takes her to Italy to live out their days. What Howells did not do in this story was pander to the melodramatic--he had no axe to grind as did Harriet Beecher Stowe; nor to the romantic--no Cooper he. His resolution, while "happy," is certainly "realistic" for his time. Rhoda's match with Olney could not be tolerated in Howells' America, however "fresh" and "pure" he believed it to be. He gave them an ending not only credible, but as real as their dilemma.

The humanistic significance of this tale lies in Howell's insistently batting down Rhoda's Puritan conscience tying down her right to personal happiness. It is almost a classical restatement in ideation of Jefferson's assertion that among unalienable rights is "the pursuit of happiness," a phrase wholly unknown to religious orthodoxy. Howells, therefore, was rooted in the idea that man can determine his own destiny.

On the other hand, the great comic realist, Mark Twain, presents the saga of a writer reaching an almost charismatic height in <u>The Adventures of Huckleberry Finn</u>, who steadily slides toward abject misanthropy culminating in <u>The Mysterious Stranger</u>. One is hard put to classify an author capable of the story of a young white boy and an older black slave defying ante-bellum society to discover brotherhood, the simple, undefiled companionship of love, but who some catastrophic years later can put into the mouth of invincible Satan words which mirror his own ultimate conviction:

> Our race lived a life of continuous and uninterrupted self-deception. It duped itself from cradle to grave with shams and delusions which it mistook for realities, and this made its entire life a sham. Of the score of fine qualities it imagined it had and was vain of, it really possessed hardly one. It regarded

itself as gold, and was only brass.[89]

Little question exists as to Mark Twain's secularism: his niche is firm among the literary heretics. But whether we are safe in declaring him a humanist is an open question. Certainly the last page of The Mysterious Stranger would qualify him for candidacy among the nihilists: Satan is speaking:

> It is true that which I have revealed to you;
> there is no God, no universe, no human race,
> no earthly life, no heaven, no hell. It is
> all a dream--a grotesque and foolish dream.
> Nothing exists but you. And you are but a
> thought--a vagrant thought, a useless thought,
> wandering forlorn among the empty eternities![90]

His elegant contemporary, Henry James, approached realism from the interiority of the experimental process, establishing an artistic technique that is only improved upon or varied by subsequent writers, but never supplanted. Aside from the technical innovations of craft which his testy, but assured genius provided, his vision was that of the intellectual, the sophisticate, the man whose empathies lay not with Howells' ordinary man-of-the-street, nor, certainly, with Mark Twain's riverboat captains. He sought the stratosphere of social aspiration and posture in which to find the germ of human striving, capacity, and shortcoming. His humanism was distinctly secular, but within his well established sense of moral oughtness against which the machinations and dramas of his characters were measured.

In this psychological approach to reality that which is real is only real as subjectively apprehended, experienced, and responded to. The impossibility, therefore, from an artistic point of view, of a narrator to be so well informed as to know the entire thought process in every mind with which he is dealing made it necessary for James to invent the device of limited omniscience, to create the illusion of the narrator's being little more knowledgeable than the reader would be. The only difference between the two is simply that of teller and listener.

Certainly this technique cast upon all of James' novels and short stories the mantle of inner directedness, as opposed to outward directedness. The abysmal labyrinth of the human heart into whose depths few have ever probed more deeply than James becomes a laboratory in which the artist experiments. He is not, as George

Eliot would be, seeking the relation of natural laws to human laws, but looking for a key to what makes the human being the mysteriously self-contradictory creature that he is. In this instance, of course, the narrative center of consciousness in James' fiction is not so much a supporter of preconceived values or a trailblazer in fashioning new ones as he is a revealer and commentator.[91] To this extent, his humanism borders on the mystical, although he never quite becomes detached from his realist assumptions, never quite seeking resolutions of the spirit beyond the practical imperative. Any number of illustrative novels come to mind. In The American an impoverished aristocratic French Roman Catholic family has treacherously dealt with the naive and bumbling Christopher Newman, an American millionaire suitor for the hand of their widowed daughter, Claire de Cintré. Put off by such betrayal of Claire, the housekeeper gives Newman a note written by the elder aristocrat accusing his wife and older son of affecting his murder. Newman has the power of revenge in his hands. Instead of exposing the culprits, he throws the note into the fireplace at the home of his friends.

Isabel Archer in The Portrait of a Lady discovers that her husband, Gilbert Osmond, is an unmitigated cad. After a series of shattering revelations she decides, nevertheless, to remain with him, to accept what life remains to her after his deceit.

And of course, Catherine Sloper of Washington Square finally realizes that her suitor, Morris Townsend, is only after her money. After twenty years of lonely, barren life she turns him down firmly, to return to her solitary existence.

In all three cases there is decision to be made upon the exposure of defect of character, upon stricture of circumstances, and upon inability to reach a happy ending, or the ultimate resolution so necessary to the Victorian. James sees mankind trapped in his own nature:

> They strike one, above all else, as giving
> no account of themselves in any terms al-
> ready consecrated by human use; to this in-
> articulate state they probably form, collect-
> ively, the most unprecedented of monuments;
> abysmal the mystery of what they think, what
> they feel, what they want, what they suppose
> themselves to be saying.[92]

22

Compromise and accommodation are all there is. Ultimacy is unpredictable beyond probabilities of character and circumstance. To this extent James is close to the modern existentialist, though hardly of the nihilistic variety. At least one commentator has made a case for James and the naturalists.[93] In both instances James agrees at least that no supernatural help can be anticipated. In the problem lies the solution. Moral grandeur is Christopher Newman's consolation for existential loss; strength of character is Isabel Archer's; Catherine Sloper's is dignity.

Naturalism. As we have noted, George Eliot's realist reign in England would not be long. Even against English literary will, naturalist forces set out to eliminate the idealist element. In presupposing a moral and spiritual being, English realism relied upon external universal guiding principle holding each man responsible for his own fate--even Fagin and Bill Sikes of Olver Twist are capable of remorse. When determinism, whether mechanistic or socio-economic, is substituted, responsibility is radically shifted from self to nonself. We no longer have English realism; it is naturalism. Now whether naturalism in England is compatible with humanism remains to be seen.

No English naturalist in the last decades of the nineteenth century became a major writer. The two most significant, however, were George Gissing and George Moore. Gissing was particularly incensed by the plight of the urban dweller, the problems heaped upon him by an unregulated, oppressive industrial society. His complaints read like a compendium of ills heard yet today: the inferior status of women, the exploitation of the poor, the tyranny of money. Such evils could not be eliminated simply by singing moral responsiblity. Their causes lay outside the victim; he was powerless before them. Influenced by the French writers, particularly Balzac,[94] the English naturalist spelled out the grim details of working-class life in a hostile environment where poverty was integral, suffering inevitable, and fate malevolent. Gissing wrote twenty-four novels to expose them.[95] His pessimism is profound.

In The New Grub Street, the title taken from the London street on which writers lived, Gissing considered nothing of worth, desert, sentiment or romance. Through a series of familial and marital relationships he brings together the two people best adapted to the brutal literary jungle, Jaspar Milvain and Amy Reardon. She possesses the mentality suitable for a calculating

23

hack. Together they succeed, a perfect, self-admiring husband-and-wife team.

With this kind of cold contempt for English realist sensitivity Gissing was never a popular writer. Yet, he foreshadowed the literary vision which would dominate the first half of the twentieth century. Here, humanism is inverted. Motivated, as many naturalists are, by injustice, Gissing manifested the reformer's zeal. By rejecting the claims of Christianity and all other religions, along with social and political creeds, he established himself as the complete secularist.[96]

His contemporary, George Moore, is difficult for some commentators to place. While borrowing much of the descriptive language of Balzac, Moore would later disavow its substance. What appeared realist in language might be naturalist in substance, or it might very well be something else. Flaubert, for example, was essentially a romantic with a flair for clinical detail. Emma Bovary is no Amy Reardon; she is <u>morally</u> responsible for her mistakes. To this extent her story resembles English realism. On the other hand, Balzac's incredible <u>Father Goriot</u>, classified by many as realism, exudes a pessimism faithfully reflected in Gissing. But in no demonstrable way is realism so utterly misanthropic. Father Goriot's reward for loving his two daughters is ruin, death, and a pauper's grave. Eugéne de Rastignac's rise from provincial to Parisian gentleman is no more deserved than Goriot's destruction. By other calculations this is naturalism. By our standards it is closer to modern nihilistic existentialism. Moore would later deny these implications in his adaptations. Much of the available scholarship wrestles with this issue.[97]

Although Enid Starkie claims that Moore's novel, <u>A Mummer's Wife</u> is the first naturalist novel in England his <u>Esther Waters</u> is more highly regarded.[98] The latter graphically illustrates Moore's uncertainty of vision:

Esther is cruelly thrown out by her stepfather complaining about too many mouths to feed. She becomes a kitchen maid at the Woodside estate. She is seduced by William, the cook's son. Although he claims to love her and wants to marry her she refuses him. He runs off with another girl. Of course, Esther discovers that she is pregnant. In shame she returns home, but is forced to leave again because of her bestial stepfather. She gives birth to a son whom she names Jackie. She meets another man, but William returns, his wife having left him. He finally convinces Esther that she should marry him. Being a compulsive gambler, he takes illegal horse-racing bets at his tavern. He is raided and ruined. He becomes tubercular and must go to Egypt for his health. He and Esther bet everything they have on a race and lose. He dies; Jackie enlists in the Army, and Esther returns to Woodside. She finds her old mistress now poor, the bulk of the estate having gone to pay racing debts. Esther is left only with the satisfaction of having given her country a fine soldier, feel-that no woman could do more. She no longer needs feel ashamed of her past.

To the extent that Moore provides no moral center, no recognizable crux of responsibility, the novel is naturalistic. Its pattern of accidental causation suggests a naturalistic tenet that men are not the supreme agents of their fate, nor are they teleologically guided by some intelligible cosmic intelligence. Esther's reactions to her misfortunes have a distinct moral tone. William is much less a Dickens-type lout than a man determined by what he is. The English realist requirement that a lesson be learned is missing; the universe is inscrutable. When confronted by the implication that he espoused the world of Balzac Moore vehemently denied it. What indeed he did accomplish in Esther Waters was an implicit cry of sympathy. Except for his naturalistic style, he might have written a sentimental novel in the tradition of Samuel Richardson.

As a humanist, then, Moore is far closer to the anthropocentric center than Gissing, fully recognizing a moral principle outside the inner vortex of individual struggle. We might dub him a secular humanist, rather than a realist or naturalist, neither of which is precise enough. In any event, he would be unquestionably a heretic.

On the American scene naturalism was more directly related to romanticism than realism, more firmly committed to idealism.[99] When Stephen Crane wrote Maggie: A Girl of the Streets, he was as indignant as a moral crusader, as passionate as a civic reformer. His naturalism consisted primarily of style, the ungilded melodramatics of slum life and family disintegration. The story itself, of Maggie, the beautiful, pure girl driven to prostitution and suicide points directly to societal cause, and implicitly affirms his conviction that it can be eliminated.[100] And in The Red Badge of Courage, Crane reacted against the glamorization of the sickly, bloody business of war--and civil war at that--but provides a

25

young man who, upon being stripped of his illusions
about the nature of war, and himself, becomes a proud,
confident bearer of the colors. What Crane achieves is
unique: with a naturalist narrative technique he
achieves the romantic's humanistic ideal without the
idealist superstructure--that guiding principle of
George Eliot. It is a naturalist humanism in a Godless
world, the key to all succeeding American naturalist
writers. In short stories such as "The Open Boat,"
Crane explores the nature of cause and effect, implicitly asking such questions as why what occurs; why those
particular four men in the boat and not three, five, or
six; why, of that four, only three make it safely to
land; and why not one of the others rather than the oil-
er? His poetry is scathing, cynical, sardonic:

A God in Wrath

A god in wrath
Was beating a man;
He cuffed him loudly
With thunderous blows
That rang and rolled over the earth
All people came running.
The man screamed and struggled,
And bit madly at the feet of the god.
The people cried:
"Ah, what a wicked man!"
And--
"Ah, what a redoubtable god!"

. . . .

I walked in a desert.
And I cried:
"Ah, God, take me from this place!"
A voice said: "It is no desert."
I cried: "Well, but--
The sand, the heat, the vacant horizon."
A voice said: "It is no desert."

. . . .

A man said to the universe:
"Sir, I exist!"
"However," replied the universe,
"The fact has not created in me
A sense of obligation."

In contrast, Frank Norris makes clear his intention
to write atavistically, biologically, and pathologically.

Man is determined by elements of his nature which in
unique individual combinations generate his own particular chemistry which manifests as his attitudes, behavior,
and psycho-social responses. This, of course, is purer
theoretical naturalism than Crane's. In McTeague, Norris presents a bull of a man with the sensitivities of
an ox, the socio-sexual drive of a satyr, and the
single-track mind of a bloodhound. In the circumstances
devised for it, McTeague's character inevitably leads
him to murder his miserly, estranged wife.

Unlike a Dickens, Norris does not suggest that
Mcteague is redeemable. Determinism is pristine.
McTeague is not better than he is because he cannot be
what he is not. Norris does not suggest that something
external to his protagonist not already within him can
be added. Yet Norris was not the pessimist that Gissing
was. He saw man's salvation in modern industrialization.
As a secularist Norris remained very much the humanist,
however much he disliked intellectuals, Pater-like aes-
theticians, and Ruskin-oriented spiritualists.101

In Theodore Dreiser the secularizing process is completed in a much more influential way. in 1900 his Sister Carrie was removed from the booksellers and not published in unemended form until 1981. Stiff-necked literary America was not ready for a young woman who sins and,
unlike Esther Waters, succeeds upon it. Dreiser's repugnance at the miserable lot of women provoked a much
more positive response than Gissing's. Carrie rises
from the sweatshop to theater stardom by the most venerable of means, the casting couch. Again, the romantic
roots of American naturalism appear clear. Quite the
opposite of the French, the American was motivated by
profound human concern, by impatience with a socio-
economic system that promised so much, but rewarded so
few.

Thus, Dreiser justifies Carrie's success by the
amoral world about her. Mrs. Hurstwood is a cold, sel-
fish, calculating prude who, upon the discovery of her
husband's liaison with Carrie, destroys him and lives
comfortably off the fruits of his labor, Her two children are spoiled and worthless, living in idle luxury
provided by their disgraced father. Drouet, Carrie's
paramour, is unmarried, enjoying his women as he sees
fit, and succeeds in his business without much ability
or drive. When she reaches the top Carrie has only
a slight regret; she is a bit lonely.

The misfortune of Clyde Griffiths in Dreiser's

27

<u>An American Tragedy</u> illustrates American naturalist dog-
ma that behavior is determined by traceable causes which
can be analyzed and removed. The pattern in Clyde's
story is as follows:

1. A boy is born in poverty and lives in familial
   alienation.
2. His behavior is that expected of a boy of the
   slums.
3. He impregnates his girlfriend, but longs for
   the world of wealth and privilege.
3. He sees a chance to enter that world through
   a rich relative.
4. The pregnant girlfriend is in the way; he
   drowns her.
5. Society catches up with him and electrocutes
   him.
6. He would do it all over again given the same
   circumstances.

In neither of these novels is the protagonist distinguished by a moral center, as neither has broken a
law greater than that broken against either. To
change them is to change the world in which they live.
Thus with Dreiser, not only has romanticism vanished,
but orthodox religious concepts have all but disappeared from the mainstream of American literature. Naturalist ideality has supplanted realism because its re-
formist attitude is more compatible with humanism, the
hope of a way out within man's exclusive control.

This faith in man himself reached its apogee at the
start of World War I. With despair and disillusion resulting from its aftermath, secular humanism would follow a slow, labored course to becoming once again, nearly a half-century later, a viable article of faith.
Within secularism, however, lay the germ of a new concept of spirituality which would be divorced from an-
thropomorphism; the traditional religious impulse would
swing from animism to animalism, to show signs currently of settling somewhere in the middle. What would manifest would be an emphasis on is-ness as opposed to
oughtness, a willingness to seek a <u>modus vivendi</u> within
an existentially delimited universe, where man is in no
elemental sense a centerpiece, but at best a coadjutor
in his own destiny, not more nor less than a participant
in the universe.

Existentialism

One of the most abused terms in modern literature

28

is "existentialism." connoting anything from humanism to
nihilism, from Christian focus on the here and now to
the revolt against Platonism. The difficulty with the
expression is its commonness. It is not an exotic coin-
age such as "noumenon" from the Greek--the opposite of
"phenomenon"--as used in Kantian philosophy to identify
an object understood purely by intuiting it. It is the
adjective of "existence," and therefore the antonym of
"essential," which is the adjective of "essence." The
distinction harks directly back to our discussion of
epistemological dualism. Plato is responsible ultimately
for the confusion.

Having made the "real" the same as "essence" Plato
separated "essence" from the material world. We have
already pointed to the untold mischief this dichotomy
has caused. But the Christians found this dualism compatible with their dualisms of heaven and earth, of
heaven and hell, of good and evil, of the saved and unsaved. In their adaptation Platonic essence becomes the
incorporeal substance of the third member of the Trini-
ty. The other two meet in the corporeality of the once
existent Christ.

Existence, then, is the material world, the sensuous and tangible reality of human experience. In es-
sentialist terms that experience is only transient and
meaningless unless it is penetrated and directed by the
"real" entering it from a dimension beyond its material
limitation. Existence is but a staging area for ultimate merger with essence which, for Christians, is eternal life in Heaven with God. What distinguishes Christian hope from similar expectation in other religions
is the primal belief that essence and existence adhere
indistinguishably in the personage of the historical Jesus Christ.[102] As long as Western men generally did not
question this assumption the epistemological conflict
engaged only isolated minds, or a few unconvinced think-
ers. The nineteenth century, however, shattered the ancient orthodox synthesis. Charles Darwin provided the
greatest impetus. In 1859 his epochal findings were
published in a dry, voluminous tome entitled On the Ori-
of the Species. Today, purged of his acceptance of La-
marck's contention that acquired traits are inheritable,
his theory of evolution is scientific dogma. This makes
of the miraculous creation of Adam and Eve little more
than charming myth, at best a poetic symbol of God's au-
thorship of life. Scientific rationalism increasingly
strained against undemonstrable essentialist-existential-
ist dualism, particularly that of the Christian scheme
where body and soul, together with spirit and flesh,

were housed in the same organism constantly at war with itself. Yet, in spite of inherent scientific optimism, the end result in many instances was despair, a principal reason for the early depreciation of George Eliot. It began to appear that there was no essence at all, that existence with all of its terrors was all there could be.

Into this miasma "The Gloomy Dane," Soren Kierkegaard, peered sixteen years before the appearance of Darwin's monumental study, profoundly shaken by the absurdity which scientific rationalism was making of Christian beliefs. Taking measure, he declared in his Journal that

> Faith therefore hopes also for this life,
> but, be it noted, by virtue of the absurd, not
> by virtue of human understanding, otherwise it
> is only practical wisdom, not faith. Faith is
> therefore what the Greeks called the divine
> madness. This is not merely a witty remark but
> is a thought which can be clearly developed.[103]

With "fear and trembling" Kierkegaard would leap over the abyss of the absurd into faith. Out of the evil of existence itself must the ultimate Christian essence be affirmed, a paradox of the will to believe. His struggle, therefore, to carve faith out of the what-is, as opposed to the what-ought-to-be, becomes the first decisively significant Christian meaning of "existential."[104]

Roman Catholic existentialist thought was early represented in Gabriel Marcel. Independent of Husserl and Martin Buber he developed his own phenomenological approach and dialogical inquiry into the nature of, and participation in, being. Born in 1889, thirty-four years after the death of Kierkegaard, he lived to become a part of the twentieth-century resurgence of French existentialism during and after World War II. Initially a mystic seeking sensory communication with others, he was converted to Roman Catholicism in 1929, and applied himself to building an existential philosophical system in Roman Catholic terms. The success of his system is questionable; in fact, modern philosophy accords little respect for his efforts which too often resemble transmogrified appeals to telepathy, clairvoyance, prophecy, and spiritualism. He fought hard, as other contemporary French existentialists with whom he directly disagreed, against the deep disillusion of defeat in World War II. As had Kierkegaard in the devastation of scientific rationalism, he discovered that essence alone is powerless to confront the awful realities of existence.[105]

Perhaps the most influential Christian existentialist of all was the late Paul Tillich. While affirming the historic Jesus, whom he called "The Christ," Tillich radically undercut all other Christian existential approaches by denying the proposition that God "exists." In fact, said Tillich, "God does not exist."[106]

Bible literalists of all stripes have grossly misread this declaration. Had they chosen to read on for another line they would have noted that Tillich added that "God is being-itself beyond essence and existence," and "that to argue that God exists is to deny him."[107]

In the next volume Tillich explained that the root of "exist" is the Latin existere, to "stand out of" something. What men "stand out of," Tillich argued, is nothingness, or nonbeing. If this be the case, then a fortiori, God does not stand out of nothingness, or nonbeing.[108]

What God is, is the "ground of being," i.e., all that exist participate in being and are thus rooted in Him while He infinitely transcends them all.[109] To this extent Tillich admirably circumvented the ball-and-chain of epistemological dualism, while accounting for the religious as a distinct phenomenon cognizable in all its manifestations, inclusive of literature and art, and for Christianity as a self-validating expression of that reality.[110] His concept of polar dimensions, in which experience was heretofore regarded as ultimately divisible--good-bad, et al.--irrevocably ties contrarieties together, so that the negative aspects can overwhelm only with the willing collapse of their polar opposites.[111] Through an in-spite-of principle Tillich proclaimed the "courage to be," an affirmation of oneself which, while equally rooted in the demonic abyss, can transcend it and participate in being-itself, and thus in God.[112]

While Tillich's language may seem unduly abstruse at first encounter, he is characteristically precise and consistent. His greatest popular impact came during the fifties and sixties, when many turned to his spiritual formulae in a recurrent era of doubt, not only of self, but of institution, country, and ultimate value. For those who harkened to his message he was able to reshape a moribund Christianity into a dynamic of fresh and meaningful vitality.

With Martin Heidegger's contrasting obsession with nothingness and death, the inherent dread of solipsistic men, we begin to trace the large representation in modern literature of those now commonplace themes of alienation, estrangement, and disenchantment. Where Tillich's affirmative outlook within a Christian framework has produced little significant literature, Heidegger's became a font of ideas delineated in much modern fiction, drama, and poetry. He replaced Tillich's "ground of being" and polar dynamics with nihilism. He denied that he was an atheist, but repudiated divinity as an ultimate cause or source of the Good. Where Tillich and other Christian existentialists called for transcendence of existence, a triumph of essence in spite of existence, Heidegger did not conceive of being as a fixed or static thing, or something that could be referred to as "it," but as an activity, an engagement with the world, a series of possibilities. These possibilities, how, ever, were rooted in the past and could only lead back to the past. What choice man had was only that choice which he had already made. Thus, existence <u>preceded</u> essence, the complete reversal of the Platonic-Christian scheme still held viable in Tillich. Man does not have a nature which determines his modes of being. He has only those restricted possibilities out of which to project himself. Transcendence can consist only of relating to other men, to the world about, a move away from one's own existence.[113]

To become aware of being, said Heidegger, required spiritual and personal qualities granted only to certain races. To be certain, he found the Germans among that chosen few, destined to be Nietzschean supermen. Their direct ancestors were the Ancient Greeks, the only other "race" to have the kiss of the gods. These rather silly flirtations with the Nazis, however, put him in disfavor with the post-World War II German regime.[114]

But it is with Jean Paul Sartre, who shared some of Heidegger's positions, notably the conviction that existence precedes essence, that we reach the most important existentialist influence on modern literature. Humiliated and disillusioned, like Marcel, by the Nazi conquest in just forty days of his beloved France, Sartre sought a way to live with total disaster without caving in. In his monumental work <u>L'Être et le néant</u> (<u>Being and Nothingness</u>, published in 1943, he reconstructed the whole Platonic-Christian value structure. While assigning a dignity to humanity unknown to the essence structure, he supplanted it with a philosophy of the real that denied the very possibility of an other-dimensional essence informing and directing an existence in which the thunder of Nazi blitzkrieg and the heel of the invader's boot could be transcended. Fortunately unlike many of his fellow existentialists, Sartre was also a literary man. His novels, plays, and short stories far better illumine his central theses.

His novel of 1938, La Nausée (Nausea), is a fundamental exposition of his theory: while writing the biography of a French nobleman at the time of the Revolution of 1789, Antoine Roquentin is suddenly overcome with nausea, an overwhelming sense of meaninglessness in himself, in life, and in the whole human enterprise. Even his body disgusts him. He records his reactions in diary form and ultimately accepts his malaise as the essence of life, an absurdity, not as Kierkegaard would have it--a paradox over which to leap into faith--but as the only substance of meaning, of the "monstrous mass" of disorder below the surface veneer.[115]

In three novels published between 1945 and 1949 under the cover title of Les Chemins de la liberté, Sartre explores the causes of the collapse of the world he loved, particularly, in the last of the trilogy, how France was betrayed. Mathieu, a soldier in defeat, knowing that France is doomed, determines to fight on and die. Firing his last round he feels cleansed and free, free of the fraud and delusion of a society ostensibly organized to preserve and nourish him. In his play, Huis Clos (No Exit) Sartre mocks the Christian idea of hell, finding it, instead, unremitting consciousness of meaninglessness, hopelessness, and boring monotony. Says Garcin, "There's no need for red-hot pokers. Hell is--other people!"

This basic theme is further explored by Albert Camus. In his book of essays, The Myth of Sisyphus, he sets out his theory of the absurd as symbolized by the hapless Sisyphus, forever condemned to roll a block of marble up a hill, and upon its promptly rolling back down to roll it up again. The Greek victim's only escape is through scorn, both for the sentence and the gods who imposed it. Camus extends this contempt to society and all of its minions in L'Étranger, perhaps one of the most important novels of the first half of the twentieth century. Where Sartre's Mathieu dies in release from a shattered ideal, Camus' stranger is guillotined in self-affirmation. Both are creatures of the absurd, but unlike the nihilist absurd, they embrace a principle of suffering in refusing a life that is not as it ought to be. One of modern literature's most moving passages records the final thoughts of Meursault, the stranger, as he awaits execution for killing an Arab in ambiguous circumstances, but without the malicious intent ascribed to him by the self-righteously hypocritical French system of justice. In Stuart Gilbert's translation the passage reads as follows:

> And I, too, felt ready to start life all over again. It was as if that great rush of anger had washed me clean, emptied me of hope, and, gazing up at the dark sky spangled with its signs and stars, for the first time, the first, I laid my heart open to the benign indifference of the universe. To feel it so like myself, indeed, so brotherly, made me realize that I'd been happy, and that I was happy still. For all to be accomplished, for me to feel less lonely, all that remained to hope was that on the day of my execution there should be a huge crowd of spectators and that they should greet me with howls of execration.

R.W.B. Lewis accuses Camus of an odd "quarrel with God . . . marked by some pretty inaccurate firing."[116] Borrowing from the title of Lawrance Thompson's book, Melville's Quarrel with God, Lewis claims to detect a God-hatred in Camus similar to that he finds in Melville.[117] Like so many of his contemporaries, Lewis states, Camus saw only one aspect of Christianity, that "unmodulated otherworldliness (or afterworldliness)" which early Protestantism took from medieval Christianity, with a God invented by Martin Luther. Not only are both dead, he concludes; they were not alive very long.[118]

Where Lewis may have some point when considering the plight of Sisyphus, he gravely misconstrues Meursault if he bases his conclusions at all on L'Etranger. Although Camus did did not discover any evidence of an existentially active God, he did not deny the principle of life. His Meursault is not so much religionless as he is existentially Godless. In whatever sense, God is ultimately symbolic, a metaphor for the unimaginable and inexpressible. Lewis commits the quite common error, especially among Christians, of equating traditional symbols with the reality to which they point. Inevitably symbols die; new symbols are required to point to, and participate in--to use the language of Tillich--the reality which does not die. As seen in these terms, Meursault little resembles an inaccurate firer. Indeed, he fires quite accurately at the effete priest seeking

"to waste his rotten prayers" on him. According to Tillich,

> A religious symbol can die only if the cor-
> relation of which it is an adequate expres-
> sion dies. This occurs whenever the revela-
> tory situation changes and former symbols
> become obsolete. The history of religion,
> right up to our own time, is full of dead
> symbols which have been killed not by sci-
> entific criticism of assumed superstitions
> but by a religious criticism of religion.[119]

What Camus saw was a sterile priestly tradition,
the natural ally of all that is designed to oppress.
The misuse of the Godly symbols throughout Meursault's
trial deserved his scorn. Yet, the transcendent principle glows from his surrender to la tendre indifference du monde.

Of course, Camus has stacked the deck. In no
sense is this a novel of action or character, determined in its outcome by one or the other. Meursault
is but an agent of dramatic ideation. By what Camus
has selected in the novel to illumine his philosophy--
the characters, scenes, events, and time--it appears
convincingly that he intended ultimate affirmation, not
negation. Recognizing that any symbol of Ultimate Re-
ality--God--remains in existential tension with death
and chaos brings us a step closer to the resolution of
the impasse of dualism, the problem increasingly being
addressed by post-existentialist writers.

Nihilism

To distinguish nihilism from secular existentialism
may seem more an exercise in neo-scholasticism than substantive enlightenment. Both are concerned with the absurd, but as Camus demonstrates, the existentialist is
committed to seeking a way out. The nihilist is committed to nothing. He denies all morality, universal order, and authority. First used as a label for certain
heretics in the Middle Ages, "nihilism" in modern times
stems from the revolt of nineteenth-century Russian writers and intellectuals--including Turgenev--against the
oppressive conditions of the czar.

Nihilistic posture is chiefly revealed in drama.
Little representation appears in the novel or systematic
philosophy, perhaps mainly because these are disciplined

forms requiring the structure which, by its very nature, nihilism repudiates. Eugene Ionesco, the contemporary playwright, is a case in point. His play, La Contratrice chauve, published in England as The Bald Prima Donna, and in the United States in 1958 as The Bald Soprano, became the prototype of the anti-play, the theater of the absurd. Aware that the nihilist absurd can never be intellectually formalized or communicated in propositional statement without utter self-contradiction, Ionesco tried to suggest it in the opposites of sense-making data. Thus language itself became a chief object of Ionesco's attack:

> To feel the absurdity of the commonplace, and of language, its falseness, is already to have gone beyond. To go beyond it we must first of all bury ourselves in it. What is comical is the unusual in its pure state; nothing seems more surprising to me than that which is banal; the surreal is here, within grasp of our hands, in our everyday conversation.[120]

In pursuit whereof Ionesco employed the following catalogue of devices:

1. Pseudo-logic.
2. Exaggeration.
3. Repetition.
4. Slapstick.
5. Farcical humor.
6. Loss of identity.
7. Proliferation of material.
8. Parodic elements.
9. Distortion of language.
10. Melodramatic surprises.
11. Cliches.
12. Nonsense syllables in dialogue.
13. Degeneration of foreign words into pure sounds.[121]

In The Bald Soprano the Smiths entertain the Martins, another married couple as devoid of meaning, individuality, and sense-making as they. A clock on the wall runs the opposite way and chimes at all hours. Dr. Ram Sewak gives the following example in his fine study of The Bald Soprano. It is after dinner:

> Mr. Smith: (Still reading his paper) Look, it says here that Bobby Watson's dead.
> Mrs. Smith: My God! poor man, when did he die?

36

> Mr. *Smith:* Why do you pretend to be astonish-
> ed? You know very well that he's been
> dead these past two years. Surely you
> remember that we attended his funeral a
> year and a half ago.
> Mrs. *Smith:* Oh, yes, of course I do remember.
> I remember it right away, but I don't un-
> derstand why you yourself were so sur-
> prised to see it in the paper.
> Mr. *Smith:* It wasn't in the paper. It's been
> three years since his death was announced.
> I remembered it through an association of
> ideas.
> Mrs. *Smith:* What a pity! he was so well presserved. [122]

Glicksberg offers the following example of gibber-
ish from the same play:

> Mr. Smith: Cockatoos, cockatoos, cockatoos,
> cockatoos, cockatoos, cockatoos, cocka-
> toos, cockatoos, cockatoos.
> Mrs. Smith: Such caca, such caca, such caca,
> such caca, such caca, such caca, such
> caca, such caca, such caca.
> Mr. Martin: such cascades of caca, such cas-
> cades of caca, such cascades of caca,
> such cascades of caca, such cascades of
> caca, such cascades of caca, such cas-
> cades of caca. [123]

Of course, Wayne C. Booth is correct to observe
that

> There are many "nihilisms" in fiction,
> from Conrad's heart of darkness to the recent
> programs of doom inspired by the ever-present
> image of that final bomb blast. All of them
> seem to face a common problem that falls on
> the borderline between aesthetics and metaphy-
> sics: Since nothingness cannot be described
> in itself, let alone dramatically, *something*
> or *someone* must always be shown doing *some-*
> *thing*, and if the action is to be grasped at
> all by the reader, it must somehow be fitted
> into a scheme of values that is intelligible
> to him . . . If, for example, we show a char-
> acter caught in a predicament that has no mean-
> ingful solution, the very terms of our literary
> success require the assumption that to be

> caught in a meaningless predicament is a
> bad thing, in which case there *is* meaning,
> however rudimentary. To write is to affirm
> at the very least the superiority of *this*
> order over *that* order. But superiority ac-
> cording to what code of values? Any answer
> will necessarily contradict complete nihilism.
> For the complete nihilist, suicide, not the
> creation of significant forms, is the only
> consistent gesture,[124]

Yet, Booth's last sentence above clearly indicates
that he must exclude the nihilist of Ionesco's stripe,
and other nihilists such as Samuel Beckett whom we
shall later look at in some detail. Obsessed with the
inevitability of death, Ionesco rips away the remaining
romantic shroud and exposes the final corruption of
flesh which, having lived purposelessly in ironic self-
contradiction, is confronted with its own unmovable impasse.

Ionesco's technique is much like that of the poets
of disenchantment, piling dissociated images upon one
another to create a clash of irreconcilably evoked
moods, and arousing in the reader--and spectator--an
awareness of disorder and meaninglessness around him
which he would not otherwise have had. This type of
nihilist, then, is not so much the negation of recep-
tiveness, by which only--he himself recognizes--can
his negations be comprehended, but of attitudes, manners, espectations, and values which his experiences
declare false and deceptive.

As perhaps the most radical of the literary heresies, the nihilistic has the greatest promise of rapprochement with orthodoxy. As Booth cogently notes,
there is no beyond for ultimate nihilism. Its nadir
is at once its zenith, At that point the utterly
helpless state becomes the state of greatest opportunity. This discovery is already evident in contemporary writing.

METHODOLOGY: LET THE WORK SPEAK FOR ITSELF

Theological critics are not the only species of
commentator who read a literary work for what they want
it to say, or not to say, rather than for what it does
say. A quite persistent variety of literary investi-
gator makes little noticeable distinction between the
author and his work. For this group all literature is
one vast autobiography. In this voyeuristic obsession

purely literary values are ignored.

On the other hand, there are the symbol seekers, those searching for occult meaning in every phrase or figure, in each line of dialogue, in every place, person, object, and incident in the work. Robert W. Stallman's analysis of Stephen Crane's novel, The Red Badge of Courage, is a case in point. In Chapter IX the narrator describes Jim Conklin's death. The last line reads as follows: "The red sun was pasted in the sky like a wafer." Stallman sees in it an analogy to the redemptive suffering of Jesus Christ:

> At Jim Conklin's death the fiercely red sun assumed the color which elsewhere in the novel symbolizes war, bloodshed and violence. Henry Fleming blasphemes against the "wafer" of the sun in this climactic moment. The sun as "wafer" represents redemption and rebirth, but it is the emblem of salvation through death--in the Army of the Lord. Henry rebels against the God of war by shaking his fist at this bloody emblem . . . Red is the color of war ("the red animal, war, the blood-swollen god") but also red is the wine of the sacrament and the red wafer is the white water saturated by the blood of Christ.

> It seems clear that Crane intended to suggest the sacrificial death celebrated in Communion and the Mass. Henry Fleming curses the God of war, who offers redemption through bloodshed.[125]

Apparently it has not occurred significantly to Stallman to account for the fact that Jim Conklin--and this Jim Conklin is the only one we have--is anything but a Christlike figure, that Stephen Crane was no believer in Christian mythology, and that as an artist he was profoundly disaffected from sacred cows. Symbol seekers frequently become so obsessed with interpretive fabric that they lose or obscure the story line. Where indeed symbol plays a principal role in the writer's intent--Blake, Yeats, Dylan Thomas--we shall assiduously seek its import.

A fourth faulty approach arises when a critic or scholar better suited for some other discipline applies the criteria of such discipline to literary works. For example, Mark Schorer and Dorothy Van Ghent have reduced the novels of Jane Austen to little more than the interplay of vicious economic forces. When speaking of Emma, Schorer remarked that "this is not simply a novel of courtship and marriage, but a novel about the

economics and social significance of courtship and marriage."[126] Indeed, "(The basic situation in all the
novels arises from the economics of marriage.)"[127] Miss
Van Ghent selects <u>Pride and Prejudice</u> to verify her like
thesis, listing in parallel columns Miss Austen's "Nar-
rowly mercantile and materialistic vocabulary in setting
up meanings."[128] In a remarkable feat of discovery,
Miss Van Ghent finds exactly eleven terms for each of
the following categories: trade, arithmetic, money, material possessions, and social integration.[129]

Our objection is not obscure; it goes to the heart
of why we read a novel about courtship and marriage,
rather than a textbook in sociology. The novelist--and
indeed the poet and dramatist--seeks to engage the
whole person, to evoke and sustain interest through his
capacity to relate in a fully personal way. While what
Schorer and Van Ghent may seek may very well be imbedded
in Jane Austen's works, her artistry, those distinctly
literary elements of craft, genre, and aesthetic dimension, is unaccounted for, a shortcoming difficult for
the genuine lover of literature to overlook.

Critics of a psychological bent, from doctrinaire
Freudians to mechanistic behaviorists, do little better,
further distorting and committing gross indecency upon
the unsuspecting writer and his works. The late Marie
Bonaparte, an early disciple of Freud, characterized
Edgar Allan Poe's literary output as motivated principally by fear of castration in all manner of conscious
and unconscious ways. She found Poe strongly both homo-
and heterosexual, waxing between an overwhelming need
for the female and the male. Her analysis of Poe's
short story, "The Pit and the Pendulum," includes the
following:

> The first of Poe's great tales, derived from
> the theme of passivity to the father, must have
> been written at a time when his paranoiac attacks
> were beginning to be persecutory; as Freud has
> shown, these are always rooted in homosexuality.

> The homosexual nature of this pendulum phan-
> tasy is sufficiently clear: the pendulum, here,
> replaces the father's penis and its movements in
> coitus. Simultaneously with the mother, the child
> within is possessed and entered--or will be--by the
> father's penis and, given its bisexuality, can
> identify itself with the mother and, in imagination,
> possess the father's penis woman-fashion.[130]

Freud, himself, perhaps inadvertently, precipitated

40

the worst of literary sins: falsification of motive, intent, or purpose. In his drive to illumine and apply a theory of psychoanlysis bearing no relationship to the character, story, and intent of Sophocles' Oedipus, Freud is responsible for the erroneous impression upon millions that the "Oedipus Complex" results from the ill-fated king of Thebes having had a sexual yen for his mother, but who had, in fact, innocently become his wife and mother of his four children. Oedipus' guilt and remorse came after knowledge as crucially distinct from conscious or unconscious desire for one's mother. His grief and self-inflicted punishment derive as much from helplessness and frustration before fate and the gods who precipitated his tragedy as from the nature of incest however unwitting and wholly unintended. But such manifest fact does not deter the psychoanalytical intrusion. For those of this persuasion literature becomes little more than a clinical data bank. But lest the reader be not adequately convinced, Miss Bonaparte adds to Poe's catalogue of horrors the woes of Oedipus:

> Poe, given the early ripening of his Oedipus Complex, as often happens with clever children, would, at an early age, identify himself with the father and, indeed, at eighteen months he did take his father's place when, in a final "fugue," David Poe deserted his children and their mother.[132]

There are, of course, valid approaches to literature. One of those is that of the "New Critics" especially concerned with the explication de texte of poetry. Centered at Vanderbilt University in Nashville, Tennessee, this extremely influential movement was nurtured by such distinguished poets and critics as Allen Tate, John Crowe Ransom, and Donald Davidson. They rebelled against the literary voyeurs, those more interested in the poet's underwear than his poetry. They divorced the poem from the poet, and sought to understand it in terms of itself, independent and isolated from the world. They were fond of such jargon as "intension," "extension," "playful ironies," and other intrinsic references to explain what to them poetry consisted of. Much criticism has been levelled at the New Critics, chiefly by the kind of critic we have deplored. It is certain, in any event, that restricting analysis to the poem itself would eliminate much of the critical babel.[133]

An equally defensible approach is commonly known as the "Neo-Aristotelian School" or the "Chicago School of Critics" originating at the University of Chicago. It is quasi-positivistic, deterministic, and artistically concerned. Fundamentally, it is an attempt to redefine Aristotle's _Poetics_ to combat the non-artistic elements of much modern criticism. The battery of scholars comprising the initial group is formidable: the late Ronald S. Crane was for years the high priest of the movement; Richard McKeon provided its philosophical base; Wayne C. Booth, a protégé of Crane's, is world-famous for his analyses of the novel; Elder Olson supplied the dramatic underpinnings, and William R. Keast focused on poetry.

As far as it goes the Neo-Aristotelian method is admirable, bringing to bear Aristotle's canons of affective intent or purport, of form and structure--beginning, middle, and end; of universal and special norms, and of ultimate resolution of artistic worth based upon ascertained and affirmed moral and spiritual value. Most of all, it is highly appreciative of _art_, without which literature would not be literature. In Aristotelian terms art may be defined as the artist's shaping, directing, and transforming of given materials according to his vision, experience, and grasp of reality. The main drawback of the Chicago approach is that much modern literature, as we have noted, has repudiated settled value and artistic structure. Nevertheless, a sound critic may yet begin with Aristotelian method to uncover what it is he is dealing with. However, once this methodology has laid a sound foundation, the vast task of determining artistic _significance_ requires an implemental approach which recognizes and accounts for the changed conditions of literary canon, value, and structural realities confronting the modern writer. Drama today frequently does not recognize a distinction between stage and auditorium, between players and audience, but rather, merges them in a single artistic effect. Equally often the novelist does not observe a "world of the novel" as distinct from the world of the reader, blending them indistinguishably. Saul Bellow's _Herzog_, of course, is a paradigm.. The poet seeks to re-create experience, to reach the reader where he lives deepest within himself, through sense-evocation in images of the inexpressibly real. In all of these instances methodological implications point beyond mere form and structure, mechanics and devices of craft; but form and craft, mechanics and device provide the indispensable clue to the ultimate meaning and value of the work. Hence, we shall always do our Aristotelian homework _before_ seeking religious significance.[134]

For our definition of religious significance we

accept the epistemological and methodological constructs of Paul Tillich, finding them unexcelled in approaching our task. Tillich sharply distinguishes <u>religion</u> from that associated with the institutional churches, finding it "an aspect of the human spirit . . .[135] the substance, the ground, and the depth of man's spiritual life . . .[136] <u>Depth</u> as used by Tillich "means that the religious aspect points to that which is ultimate, infinite, unconditional in man's spiritual life."[137] Religion itself, then, is "ultimate concern."[138] In commenting on the aspect which consumes so many of the orthodox critics of literature, Tillich declares that "the glory of what we call religion "lies in its giving us "the experience of the Holy, of something which is untouchable, awe-inspiring, an ultimate meaning, the source of ultimate courage."[139] Its shame, he continues, lies in the opposite direction:

> It makes itself the ultimate and despises the secular realm. It makes its myths and doctrines, its rites and laws into ultimates and persecutes those who do not subject themselves to it. It forgets that its own existence is a result of man's tragic estrangement from his true being. It forgets its own emergency character.[140]

And in the daazzlingly precise paragraph below, Tillich sets out the central theme of our analysis:

> This is the reason for the passionate reaction of the secular world against religion, a reaction which has tragic consequences for the secular realm itself. For the religious and the secular are in the same predicament. Neither of them should be in separation from the other, and both should realize that their very existence as separated is an emergency, that both of them are rooted in religion in the larger sense of the word, in the experience of ultimate concern. To the degree in which this is realized the conflicts between the religious and the secular are overcome, and religion has rediscovered its true place in man's spiritual life, namely, its depth, out of which it gives substance, ultimate meaning, judgment, and creative courage to all functions of the human spirit.[141]

Thus, we have made the following classification of the writers in our study, according to orthodox terminology:

The Heretics

The mystical humanists

William Butler Yeats
James Joyce
D.H. Lawrence
Eugene O'Neill
Dylan Thomas

The Social Humanists

George Bernard Shaw
Archibald MacLeish
William Faulkner
Ernest Hemingway
Saul Bellow

The Nihilists

Robinson Jeffers
Samuel Beckett

The Orthodox

The Roman Catholic

Graham Greene
Flannery O'Connor

The Anglican

T.S. Eliot
W.H. Auden

[1]*Modern Literature and the Death of God* (The Hague: Martinus Nijhoff, 1966), pp. 3-36. See also Glicksberg's earlier volume, *The Self in Modern Literature* (University Park, Pa.: The Pennsylvania State University Press, 1963), pp. 3-11.

[2]*The Modern Novel in America: 1900-1950* (Chicago: Henry Regnery Company, 1951), p. vii.

[3](Ithaca, N.Y.: Cornell University Press, 1970).

[4]*On Native Grounds: An Interpretation of Modern American Prose Literature* (New York: Reynal & Hitchcock), pp. vii-xii.

[5]*Modern Poetry and the Tradition* (New York: Galaxy-Oxford University Press, 1965), pp. 69-109.

[6]*The Playwright as a Thinker: A Study of Drama in Modern Times* (New York: Meridian Books, Inc., 1958), pp. 1-22.

[7]Eds., *Twenty-Five Modern Plays*, 3rd ed. (New York: Harper & Brothers, 1953), pp. vii-xix.

[8]*Man in Modern Fiction: Some Minority Opinions on Contemporary American Writing* (New York: Random House, 1958), and *Books with Men behind Them* (New York: Random House, 1962).

[9]*The Prophetic Voice in Modern Fiction* (New York: Haddam - House Association Press, 1959).

[10]*Christ and Apollo: The Dimension of the Literary Imagination* (New York: New American Library, 1963).

[11]*Poetry and Prayer* (New Brunswick, N.J.: Rutgers University Press, 1967).

[12]The cacophany of mutually contradictory theological criticism of literature is illumined by Vernon Ruland, who devotes the whole of Chapter II of his book *Horizons of Criticism: An Assessment of Religious-Literary Options* to citing the errors of his fellow theological critics, before launching into his own in Chapter

III, "Themes and Fallacies in Religious-Literary Criticism" (Chicago: American Library Association, 1975), pp. 13-52.

[13]The theories of Hippolyte Taine as expressed in his introduction to *Histoire de la litterature anglais* (1863-64), finding the causes of vice and virtue to be as determinable as for "vitriol and sugar;" the Goncourt brothers' novel *Germini Lacerteux* (1864)-- the case history of a servant girl--and their massive *Journal* (1851-1896), which frequently reflects a Sartre-like nausea; and Emile Zola's *Le Roman experimental* (1880), which became the naturalist manifesto, provided a theoretical base and model for literarary reaction against a universe perceived to be as hostile as that which confronted the existentialists in the 1930's and 1940's, whose chief achievement was World War II. Both movements were reactions against profound despair.

[14]*A Study of the History of an Idea* (New York: Torchbooks-Harper & Row, 1960), pp. 99-143.

[15]*Ibid.*, pp. 183-207.

[16]·Yet, Scott cannot resist quibbling with the New Critics and other contemporary literary theorists who demand that the work of art be approached primarily as that, before being subjected to the incursions of those seeking anything but art. See *Modern Literature and the Religious Frontier* (New York: Harper & Brothers, 1958), pp. 22-30/

[17]"Introduction: Theology and the Literary Imagination," in *Adversity and Grace: Studies in Recent American Literature*, ed. Nathan A. Scott, Jr. (Chicago: University of Chicago Press, 1968), p. 17.

[18]*Horizons*, p. 4.

[19]"Religion and Literature: An Essay on Ways of Reading," trans. Melvin Zimmerman, in *Mansions of the Spirit: Essays in Literature and Religion*, ed. George A. Panichas (New York: Hawthorn Books, Inc., 1967), p. 70. Reference to *Varouna* is to a novel by Julian Green, which Moeller states "reveals this Christian profundity." See p. 73, n. 28.

[20]"A Question: What Does One Mean by 'Religious Literature'?" in *Mansions of the Spirit*, p. 80.

[21]*Christ and Apollo: The Dimensions of the Literary Imagination* (New York: New American Library, 1963), p. 161.

[22] *Ibid.*, p. 183.

[23] *Systematic Theology I* (Chicago: University of Chicago Press, 1951), pp. 11-12.

[24] Ed. Robert C. Kimball (New York: Oxford University Press, 1959). See particularly Chapter IV, "Aspects of a Religious Analysis of Culture," pp. 40-51; and Chapter VI, "Protestantism and Artistic style," pp. 68-75. In *Modern Literature and the Death of God*, on p. 15, Glicksberg quotes a highly relevant passage from p. 70 of *Theology of Culture*:

> Whatever the subject matter which an artist chooses, however strong or weak his artistic form, he cannot help but betray by his style his own ultimate concern, as well as that of his group, and his period. He cannot escape religion even if he rejects religion, for religion is the state of being ultimately concerned.

[25] *Literature and Religion: A Study in Conflict* (Dallas: Southern Methodist University Press, 1960), p.8.

[26] *Religion and Literature* (New York: Oxford University Press, 1971), p. 135.

[27] *Loc. cit.*

[28] A novel first published in 1933, then in 1934 as *Man's Fate*. It traces the rise and fall of a handful of revolutionary characters engaged in a human drama in which man chooses his own life, and is considered to be the sum of his acts--an idea later adopted by the French existentialists. The now widely used expression, "human condition," was taken from Blaise Pascal's *Pensées* where the condition of man is like the fate of prisoners who see one of their number murdered before their very eyes each day. Thus, Pascal saw man bound to an ever-present consciousness of his mortality. But for Pascal redemption was in the grace of Christ; for Malraux, only transcendence. There is no salvation. See James Robert Hewitt, *André Malraux* (New York: Frederick Ungar Publishing Co., 1978), pp. 30-48.

[29] For a discussion of the book and the play see Gabriel Vahanian, *The Death of God: The Culture of Our Post-Christian Era* (New York: George Braziller, 1961), pp. 122-34.

[30] Few, if any, of the Psalms were written by David, or other

patriarchs mentioned in the titles The Psalter is a special collection of psalms begun about 400 B.C. and completed about 100 B.C.
See Robert H. Pfeiffer, *The Books of the Old Testament*, an abridge-
ment of the author's *Introduction to the Old testament* (New York:
Harper & Brothers, 1948), pp. 193-206.

[31]Neo-Platonism is the philosophical source of the Christian
denial of the senses, the work of Plotinus and Origen in the third
century A.D., culminating in Augustine of Hippo in the fourth and
fifth centuries. It is an absolute, body-defying distortion of
original Platonism whose motivating principle was *transcendence*,
not rejection, of the senses. Plotinus espoused a mystical asceticism which wholly eliminated materiality. He had such a repugnance
for his own body that only by stealth could a portrait of him be
made--nothing could be more unreal than an image of an image. For
Origen only "God" had *being*, "God" apprehended as an abstraction
quite removed from the corporeality of a Saviour-God in the flesh
which, when He was sent, was commissioned for those only who could
not reach Origen's exalted level of spiritual communication. It
remained for Augustine to wrestle specifically with the sexual, a
struggle reaching paranoid proportions of intensity, and setting
the Christian attitude toward the sensual (and sensuous) for centuries to come. See Philip Merlan, *From Platonism to Neo-Platonism*,
2nd ed., rev. (The Hague: Martinus Nijhoff, 1960), p. 2; Thomas
Whittaker, *The Neo-Platonists*, 4th ed. (Hildesheim: Georg Olms
Verkagsbuchhandkung, 1961), pp. 26-33; and Kenneth S. Latourette,
A History of Christianity (Harper & Brothers, 1953), pp. 148-51.
See also n. 33 *infra*, pp. 49-50.

[32]Among the most reprehensible characterizations of the religious is that of Norman O. Brown, a doctrinaire Freudian psy-
cho-analyst: religion is the result of a longing in the post-geni-
tal state of repression to return to the pre-genital state in order to escape the strictures of time and space which comprise historic reality. See generally *Life against Death: The Psychoanalytic Meaning of Death* (Middletown, Conn.: Wesleyan University Press,
1959), and especially pp. 23-29, pp. 110-34.

Bronislaw Malinowski approached religion on a functional basis, attempting to explain the religious in terms of individual
purpose manifested on a social basis. Accordingly, he held that
all culture has a biological basis, and that religious manifestations arose out of the effort to satisfy them. See *Magic, Science
and Religion and Other Essays* (Garden City, N.Y.: Doubleday and
Co., 1955), pp. 27-36; Audrey I. Richards, "The Concept of Culture
in Malinowksi's Work," and Ralph Piddington, "Malinowski's Theory
of Needs," both in *Man in Culture: An Evaluation of the Work of
Bronislaw Malinowski*, ed. Raymond Firth (London: Routledge and Kegan Paul, 1957), pp. 17-92.

Emile Durkheim, the pioneer in sociology, found religion to be based on a symbolic understanding of life, with totemism the earliest expression of the group giving reality to itself, in the sense that it was greater than any one individual in it, or any individual need. See *The Elementary Forms of Religious Life: A Study in Religious Sociology*, Trans. John Ward Swain (London: George Allen and Unwin, Ltd., n.d.), p. 94, n. 94, and p. 417.

Joachim Wach expressed the theory that "In opposition to the popular preoccupation with the quest for the function of religion, it is necessary to stress the search for the nature of religion." See *The Comparative Study of Religions*, ed. J.M. Kitagawa (New York: Columbia University Press, 1958), p. 27; also Wach's *Sociology of Religion* (Chicago: University of Chicago Press, 1958), p. 5, for the interrelation of religion and culture (*cf.* Tillich's *Theology of Culture*, see no, 24, *supra*, p. 47), and as between forms of expression of the religious experience.

Mircea Eliade, the distinguished historian of religion, poses a thesis that man does not wish to live in historical time, and seeks through religion to escape. See *The Myth of the Eternal Return*, trans. Willard R. Trask (London: Routledge and Kegan Paul, 1955), *passim;* and *The Sacred and the Profane: The Nature of Religion*, trans. Willard R. Trask (New York: Harcourt, Brace and Co., 1954), pp. 104-13.

Andrew Lang took exception to all of these views long before they were formulated. Philology contains the answer to the nature of religion. He specifically denies a universal evolutionary hypothesis, taking exception to Max Muller. See *Modern Theology* (Longmans, Green, and Co., 1897), pp. 120-21.

[33]As implied in n. 31, *supra*, p. 48, a dualistic impasse was reached in the West in the third century A.D. when the Neo-platonists confused authentic Platonism in a highly syncretistic adaptation to Christianity. However, St. Paul anticipated them by two centuries.

When it became doubtful that the Second Coming would take place soon, the early Christians were compelled to seek accommodation in *this* world. For a cosmogony remarkably free of philosophical abstraction, nascent Christianity discovered that to compete with older, more established religions it would have to develop a system of thought as philosophically complete as theirs, in addition to its unique doctrine of salvation. With Paul's having attempted the impossible task of being "all things to all men," (1 Cor, 9:22), the new religion acceded slowly to being earthbound, and looked to the philosophical systems of its first gentile converts, the Greeks, for conceptual forms. Paul's dualism, nevertheless, was not that of Plato's distinction between the reality of *idea* and the *apparency* of materiality, but of irreconcillable hostility between ultimate evil and ultimate good. Plato's dualism is ontological. Idea, essence, and the real are one, while sense experience can only be impression. Perception, however, is not helplessly penumbral because the soul is mediator of the idea-real to the world of the senses. Being immaterial, the soul is cognate with, and through reason apprehends, the idea; being imprisoned in the body, it is cognate with, and through the senses apprehends, the sensible world. Universal idea, as hypostasized into particulate generic ideas, is efficient cause, or the energy of the material world, giving it life, growth, and teleological significance. In this sense all things participate in *being*, and are intelligently moved toward a divinely ordained purpose represented in the supremacy of absolute good in the universal idea. The metaphor to express this reality is *God*, a concept wholly alien to the initial Christian proclamation of an anthropomorphic deity.

The senses are centrally important in Platonic dualism, but they are ultimately insignificant. What reason can know is at first what the senses can perceive. Absolute knowledge is possible because it is absolute being. In the material universe it is imperfectly manifested. Only upon the attainment of absolute idea-reality may the senses be dispensed with; at that point materiality becomes the merely apparent. Thus, Plato charts a path *not* through rejection of materiality, but through transcendence of it, the difference between ontic resolution of the conflict between real and unreal, and the irresolution of dual polar conception--good and evil--which augurs no ultimate compromise.

Paul offered the hard-pressed Christian neophyte, trapped between the two forces waging eternal battle over him, no escape except through total rejection of, rather than Platonic transcendence of, the Satanically ruled world. In Eph. 6:12 he wrote "For we are not contending against flesh and blood, but against the principalities, against the powers , against the world rulers of this present darkness, against the spiritual hosts of wickedness in the heavenly places." (RSV)

Where Plato found the soul pre-existent and immortal, and only temporarily housed in an existential form before reappearing in another form, Paul held the soul either eternally damned or saved by what happened *entirely* in this world. Thus, Neo-Platonism was invented to make Platonic idealism compatible with the Christian idea of utter cosmic estrangement. Again, see n. 31 *supra*, p. 48. As now revised, the material world is in a fallen state, and is but a proving ground for divine wrath against the pre-existent evil spirits. The material body, a form created for punishment, is *per se* polluted, from which a purified soul must extricate itself. The stage is set for the Christian war against the flesh, the senses, the very elements of creatureliness by which art is created, a conflict at times reaching nearly schizoid proportions, echoing currently in no less intensity.

See Plato's *Republic* and *Phaedrus*. These dialogues carefully spell out the limit of the senses and their function in the economy of the ideal. Plato's famed rejection of poets is highly qualified; it is not unconditional. Socrates proclaims that the poet who can "educate men and make them better" would be welcome in the ideal state. See p. 12 *supra* on Sidney.

[34] *Ideas: General Introduction to Pure Phenomenology*, trans. W.R. Boyce Gibdon (New York: Collier Books, 1962), p. 6.

[35] For a succinct layman's summary of Husserl's work see "Phenomenology," *Encyclopaedia Britannica: Macropaedia*, 1974 ed.

[36] 2nd ed. (London: Geoffrey Cumberlege--Oxford University Press, 1952), pp. 1-40.

[37] *Religion in Essence and Manifestation*, I, trans. J.E. Turner (New York: Harper & Row, 1963), 23.

[38] *Ibid.*, 23-4.

[39] See the discussion on Joyce, *infra*, pp. 9-11 and pp. 83-95.

[40] *The Prophetic Voice in Modern Fiction* (New York: Haddam-House Association Press, 1959).

[41] *Ibid.*, pp. 25-6.

[42] *Ibid.*, p. 50.

[43] *Ibid.*

[44] *Ibid.* The novel which Mueller has chosen as paradigmatic of each of his five remaining themes fares little better:

Fall:	*The Fall*, Albert Camus.
Judgment:	*The Trial*, Franz Kafka.
Suffering:	*The Sound and the Fury*, William Faulkner.
Love:	*The Heart of the Matter*, Graham Greene.
Remnant:	*A Handful of Blackberries*, Ignazio Silone.

[45] See *A Portrait of the Artist as a Young Man: Text. Criticism and Notes*, ed. Chester G. Anderson (New York: Viking Critical Library-Viking Press, 1968), pp. 243-4, where Stephen disavows Protestantism. *Infra*, p. 94.

[46]"Theology and Imagination," II, *Thought: The Fordham University Quarterly*, Spring, 1954, 10.

[47] *Ibid.*

[48]*Portrait*, p. 171.

[49]*Christ and Apollo: The Dimensions of the Literary Imagination*, p. xii.

[50]Act II, sc. iii.

[51]*The Elizabethan World Picture* (1953: rpt. New York: Vintage Books, N.D.), p. 3.

[52]*Defence of Poesy*, English Literature Series, ed. Dorothy M. Maccardle (1919; rpt, London: MacMillan & Co., Ltd., 1963), p. 3. See also n. 33 *supra*, pp. 49-50.

[53]See Kenneth Scott Latourette, *A History of Christianity* (New York: Harper & Brothers, 1953), p. 659.

[54]For a novel-like account of Petrarch as "The Father of the Renaissance," see Will Durant, *The Renaissance: A History of Civilization in Italy from 1304-1576 A.D.*, Vol. V of *The Story of Civilization* (New York: Simon and Schuster, 1953), pp. 3-15. For a scholarly discussion of Petrarch's spiritual and human conflicts see J.H. Whitfield, *Petrarch and the Renascence* (Oxford: Basil Blackwell, 1943), pp. 52-73.

[55]See Whitfield, Chap. V, for a discussion of Petrarch's legacy of humanist education, pp. 94-115.

[56]Latourette, pp. 661-2.

[57]Luther's specific contribution to humanism is discussed by Conrad Bergendoff in "Lutheran Church in the Americas," *Encyclopedia Americana*, 1959 ed.

[58]This quip-like oversimplification is suggested by the distinction technically made between Deism and Theism. The latter posits a theory of active intervention by God into the affairs of men. In actual practice many Deists were not as completely mechanistic as the bare theory might suggest. Deism's inestimable

contribution to many political and social ideas Americans and Englishmen take for granted cannot be overstated. As a metaphysical
concept today it has little currency. Modern humanists have virtually pre-empted Deistic principles. In religion Deism survives
in some Unitarians and Universalists. The literature is large and
unsystematized, frequently discursive and abstruse. For a succinct
reliable summary see "Deism," *Encyclopaedia Britannica*. 1974 ed.

[59]Pope interpreted Leibnitz's philosophical construct of "the
best of all possible worlds" to mean that the world, as is, could
not be improved upon; that being "perfectly" made, the universe
contained its own regulatory principle inherent in the natural
order. The glaring defect in Pope's construction was his failure
to account for evil, and for tragedy which had so consumed the
classical Greeks whom he so admired and whose literature he tried
to emulate. Aristotle, in particular, fared as badly in his understanding as Leibnitz. In the *Essay on Man* Pope wrote

> Nature and Homer were, he found, the same
> Convinc'd, amaz'd, he checks the bold design:
> And rules as strict his labour'd work confine
> As if the Stagirite [Aristotle] o'erlook'd each line
> Learn hence for ancient rules a just esteem:
> To copy nature is to copy them.   [Pt. 1, II, 135-50]

This passage is nonsense. Neither Homer nor Aristotle laid
down rules. Aristotle simply studied how poetry (drama) of his
and past ages was put together, relying heavily on Sophocles--
apparently from what is left of works now lost--and described
origins, functions of parts, characterizations, and artistic significance. What had been supremely human in Aristotle became
rigid, formalized intellection in Pope, the kind of ultimate
smothering of the creative impulse which led to the romantic revolt.

[60]*Essay on Man*, Epis. II, 1, 2.

[61]The vast, fascinating panorama of Anglo-American Puritanism has never been fully revealed by any one man. Perhaps the
most decisive movement in Anglo-American religious history, it
has penetrated down to the warp and woof of the modern literary
struggle. Originally, Puritans wanted to "purify" the Church of
England of all remaining traces of papistry, formal hierarchical
structure, ritual, and vestment. They were soon joined by others who are more properly called Separatists because they wanted
utter separation from the Church of the realm. Like severed
starfish, they spawned competing sects. The name "Puritan,"
however, stuck to them all. Among scholars who, together, have
exhaustively chronicled much of the positive and negative aspects of the Puritan movement are the following: William Haller,

The Rise of Puritanism, Or, the Way to the New Jerusalem as Set Forth in Pulpit and Press from Thomas Cartwright to John Milton, 1570-1643 (Philadelphia: University of Pennsylvania Press, 1972) and *Liberty and Reformation in the Puritan Revolution* (New York: Columbia University Press, 1967); Perry Miller, *The New England Mind: The Seventeenth Century* (New York: The Macmillan Co., 1939) and *The American Puritans: Their Prose and Poetry* (Garden City: Anchor-Doubleday & Co., 1956). Perry Miller authored a number of other volumes on the American Puritans. His scholarship, reputedly that of an atheist, is unparallelled. For the secular aspects see Max Weber, *The Protestant Ethic and the Spirit of Capitalism*, trans. Talcott Parsons (New York: Charles Scribner's Sons, 1958); Ernst Troeltsch, *Protestantism and Progress: A Historical Study of the Relation of Protestantism to the Modern World*, trans. W. Montgomery (Boston: Beacon Press, 1966).

[62]Frequently, both Deism and early Romanticism are referred to as being forms of *Naturphilosophie*, a German development espoused by Goethe and Schelling in which all aspects of human feeling, thinking, seeing, and doing were united in a repudiation of the Newtonian tradition of mathematics and experimental science. A succinct but adequate summary of *Naturphilosophie* is found in "Science, History of," *Encyclopaedia Britannica: Macropaedia*, 1974 ed.

[63]For a study of the life, work and romantic theorization of Coleridge, see E.K. Chambers, *Samuel Taylor Coleridge: A Biographical Study* (Oxford: Oxford University Press, 1950). Coleridge's "imagination" and "fancy" depend upon a reality as transformed by individual experience.

[64]Glicksberg, *Modern Literature and the Death of God*, p. 67.

[65]A summary of Blake is provided by Hazelton Spencer *et al.*, *British Literature 1800 to the Present*, 3rd ed. (Lexington, Mass.: D.C. Heath and Co., 1974), II, 17-38.

[66]Probably the best known of several such poems is the following:

> If ever two were one, then surely we.
> If ever man were lov'd by wife, then thee;
> If ever wife was happy in man,
> Compare with me ye women if ye can.
> I prize thy love more then whole Mines of gold,
> Or all the riches that the East doth hold.
> My love is such that Rivers cannot quench,
> Nor ought but love from thee, give recompense
> Thy love is such I can in no way repay,

The heavens reward thee manifold I pray.
Then while we live, in love lets persever,
That when we live no more, we may live ever.

See *The Works of Ann Bradstreet in Prose and Poetry*, ed. John Harvard Ellis (Gloucester, Mass.: Peter Smith, 1962), p. 394.

[67]"Fenimore Cooper's Literary Offenses," *Selected Shorter Works of Mark Twain*, ed. Walter Blair (Boston: Houghton Mifflin Company, 1962), pp. 227-38.

[68]See Arvid Shulenberger, *Cooper's Theory of Fiction: His Prefaces and Their Relation to His Novels*, University of Kansas Publications Humanistic Studies, No. 32 (New York: Octagon:Farrar, Straus and Griroux, 1972).

[69]See Chap. VI, *The Scarlet Letter*. See n. 104 *infra*, p.137.

[70]As quoted by Richard P. Adams, "American Renaissance: An Epistemological Problem" in *Romanticism and the American Renaissance: Essays on Ethos and Perception in the Age of Emerson, Thoreau, Hawthorne, Melville, Whitman and Poe*, ed. Kenneth Walter Cameron (Hartford: Transcendental Books, 1977). p. 4.

[71]In a chapter entitled "Divine Depravity" Lawrance Thompson accuses Melville of blasphemy and roundly castigates the whole conception, writing, and execution of the story of Billy Budd. See *Melville's Quarrel with God* (Princeton: Princeton University Press, 1952), pp. 354-414.

[72]See Latourette, pp. 1018-1035.

[73]For Carlyle's specific contribution to realist theory see Ioan Williams, *The Realist Novel in England: A Study in Development* (London: The Macmillan Press, Ltd., 1974), pp. 96-111.

[74]*Ibid.*, p. 124.

[75]Carlylean ideality in *Dombey and Son* is discussed by Michael Goldberg in *Carlyle and Dickens* (Athens, Ga.: University of Georgia Press, 1972), pp. 45-58.

[76]*Ibid.*, p. 45.

[77]Williams, p. 139.

[78] *Ibid.*, p. 171.

[79] *Ibid.*, 173.

[80] *Ibid.*

[81] Everett Carter, *Howells and the Age of Realism* (Philadelphia: J. B. Lippincott Co., 1954), p. 195.

[82] "Criticism and Fiction" in *The American Tradition in Literature*, 3rd ed., eds. Sculley Bradley *et al.* (New York: W.W. Norton & Co., 1967), p. 1118.

[83] *Ibid.*

[84] *Ibid.*, p. 1119.

[85] *Ibid.*, p. 1125.

[86] *Ibid.*, p. 1124.

[87] *Plesy v. Ferguson*, 1896. Segregation of blacks by this decision would be the law of the land until *Brown v. The Board of Education of Topeka*, 17 May 1954 held that segregation in the public schools violated the Constitution of the United States.

[88] *The Shadow of a Dream* and *An Imperative Duty*, ed. Edwin H. Cady (New Haven: College & University Press, 1962), p. 145.

[89] *Selected Shorter Writings*, p. 383.

[90] *Ibid.*, p. 388.

[91] See his *Art of the Novel: Critical Prefaces*, intro. Richard P. Blackmur (New York: Charles Scribner's Sons, 1937). James revised much of his work years after initial publication, seeking always to improve his artistic grasp. But the very nature of psychological realism does not permit an impression received at one moment to remain in the author's mind unaffected by time and further experience.

[92] Quoted by James Baldwin to introduce his sensationalistic novel, *Another Country* (New York: Dell Publishing Co., 1962).

[93] Lyall H. Powers, *Henry James and the Naturalist Movement* (East Lansing: Michigan State University Press, 1971).

[94] See Harry Levin, *The Gates of Horn: A Study in Five French Realists* (New York: Oxford University Press, 1963). Here again, the term "realist" is confused with "naturalist." This study is necessary to understand English response to French theorists.

[95] See generally Pierre Coustillas, ed. *George Gissing: Essays & Fiction* (Baltimore: The Johns Hopkins University Press, 1970). An excellent study.

[96] *Ibid.*

[97] George Moore has excited considerable recent scholarship. The following are of particular help in understanding his art: Janet E. Dunleavy, *George Moore: The Artist's Vision, the Story-teller's Art* (Lewisburg: Bucknell University Press, 1975). See especially Chap. IV, "*A Mummer's Wife*: Zola's Imperfect Richochet," pp. 63-85; Walter D. Ferguson, *The Influence of Flaubert on George Moore*, (Philadelphia: N.P., 1934); Enid Starkie, "George Moore and French Naturalism," in *The Man of Wax: Critical Essays on George Moore*, ed. Douglas A. Hughes (New York: Alfred A. Knopf, 1930), pp. 61-74.

[98] Starkie, p. 66.

[99] See Donald Pizer, *Realism and Naturalism in Nineteenth-Century American Literature* (Carbondale: Southern Illinois University Press, 1967), pp. 88-98.

[100] *Ibid.*, pp. 121-31.

[101] *Ibid.*, pp. 99-107.

[102] The early battles over the substance of Jesus, whether he was of "like" substance, ὁμοιούσιον (*homoiousion*), or of the "same" substance, ὁμοούσιον (*homoousion*), with God, were ferocious over the middle iota, that Greek letter which has come down to us in expressions such as "They have not budged one iota!"

[103] *Fear and Trembling* and *Sickness Unto Death*, trans. with intro. and notes Walter Lowrie (Garden City: Doubleday Anchor books, 1954), p. 10.

[104] *Ibid.*, pp. 22-132. The Old Testament account of God's command to Abraham that he sacrifice his son Isaac (Gen. 22:1-18) provides Kierkegaard with an illustration of his concept of the absurd and the paradoxical:

> If Abraham had merely renounced his claim to Issac and had done no more, he would in this last word be saying an untruth, for he knows that God demands Isaac as a sacrifice, and he knows that he himself at that instant precisely is ready to sacrifice him. We see then that after making this movement he made every instant the next movement, the movement of faith by virtue of the absurd . . . For my part I can in a way understand Abraham, but at the same time I apprehend that I have not the courage to speak, and still less to act as he did . . . So either there is a paradox, that the individual as the individual stands in an absolute relation to the absolute/or Abraham is lost." [sic] (pp. 128-29)

[105] A summary of Marcel's philosophy is provided by J.V. Langmead Casserly in "Gabriel Marcel" in *Christianity and the Existentialists,* ed. Carl Michalson (New York: Charles Scribner's Sons, 1956), pp. 74-96. For his own summary see "An Outline of a Concrete Philosophy from *Creative Fidelity*," in *The Existentialist Tradition: Selected Writings,* ed. Nino Languilli (Garden City: Anchor-Doubleday, 1971, pp. 332-57).

[106] *Systematic*, I, 205.

[107] *Ibid.*

[108] *Systematic Theology*. (Chicago: The University of Chicago Press, 1957), II, 20.

[109] *Systematic*, I, 238: "Since God is the ground of being, he is the ground of the structure of being. He is not subject to this structure; the structure is grounded in him. He *is* this structure, and it is impossible to speak about him except in terms of this structure. God must be approached cognitively through the structural elements of being-itself. These elements make him a living God, a God who can be man's concrete concern. They enable us to use symbols which we are certain point to the ground of reality."

[110] In *The Courage to Be* Tillich shows an understanding of contemporary art and literature extraordinary for theological critics

(New Haven: Yale University Press, 1954), pp. 142-54 In conjunction with his discussion of "the courage of despair" see Chap. IV of *Theology of Culture* in which Tillich places the Christian church within culture as integral, whose function is not apart from it; ed. Robert C. Kimball (New York: Oxford University Press, 1959), pp. 40-51.

[111]*Systematic*, I, 174-86. Three pairs of polarities express the basic ontological structure: individuality (*not* individuation) and universality; dynamics and form; freedom and destiny.

[112]*The Courage to Be*, 32-39.

[113]For a summary see Erich Dinkler, "Martin Heidegger," in *Christianity and the Existentialists*, pp. 97-127.

[114]See Sidney Finkelstein, *Existentialism and Alienation in American Literature* (New York: International Publishers, 1965), pp. 97-127.

[115]*Ibid.*, pp. 135 *et seq.*

[116]*The Picaresque Saint: Representative Figures in Contemporary Fiction* (Philadelphia: J.B. Lippincott Co., 1959), p. 78.

[117]*Ibid.*, p. 301, n. 23.

[118]*Ibid.*, pp. 78-9; pp. 301-02, n. 24. Lewis quotes a few of Luther's "notorious" comments such as "The nature of God demands that He should at first destroy and annihilate everything that is in us."

[119]*Systematic*, I, p. 240.

[120]As quoted by Ram Sewak Singh, *Absurd Drama, 1945-1965* (Delhi, India: Haryiana Prakashan, 1973), p. 63.

[121] *Ibid.* See Charles I. Glicksberg, *The Self in Modern Literature* (University Park, Pa.: The Pennsylvania State University Press, 1963), p. 108, where the same catalogue is made.

[122]Singh, p. 60.

[123]Glicksberg, *The Self in Modern Literature*, p. 110.

[124]*The Rhetoric of Fiction* (Chicago: The University of Chicago Press, 1961), pp. 297-98.

[125]*Stephen Crane: A Biography* (New York: George Braziller, 1973), pp. 173-74.

[126]"The Humiliation of Emma Woodhouse," in *Jane Austen: A Collection of Critical Essays,* ed. Ian Watt (Englewood Cliffs, N.J.: Prentice-Hall, 1963), p. 101.

[127]*Loc. cit.*

[128]*The English Novel: Form and Function* (New York: Harper-Torchbooks, 1953), p. 109.

[129]*Ibid.*

[130]*The Life and Works of Edgar Allan Poe: A Psycho-Analytic Interpretation,* foreword Sigmund Freud, trans. John Rodher, 1st Eng. ed. (London: Imagi Publishing Co., 1949), pp. 589-90.

[131]*The Basic Writings of* ... trans. ed. & introd, A.A. Brill (New York: The Modern Library, 1938), p. 906.

[132]Bonaparte, p. 88.

[133]See W.K. Wimsatt, Jr., *The Verbal Icon: Studies in the Meaning of Poetry* (New York: The Noonday Press, 1958), pp. 146-49, for an attempt to explain what Allen Tate meant by some of his critical terms. See also Yvor Winters, *The Anatomy of Nonsense* (Norfolk, Conn.: New Directions, 1943), pp. 168-228. for an extended analysis of John Crowe Ransom.

[134]Perhaps the sharpest criticism of the Chicago Aristotelians has come from W. K. Wimsatt, Jr. in his *Verbal Icon,* pp. 41-65, "The Chicago Critics: The Fallacy of the Neoclassic Species." As the modern critical task at best is eclectic, one needs not feel compelled to accept the ultimate direction or value of any given critical stance in order to make use of that which is helpful. Consistency and cohesion of critical effort do not require monolithic rigidity. In an excellent discussion Eugene Goodheart has tried to determine why modern critical standards are declining. See *The Failure of Criticism* (Cambridge: Harvard University Press, 1978).

[135]*Theology of Culture,* p. 5.

[136]*Ibid.,* p. 8.

[137]*Ibid.,* p. 7.

[138]*Ibid.,* pp. 7-8.

[139]*Ibid.,* p. 9.

[140]*Ibid.*

[141]*Ibid.*

THE "HERETICS"

CHAPTER II: THE MYSTICAL HUMANISTS

WILLIAM BUTLER YEATS: THE HETERODOX PLATONIST

Yeats referred to himself as a heterodox mystic. As such, he was a model of the dualistic split which occupies much of our Preliminary Considerations. However, he denied having a mystical intent in setting out his concepts in A Vision, that attempt to systematize the myths in terms of which his poetry and plays must be read to be understood. Nevertheless, he sought to compromise between his two great divisions of mystical experience, the objective and the subjective. F.A.C. Wilson describes the distinctions as lying between T.S. Eliot's objective "Christian procedure of purification through renunciation" of "human inadequacy and impurity" and Yeats' subjective mysticism achieved through the opposite means of self-sufficient joy.[1]

The sometimes baffling nature of Yeatsian poetry and drama can be approached from its phenomenological aspect with as much promise of comprehension as from any other. Where studies abound showing the ambivalence of Yeats' attitude toward Christianity,[2] his primary conviction of the immortality and perfectibility of the human soul,[3] and the ambiguity of his symbology,[4] few seem to appreciate the structure itself of Yeats' religious experience revealed in his poetry and drama. Fundamentally, it is cognizable in categorical Platonic ideality, in the authentic, original distinction between the world of appearance and the world of reality. He was never able to accept the Christian attempt to fuse the two in Jesus Christ at the expense of discrete personal reality, to engraft the thought processes of the Greek to the oriental mysticism of the Hebrew with little or no accounting for the Anima Mundi. Once again it may not be amiss to re-emphasize the crucial distinction between Plato's concept of, and place for, flesh in his scheme of ultimate transcendence, and that of Plotinus and succeeding Neo-Platonists who rejected flesh outrightly. The orthodox Christian's insistence upon elimination of the subjective element of individual vision which varies from the received objective elements rules out, as invalid, any contrary experience. To Yeats this was intolerable, as it relegated all post- and pre-Christian religious experience to the realm of falsehood and heresy; it invalidated individual, per-

sonal mystical apparatus, and it stultified all further
revelatory experience outside its narrow restrictions.

As a poet, therefore, Yeats had the immense problem
of finding imagerial means to communicate the depth of
his vision, a description tantamount to the revelatory
nature of his religious experience. The problem was one
of antipodes, one which reflected his lifelong effort to
resolve the riddle of the antinomies. In effect, he was
required to invent poetic means for a reality which had
no language. How can the experience of the divine, for
example, be communicated except by metaphor appealing
directly to the senses and the emotions, to those fleshly habiliments without which no reality is apprehensible?

The hiatus comes in the orthodox Christian's mind,
of course, when his reality admits of only one objecti-
fied mythological system, and refuses to countenance
any other, such as the Hindu, the pre-Christian Greek,
or the astrological from all of which Yeats freely borrowed in his search for image, figure, metaphor, and
concept to compile a body of myth adequate to his experience.

An invented system such as Yeats' does not presup-
pose an a priori ground for validity in any phenomenological sense. It is sufficient that it contain intelligible reference points for the imagery used to evoke
the poet's vision, his experience of the divine as it
reveals itself to him.

In 1914, eleven years before A Vision appeared in
print, Yeats published two poems complementing each
other. They indicate what was to come:

The Magi

Now as at all times I can see in the mind's eye
In their stiff, painted clothes, the pale unsatis-
    fied ones
Appear and disappear in the blue depth of the sky
With all their ancient faces like rain-beaten stones,
And all their helms of silver hovering side by side,
And all their eyes fixed, hoping to find once more,
Being by Calvary's turbulence unsatisfied,
The uncontrollable mystery on the bestial floor.

The Dolls

A doll in the doll-maker's house

Looks at the cradle and bawls:
"This is an insult to us."
But the oldest of all the dolls,
Who had seen, being kept for show,
Generations of his sort,
Out-screams the whole shelf: "Although
There's not a man can report
Evil of this place,
The man and the woman bring
Hither, to our disgrace,
A noisy and filthy thing."
Hearing him groan and stretch
The doll-maker's wife is aware
Her husband has heard the wretch,
And crouched by the arm of his chair,
She murmurs into his ear,
Head upon shoulder leant:
"My dear, my dear, O dear,
It was an accident."[5]

Aside from Yeats' note that the imagery of the poems
was suggested by the blue sky,[6] it evokes overwhelming
hostility to Christian irresolution of the antinomian
aspects of existence so superbly handled much later by
Paul Tillich. "The uncontrollable mystery on the bestial floor," invokes the nativity scene as wholly incompatible with "Calvary's turbulence." Doubtless,
Yeats was familiar with Roman Catholic fondness for depicting the newly born Divine Child sitting upright,
unaided by his duly reverent mother, anachronistically
holding rosary beads, and with two sturdy fingers giving
the blessing to all. The magi of the poem, having sought
in the stars signs of this miraculous occurrence, find
centuries later little evidence of the yet awaited promise. Instead, they have the crucifixion. The poet sees
no resolution of the tension between hope and reality,
no indication in the objective orthodox stance of a
translation into substance. What irony the poet finds
subjectively in "their ancient faces like rain-beaten
stones, / And all their helms of silver hovering side
by side"! What within the birth event can these yet
expectant wise men find to compensate for the lingering
horror of execution? Frozen into celestial space, they
are at once an accusation and a judgment of orthodox
futility.

As reflected in "The Dolls" it is not, certainly, a
Yeatsian ploy on the newly recurrent theme of the death
of God, but rather, a further indictment of the lack of
evidence of immortality and perfectibility for men in
the man-God event. The dolls, on the other hand, _are_

perfectly made. They neither grow old, die, nor decay.
Thus, they are outraged to have shoved upon them a human "doll" which cannot share their incorruptibility--
an incorruptibility which includes their doll-like bod-
ies. The child in this cradle is not unlike the child
in the crib "on the bestial floor," no harbinger of
glad tidings; indeed, "A noisy and filthy thing." Even
the Holy Child had bodily functions which required moth-
erly attention--which, of course, the dolls had not.
And dolls were the business of the doll-maker. To make
them unhappy ran counter to his whole purport. "My
dear, my dear," his wife laments on his shoulder, "It
was an accident." Does the cry "rise to a glorious
pun" as John Unterecker declares?[7] Or is it an almost
bitterly ironic jab at the Holy-Baby myth upon which
orthodoxy stands? In both instances the child is a dis-
ruption, an augur of evil, "Although / There's not a
man can report / Evil of this place." In like manner,
the doll-maker stands in relation to the divine maker
of the child sought by the Magi. The doll-maker does
his work in a manner superior to God. When he apes
God's work it is a mistake. In Unterecker's sense, it,
too, is "an accident."

    At so early a stage Yeats had yet to develop a sys-
tem of myth of his own. Thus, these two poems are
stark rejections of Christian claims without alternative. By 1939, however, Yeats' imagery reached full
flower. His poem of that year, "A Nativity," dealing
with a like theme, evokes a far different sensation:

                What woman hugs her infant there?
                Another star has shot an ear.

                What made the drapery glisten so?
                Not a man but Delacroix.

                What made the ceiling waterproof?
                Landor's tarpaulin on the roof.

                What brushes fly and moth aside?
                Irving and his plume of pride.

                What hurries out the knave and dolt?
                Talma and his thunderbolt.

                Why is the woman terror-struk?
                Can there be mercy in that look?[8]

    Here, birth of promise is indeed fulfilled, not in
the cold futility of orthodox waiting, but in artistic

genius, the very creative principle itself.

"The woman hugging her infant there" does not refer to Mary and the Christ child, but "Another star has shot an ear." The almost snide image suggests the Star of Bethlehem regarded here as little more than a falling star leaving a path of irridescent fragments behind it. Where the fabled infant has yet to deliver upon his promise, Delacroix, Landor, Irving, and Talma have flowered.

Ferdinand-Victor Delacroix, one of the greatest of French romantic painters, is in the poem a fulfillment of immortal promise: the ironic twist of "Not a man but Delacroix." The Christ figure is but a phase in cyclical historical movement.[9]

Walter Savage Landor was an anti-romantic classicist of the first half of the nineteenth century, suggested in the lines "What made the ceiling waterproof? / Landor's tarpaulin on the roof." "Romantic" rain leaked, drenched, and washed away; the tarpaulin (classicism) conserved and protected. In A Vision Yeats finds Landor "antithetical" to the prevailing current. For this reason he is dumped with the unlikely pair of Dante and Shelley in "Phase Seventeen" as examples of "Daimonic" man whose will is breaking up into fragments, each of which seeks images rather than ideas which the intellect attempts in vain to synthesize.[10] This antithetical phase is but one in the system of A Vision, but it demonstrates Yeats' lack of concern for neat literary categories. Dante, concerned to construct a mythology out of thirteenth-century Roman Catholic dogma and widely believed legend, and Shelley, the nineteenth-century romantic who sought to establish a new reality of the untrammelled heart and feeling--or in Yeatsian terms, the subjective influx of divine power--are coupled with a poet associated with vicious attack on the romantic through fictitious classical figures. In "A Nativity" their contrariety heightens the "nativity" of genius as opposed to the sterility of the Christ child.

Very little ascriptive light is shed upon these somewhat obscure references by Yeats' own notes or the opinions of his wife. Neither are the commentators of much help. But John Unterecker, together with A. Norman Jeffares, agrees that the woman of "A Nativity" in the last couplet is "terror-struck" because she has been divinely "had." In this respect she is the ironic epitome of the women in "The Mother of God," "Leda the Swan," and "Wisdom."[11] Yeats said that the image of a

69

star "shooting an ear" derived from his memory of a Byzantine mosaic of the Annunciation, with a line drawn from a star to the ear of the Virgin: "She conceived of the Word, and therefore through the ear a star fell and was born.12 In "A Nativity" the first and last couplets become sheer mockery. The woman's terror is compounded by fear of being again the object of divine futility instead of being the mother of a Delacroix, Landor, Irving or Talma. For this bitter prospect she has no mercy.

"The Mother of God," first appearing in 1931, dramatically reflects Yeats' romantic rebellion against the cold classicism of Aristotelian dogma. This poem is an epitome of his rejection of ill-explained heavenly purpose at odds with, or even hostile to, the purely human. The motherhood has no warmth, tenderness, motherliness, nor fleshliness. It results, instead, from

> The threefold terror of love: a fallen flare
> Through the hollow of an ear;
> Wings beating about the room
> The terror of all terrors that I bore
> The Heavens in my womb.

But, asks the mother

> Had I not found content among the shows
> Every woman knows,
> Chimney corner, garden walk,
> Or rocky cistern where we tread the clothes
> And gather all the talk?

Then she ponders:

> What is this flesh I purchased with my pains,
> This fallen star my milk sustains,
> This love that makes my heart's blood stop
> Or strikes a sudden chill into my bones
> And bids my hair stand up?

The element common to all of these poems is the poet's rejection of the orthodox chasm between the mortal and the immortal, between earthly destruction and heavenly salvation. The duality is complete. No reconciliation is possible. But no romantic poet will accept it. Yeats' _Vision_, sometimes scientifically or factually questionable, provides his mystical union of these opposites in a heterodox dialectic reflected in and operative through mortality. This mystical element is crucial in grasping Yeats' intent. His eclectic borrowings represent his attempt to account for the substratum of universal oneness of human experience. He was, in fact, the mystical brother of William Blake whom he defined as

> a man crying out for a mythology, and trying
> to make one because he could not find one to
> his hand. Had he been a Catholic of Dante's
> time he would have been well content with
> Mary and the angels; or had he been a schol-
> lar of our time he would have taken his sym-
> bols where Wagner took his, from Norse myth-
> ology; or have followed, with the help of
> Professor Rhys, that pathway into Welsh my-
> thology which he found in Jerusalem; or have
> gone to Ireland and chosen for his symbols
> the sacred mountains, along whose sides the
> peasant still sees enchanted fires, and the
> divinities which have not faded from the be-
> lief, if they have faded from the prayers,
> of simple hearts; and have spoken without
> mixing incongruous things, because he spoke
> of things that had been long steeped in emo-
> tion; and have been less obscure because a
> traditional mythology stood on the threshold
> of his meaning and on the margin of his sa-
> cred darkness. 13

The parent term of myth is the Ancient Greek μῦθος which literally means "a word." Generally it is trans-lated to mean a "fiction," "fable," or "falsehood." The latter meaning occurs five times in the koine (demotic Greek) of the New Testament, four in the context of Paul's letters, directed chiefly against Paul's former faith--"the Jewish myths" (Ιουδαϊκοις μύθοις), as he calls his repudiated beliefs in Titus 1:14.

This pejorative usage in the New Testament contrasts with Homeric and Platonic usage to mean, in the chiefly Ionic dialect of the Iliad, simply a "word" or "speech," and in the Attic Greek of Plato's Timaeus, a "fable" or "legend." Plato's meaning is the one which Yeats as-signs to mythology, the poetic embodiment of the reli-gious and cultural values of a people. The distinction between Pauline and classical Greek usage is the same as the modern: the telling of a story to deceive, as op-posed to the telling of a story to enlighten.

This distinction is not accidental. Paul purported to have the whole truth encapsulated in his own private revelation from which there was to be no deviation, ad-

71

dition, or emendation, thus beginning the ferocious
battle of heresy which plagues all branches of the faith
to this moment. Yeats was unable to adjust himself to
the pretentious exclusivity of the orthodox whose endless intramural squabbles make a mockery of any claim
to a closed revelatory process.

    The life of any revelation is entirely dependent up-
on the viability of the myth embodying it, and the myth
is absolutely dependent upon its symbols. When symbols
die the myth they comprise also dies. The poet for
whom the ancient symbols of a closed myth have died
finds himself confronting realities for which he has no
adequate evocative means. He cannot re-invent the myth,
nor use its lifeless symbols for his own revelation.
Symbolic power is evoked, never created. But a new myth
is invented with symbols pointing to and participating
in the constant re-informing process of a new revelation, and captured in poetry. The Platonic poet, such
as Yeats, therefore, must evoke his experience of the
essential through the existential without diminishing
the sphere of either. Like Blake, he may search for
symbols in his own national mythology of the past, in
other cultures, and in a new mystical sense attempt to
weld them in a new poetic.

    Any such effort is hazardous and uncertain. The po-
et's vision may not be shared by many others, especially during and after his lifetime. But the nature of
the poetic, so intensely individualistic, is not subject
to mass validation. The mystical process, nevertheless,
is phenomenologically little different from any other
spiritual phenomenon. To say that Yeats' vision lacks
the authenticity of received canon is to say precisely
what he vehemently rejected, that the age of revelation
is over. His response is graphic in "The Second Coming"
from his mythological Michael Robartes and the Dancer:

                Turning and turning in the widening gyre
                The falcon cannot hear the falconer;
                Things fall apart; the centre cannot hold;
                Mere anarchy is loosed upon the world,
                The blood-dimmed tide is loosed, and everywhere
                The ceremony of innocence is drowned;
                The best lack all conviction, while the worst
                Are full of passionate intensity.

                Surely some revelation is at hand;
                Surely the Second Coming is at hand.
                The Second Coming! Hardly are those words out
                When a vast image out of Spiritus Mundi

Troubles my sight: somewhere in the sands of the
   desert
A shape with lion body and the head of a man,
A gaze blank and pitiless as the sun,
Is moving its slow thighs, while all about it
Reel shadows of the indignant desert birds.
The darkness drops again; but now I know
That twenty centuries of stony sleep
Were vexed to nightmare by a rocking cradle,
And what rough beast, its hour come round at last,
Slouches towards Bethlehem to be born?

Between 1887 and 1938 Yeats experienced much of the
history of the world as a horrendous reminder of his
own worst fears about the fate of the Christian era. In
his Autobiography published in book form a year before
his death in 1939 he wrote

> I was unlike others of my generation in one
> thing only. I am very religious, and deprived
> by Huxley and Tyndall, whom I detested, of the
> simple-minded religion of my childhood, I had
> made a new religion, almost an infallible church
> of poetic tradition, of a fardel of stories, and
> of personages, and of emotions, inseparable from
> their first expression, passed on from generation
> to generation by poets and painters with some help
> from philosophers and theologians. I wished for
> a world where I could discover this tradition per-
> petually, and not in pictures and in poems only,
> but in tiles round the chimney-piece and in the
> hangings that kept out the draft. I had even cre-
> ated a dogma: "Because those imaginary people are
> created out of the deepest instinct of man, to be
> his measure and his norm, whatever I can imagine
> those mouths speaking may be the nearest I can go
> to trust."14

But looking back to the four years of 1887 to 1891,
he declared that he had not had "the courage of [his]
own thought: the growing murderousness of the world."15
He then quoted the first stanza of "The Second Coming,"
written some thirty-two years later, to reflect the
world of that time. In a letter to Ethel Mannin in 1938
he quoted "The Second Coming" to reflect his growing
concern about Fascism.16 Thus, this poem does not share
the hope of A Vision.

When he wrote A Vision Yeats had anticipated a new
post-Christian era to succeed the presently ensuing two-
thousand-year reign of the "Objective" (Primary) Christ

in a "subjective" (Antithetical) age, providing a new
god who will be "Subjective"--where personality is upper-
most--to reign in an "Objective" (Primary) world. In
his last years Yeats perceived the holocaust which began with Hitler's invasion of Poland within eight months
after his death. Unlike T.S. Eliot, Yeats was infinitely of the world and intoxicated by it. Its dilemma was
his fate; its fate his fate. Thus, it is not surprising
that "The Second Coming" is, as Yeats observed, his most
important poem. It is both a prophecy and a revelation,
at once Yeats' poetic evocation of the very world horrors we now experience, and his perception of the futility of orthodox hope of "Objective" or "Subjective" salvation.

The manner in which "The Second Coming" achieves
this result is remarkable:

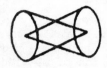

"Turning and turning in the widening gyre." "Gyre"
is a favorite figure of Yeats to explain his vision of
the subjective and objective life and to indicate the
spiritual history of the world, represented as one cone
inverted into another. Stating that "the mathematical
figure is an expression of the mind's desire," Yeats
went on to exxplain that

> In other words, the human soul is always mov-
> ing outward into the objective world or inward
> into itself; & this movement is double because
> the human soul would not be conscious were it
> not suspended between contraries, the greater
> the contrast the more intense the consciousness.
> The man, in whom the movement inward is stronger
> than the movement outward, the man who sees all
> reflected within himself, the subjective man,
> reaches the narrow end of a gyre at death, for
> death is always, they contend, even when it seems
> result of accident, preceded by an intensification
> of the subjective life; and has a moment of revela-
> tion immediately after death, a revelation which
> they describe as his being carried into the pres-
> ence of all his dead kindred, a moment whose ob-
> jectivity is exactly equal to the subjectivity of
> death. The objective man on the other hand, whose
> gyre moves outward, receives at this moment the
> revelation, not of himself seen from within, for

74

that is impossible to objective man, but of
himself as if he were somebody else. This figure is true also of history, for the end of
an age, which always receives the revelation
of the character of the next age, is represented by the coming of one gyre to its place of
greatest expansion and of the other to that
of its greatest contradiction. At the present
moment the life gyre is sweeping outward, unlike that before the birth of Christ which was
narrowing, and has almost reached its greatest
expansion. The revelation which approaches
will however take its character from the contrary movement of the interior gyre.[17]

"The falcon cannot hear the falconer." According
to Jeffares, the origin of Yeats' falcon imagery may be
Dante's Geryon, but in "The Second Coming" it stands for
Christ, the falconer unable to reach man and his present civilization.[18] This turn of events is expectable
in Yeats' thought since it anticipates the soon end of
the era ushered in by Christ nearly two thousand years
ago. The rest of the stanza presents the signs: "Things
fall apart, the centre cannot hold; / Mere anarchy is
loosed upon the world," and "The blood-dimmed tide is
loosed. . . ." As promised by A Vision the Second Coming should herald itself with signs of the re-birth of
individual men in all of the dignity the poet's romantic heart yearned for. The spiritual signs the poet
does see, however, are chilling. The ageless Sphinx, a
monstrous "shape with lion's body and the head of a
man, / A gaze blank and pitiless as the sun, / Is moving
its slow thighs, while all about it / Reel shadows of
the indignant desert birds." Unterecker sees a double
meaning in the image of the Sphinx compounded of the
beast of the Apocalypse (cf. Rev. 13) and Matthew's
prophecy of a spectacular return (chap. 24).[19] It would
seem, however, more consistent with the tenor of the poem to suggest that the beast which "Slouches towards
Bethlehem to be born" is triumphant, rather than vanquished as promised by Revelation. Unterecker may see
this result and intend his interpretation as sheerest
irony. The poet's bitterness in disappointment is unrelieved. It is certain that he intends the deepest
of irony, at once suggested in the title. Twenty centuries of waiting have been only "twenty centuries of
stony sleep" for the "rough beast, its hour come at
last." Had some magic supposed to have inhered in the
Bethlehem manger to prevent the awakening of the desert
beast? What manner of horror awaits us as that beast
seeks the same stable for ushering in the new era?

And, of course, in such shattering poetic evocation we discern Yeats' genius. No historian nor theologian can deny its efficacy. If orthodox soteriology remains confident in its endlessly delayed expectation of the millenium, the poet's perception is more faithful to the actual state of the world.

In one of his last poems he confirms that perception, using again his image of gyres, but not completely as bleakly. He sees no Second Coming different from that which he has prophesied, but he can in some measure celebrate the return of the cycle, both the things he rejoices in and those he does not. It is not a return to the optimism of A Vision, but to a sober appraisal of a world in which he is yet much a part of and a participant in:

> The gyres! the gyres! Old Rocky Face, look forth,
> Things thought too long can be no longer thought,
> For beauty dies of beauty, worth of worth,
> And ancient lineaments are blotted out.
> Irrational streams of blood are staining earth;
> Empedocles has thrown all things about;
> Hector is dead and there's a light in Troy;
> We that look on but laugh in tragic joy.
>
> What matter though numb nightmare ride on top,
> And blood and mire the sensitive body stain?
> What matter? Heave no sigh, let no tear drop,
> A greater, a more gracious time has gone,
> For painted forms of boxes of make-up
> In ancient tombs I sighed, but not again;
> What matter? Out of cavern comes a voice,
> And all it knows is that one word "Rejoice!"
>
> Conduct and work grow coarse, and coarse the soul
> What matter? Those that Rocky Face holds dear,
> Lovers of horses and women, shall,
> From marble of a broken sepulchre,
> Or dark betwixt the polecat and the owl,
> Or any rich, dark nothing disinter
> The workman, noble and saint, and all things run
> On that unfashionable gyre again.

In two short plays Yeats explores the antithetical concepts of Christ and his mission. Modelled on the Japanese Noh plays,[20] they are brief dramas of ideas. The first, Calvary, dwells upon Christ's inability to save Lazarus and Judas from intellectual despair, three Roman soldiers for whom his dying is in vain, and three birds: Heron, Eagle, and Swan. In explaining the play,

Yeats' mythic spokesman, Robartes, says that

> Christ only pitted those whose suffering is
> rooted in death, in poverty, or in sickness,
> or in sin, in some shape of the common lot,
> and he came especially to the poor who are
> most subject to exterior vicissitude.[21]

The first we learn of those not included in this lot
is sung by the second of three musicians: "God has not
died for the white heron." The implication in this
thrice-sung announcement is simply that the heron is not
in need of being saved. The purpose, said Yeats, is to
contrast objective self-sufficient loneliness with
Christ's which is not.[22]

Lazarus then complains of having been raised from
the dead. In death he had found the solitude that had
eluded him in life. Now, he "must go search / Among
the desert places where there is nothing / But howling
winds and solitary birds."

The freedom which Lazarus had found in death is
sharply contrasted to Christ's inability to turn this
life into something equal to, or better, a theme we
shall meet again in D.H. Lawrence's The Man Who Died.
In a similar sense, Judas, who never doubted Christ's
divine claims, nor his miracles, justifies his betrayal
by fear of eternal bondage to a God whose "Father put
all men into [his] hands":

> That was the very thought that drove me wild,
> I could not bear to think you had but to whistle
> And I must do; but after that I thought
> Whatever man betrays Him will be free;
> And life grew bearable again. And now
> Is there a secret left I do not know,
> Knowing that if a man betrays a God
> He is the stronger of the two.

In typical Yeatsian irony Christ's protests are impotent, though he claims that Judas' betrayal of him
"was decreed that hour / When the foundations of the
world were laid." In supreme mockery Judas taunts him
with the Yeatsian poetic truth: "You cannot even save
me."

The three Roman soldiers further goad him with their
desire for nothing, "three old gamblers" who dance the
dance of the dice-throwers for him before he dies. The
play ends with the three musicians once more singing

77

about the birds.

Helen H. Vendler interprets the play within the terms of Yeats' double gyres as "the interaction of objective and subjective life."[23] Judas remains bound to Christ in spite of his betrayal, and the soldiers remain involved however much they disdain him. At the same time Christ is bound by himself and his pretensions, being both man and God.

The play is generally accepted as the agony of Christ re-living his Passion. The _primary_ and _antithetical_ elements of Christ's double nature are seen by Jeffares and Knowland as "the consequences of His incarnation which include a world that is opposed to Him."[24] While these interpretations are faithful to Yeats' plan of approach, they seem hardly to bear decisively upon the consistent Yeatsian attitude of rejection of the Christly gyres, as a matter of poetic faith. They are fatally composed of two equally contradictory substances, dualism at its worst. Christian history is linear, calculating time in the chronology of its own mythology: creation, fall, redemption, and millenium. It presupposes a divine timetable, and summarily, even ferociously, resists the possibility of miscalculation or change of any kind. Yeats poured scorn upon it. He was scandalized by orthodox Christianity's ignorance and sweeping presumptuousness in applying its closed system to the remainder of mankind. But only in its exclusive linear dualism can the incompatible locked gyres be perceived so brilliantly, only in so resolutely separated subjectivity and objectivity can the failures of Christ's missions be so obvious. Thus, the Christ of _Calvary_ is trapped in a gigantic fraud: He can neither transcend his humanity, nor bring to bear his Divine Power.

In about 1720 Giambattista Vico observed that Western civilization had passed through stages similar to those of the Graeco-Roman world. In the twentieth century Oswald Spengler broadened the observation. Thus, cyclical or recurrent theories of history justified Yeats' disdain for Christian lineal claims. In this sense Lazarus' desire to remain dead is considerably more than a morbid reflection. As Leonard E. Nathan sees it, Jesus "is a protagonist agonizingly fixed in His historical role and has no hope of fulfilling tragic experience."[25] Succinctly put, Christ's lot is "unmitigated horror."[26]

In _The Resurrection_ Yeats explores the arch-conflict among the Jewish, Greek, and Christian religions, expos-

78

ing them to be as mutually incompatible discretely as manifestly they are in Christian syncretism. In perhaps as brilliant a stroke as modern drama has produced he pinpoints the dilemma in such a way that his whole visionary scheme is illumined. Of the four versions of The Resurrection we quote from the first Adelphi version of the Variorum edition which includes a Syrian character rather than an Egyptian.[27] Three speakers, the Hebrew, the Greek, and the Syrian, symbolize the Christian problem: confrontation of faith by reason. During their opening conversation the Greek laughs at the solemnity with which the Hebrew greets Calvary and the huddled, apprehensive disciples remaining. The Hebrew demands to know whether he has gone out of his mind. The Greek replies,

> No, no. I am laughing because they thought they were nailing the hands of a living man upon the Cross, and all the time there was nothing there but a phantom.

The Hebrew insists: "I saw hum buried." The philosophical Greek stands pat:

> We Greeks understand these things. No god has ever been buried, no god has ever suffered. Christ only seemed to be born, only seemed to eat, seemed to sleep, seemed to die. I did not mean to tell you until I had proof.

The Greek promises his proof before nightfall, but the Hebrew is scornful. The Greek retorts, "No Jew can understand these things." Not to be convinced, the Hebrew responds with Jewish faith, rationally about midway between Greek and Christian:

> It is you who do not understand. It is I and those men in there, perhaps, who begin to understand at last. He was nothing more than a man, the best man who ever lived. Nobody before him had so pitied human misery. He preached the coming of the Messiah because he thought the Messiah would take it all upon himself. Then some day when he was very tired, after a long journey perhaps, he thought that he himself was the Messiah. He thought it because of all destinies, it seemed the most terrible.

The Jew informs the Greek that the Messiah was prophesied to be born of a woman, to which the Greek objects. He calls it "the most terrible blasphemy." Cur-

iously, the Hebrew repeats the heart of the Christian
message, that God must be born as a man in order to take
away the sins of man. The Greek rejects this argument:
Every man's sins are his property. Nobody has a right
to them." He thinks the whole scheme is morbid: "That
makes me shudder. The utmost possible suffering as an
object of worship!" He chides the Hebrew for having no
statues which, In Greek sense, are the means by which
spiritual reality may be apprehended by the senses. The
Hebrew God, of course, had early forbidden them.

What the Greek is uttering is one of the earliest
heresies, Docetism, which held that Christ's apparent
body was a mere phantasy, and that he only appeared to
have died on the Cross. The belief was suported by the
rationale that the absolute can never unite with the finite, and that matter is evil forever in conflict with
the spiritual.[28] The early Christian fathers such as
Athanasius, Nestorius, and Cyril battled each other
over the issue, condemned and rejected each other, and
in general bore abject precursory witness to the reasons behind Yeats' two-millenia-later reaction.

The Jew, whose faith has no demi-god, semi-god, nor
divine-human God whose elements are in equal stasis--
and whose angels, unlike the Christian, have gender,
the masculine, in fact, fully capable of sexually exciting some of the men at Sodom--accepts all of Christ's
claims except those of divinity and messiahship. Christ
can only be a man to the Hebrew. God is One and oper-
ates through appointees and hired help, not co-equals.
The Messiah in Jewish belief has not come. Christ,
then, can only be a sincere imposter.

Through the contrast of Dionysian revelers, who comprise a symbol of the parallel relation of pagan rituals
to Christian, the Hebrew turns his thoughts again to the
ancient riddle of what and who the Messiah is. As he
contemplates, the Hebrew is not sure he wants the Messiah to come. The reasons are pure Yeats: the everlasting
distrust of the linear interpretation of history, and a
divinity which docetically rejects flesh:

> I am glad that he was not the Messiah; we
> might all have been deceived to our lives' end,
> or learnt the truth too late. One had to sac-
> rifice everything that the divine suffering
> might, as it were, descend into one's mind and
> soul and make them pure . . . One had to give
> up all worldly knowledge, all ambition, do noth-
> ing of one's own will. Only the divine could

have any reality. God had to take complete possession. It must be a terrible
thing when one is old, and the tomb round
the corner, to think of all the ambitions
one has put aside; to think, perhaps, a
great deal about women. I want to marry
and have children.

Having been sent by the Greek to learn of the events
following the Crucifixion, the Syrian returns with news
that the women proclaim that they have seen the tomb empty and the Christ risen. The Hebrew must, of course,
reject this news. Humanity cannot rise. (Such monumental vanity belongs with the ancient pharoahs.) The
docetic-persuaded Greek can believe it, as resurrection
is proof of the apparent nature only of Christ's body.
At this point, the Christian yoking together of the two
views hangs in suspension. For this reason the Syrian
must assert the evidence: "He is no phantom. We put a
great stone over the mouth of the tomb, and the women
say that it has been rolled back." The course of the
ensuing argument is surely predictable, with none of the
three views more convincing than the others. Nevertheless, the Syrian leaps into his faith in spite of whatever rational objection he hears. Laughing. he demands,
"What is human knowledge?" The Greek responds quite
practically: "The knowledge that keeps the road from
here to Persia free from robbers, that has built the
beautiful humane cities, that has made the modern world
that stands between us and the barbarians." The Syrian
insists on something outside of knowledge, suggesting
the powerlessness of reason in the face of the irrational. Seeing no more humor in the Syrian's laughter than
he did in the Greek's, the Hebrew ruefully contrasts the
pagan rites of cyclical rebirth of their gods to the
eternal death of "our God." Then, Christ appears. The
Greek sees a phantom; the Hebrew, a man whom he touches
and discovers a beating heart. It is too much for him.
He screams. Christ goes into the inner room. The Syrian describes how the disciples examined him. In this
turn of events the Greek sees the death of man. If a
phantom is to be man's ruler, man must die:

O Athens, Alexandria, Rome, something has
come to destroy you. The heart of a phantom
is beating. Man has begun to die. Your words
are clear at last, O Heraclitus. God and man
die each other's life, live each other's death.

The reference to Heraclitus caps Yeats' purport
here. A philosopher in Ephesus about 540 B.C., Heracli-

tus evinced a gloomy outlook on life, but attempted to
explain what λόγος, or reason meant, which, he said,
most men misunderstood. It was the universal principle
by which all things were interrelated. Opposites, he
declared, define each other. Balance and order are
achieved in the corresponding influence of polar dimensions upon each other, a philosophy as we have seen, to
find its way into Paul Tillich's system. It is the destruction of this principle that the Greek sees in the
phantom with a beating heart. The play ends with two
songs, the second of which as follows:

> Everything that man esteems
> Endures a moment or a day,
> Love's pleasure drives his love away,
> The painter's brush consumes his dream;
> The herald's cry, the soldier's tread
> Exhaust his glory and his might:
> Whatever flames upon the night
> Man's own resinous heart has fed.

Thus, Yeats has sharply etched his life-long conviction that Christianity has forever put body and soul
at war. The fatal dualistic spirit is unable to distinguish between the earthly good and the spiritual demand, between essence immanent in matter and the tempor-
ality of life.

His significance to modern literature is critical.
Understanding his religious outlook prepares us to understand the religious dimension of succeeding British
and American writers. As a poet, Yeats was committed
to existence; as a religious man he was rooted in essence. The effort to re-unite the two--in his case within a pristine Platonic scheme--is an artistic aim he
has shared with others, from Petrarch to the present
writer. Unable to make the Kierkegaardian leap of a T.
S. Eliot, Auden, or Greene, he could not, nevertheless,
relinquish his deepest religious convictions. His artistic modus vivendi was comprised of profoundest participation in the human condition and in his spiritual
reach beyond the stars.

JAMES JOYCE: THE ROMAN CATHOLIC REBEL

Religiously, James Joyce stood opposite Yeats: the
Irish recalcitrant seeking expression of his soul in
art as distinct from the Irish skeptic searching for a
new myth in which to find his soul. Instead of invent-
ing esoteric symbolism with which to express inner reality, Joyce plunged into the senses themselves made
the experiential equal of whatever higher reality conducted through them. In this aspect Joyce is of utmost
importance to modern literature.

The scandal of the artist since the Renaissance has
been the orthodox religious hostility to the language
of art. Torn between the two, the artist must decide
whether to surrender to proscription or to glory in the
flesh. William T. Noon, the Jesuit commentator, makes
a sharp distinction between the experience of art and
the experience of faith:

> Some of Joyce's commentators tend to blur
> the distinction between his achievement in art
> and the success-failure of his religious life
> of supernatural faith. Joyce for himself saw
> the difference. Faith in art is grounded on
> the grace of art; no one just manufactures se-
> rious art. Religious faith is grounded on an-
> other kind of grace.[29]

We confront here a dramatic example in Roman Catholic theological criticism of the vast distinction between religious significance and theology, between theology and art. In Noon's schemata art is merely functional, and when properly directed, only an aspect of
the ultimate goal of faith. Yeats, we recall, precisely rejected this secondary significance assigned to art.
Both he and Joyce sought in art to compensate for dead
myth and dying symbol, rejecting the Roman Catholic
claim that the myth and symbol of grace are the same as
grace itself. Noon insists, notwithstanding, that the
primary function of art is to pursue the Christic ana-
logue--represented in our study by Graham Greene and
Flannery O'Connor.

Phenomenologically, there can be no intelligible
distinction between the artistic process and that by

83

which grace is cognizable. The young man of _Portrait_ lost his faith, but not his epiphanies. Joyce himself repudiated Roman theology, but remained steeped in its mortal and spiritual distinctions. But in support of his position Noon cites Jacques Mercanton, Joyce's good friend. However, the full citation from Mercanton supports our contention, instead. In a conversation on Christmas Eve, Joyce refers to Molly of _Ulysses_ as "Madonna Bloom." Mrs. Joyce exclaims "He is always blasphemous!" Mercanton writes that

> The comparison is perhaps sacrilegious, but perfectly orthodox: Madonna Bloom is the mother of all the vices, just as the Virgin is the mother of all the virtues. Together they make the world go round.

> He was joking; yet the sense of what he said was seriously intended. Although a connoisseur of blasphemies, he remained always within the most orthodox frame of reference, his mind curiously closed to every form of heresy in the moral as in the religious order.[30]

In spite of his construction of this incident, Noon cannot escape the fact that as Glicksberg discerns, Joyce violently rejected the Roman Church.[31] Its very vestiges clinging to him are an indication of how deeply it had impressed itself upon him. Noon sees but a rebellion against the Jesuits.[32] What Noon misses is put by Glicksberg about as eloquently as any commentator today:

> Since he is neither a theological propagandist nor a priest, the poet [in the Aristotelian sense which includes novelists] instinctively rebels against any force which would exploit him for ends not inherent in his calling. His function is not to convert but to reveal. He writes not out of a body of fixed beliefs but out of his deeply felt vision of life . . . he is enchanted with the phenomenal world, the flow of time, the stuff of human experience, human passion, human joy and sorrow. If in responding to the world of experience in all its immediacy and variousness he gives utterance to profound religious intuitions, these are not of an orthodox case. Ingrained doubt as to the existence of God is today an inescapable condition of religious faith . . . The modern poetic consciousness, as it unburdens itself of its charged

sensibility, its deep sense of irony, its conception of change, cannot continue to exploit
the myths and metaphors of a Christianity that
is no longer relevant to the context of reality.[33]

What Joyce purported was inherently heretical: the
elevation of art to the holy. Chapter IV of <u>Portrait</u>
is set against the whole panoply of orthodox Christian
concept of woman. Although we have alluded in our "Preliminary Considerations" to Stephen's epiphany at the
rivulet, it bears full citation here with some further
comment:

> A girl stood before him in midstream, alone
> and still, gazing out to sea. She seemed like
> one whom magic had changed into the likeness of
> a strange and beautiful seabird. Her long slen-
> der bare legs were delicate as a crane's and
> pure save where an emerald trail of seaweed had
> fashioned itself as a sign upon the flesh. Her
> thighs, fuller and softhued as ivory, were bared
> almost to the hips where the white fringes of her
> drawers were like featherings of soft white down.
> Her slateblue skirts were kilted boldly about her
> waist and dovetailed behind her. Her bosom was
> as a bird's, soft and slight, slight and soft as
> the breast of some darkplumaged dove. But her
> long hair was girlish: and girlish, touched with
> wonder of mortal beauty, her face.[34]

As any Freudian would be eager to point out, the imagery is as sexually suggestive as that in any gentleman's bedside reader. Such an approach, certainly, ob-
viates Joyce's spiritual intentions. A "blasphemer"
such as Joyce, says Glicksberg, "acknowledges the existence [read <u>reality</u> here] of God even as he curses
him."[35] It becomes clear, then, why Joyce insisted upon the religious vocation of art, while rejecting the
Roman vocation, why in elevating flesh he never lost the
clear distinction between virtue and vice.

What Fathers Noon and Lynch cannot countenance is
the direct, uncompromising denial of an art-less theology. It is striking to note Joyce's implicit rejection of Plotinian Platonism which, since Augustine, is
at the heart of Roman dogma. Today, literature is of
vital importance in the Roman hierarchy of essential
studies, serving as textbook grist for the application
of theological corrective, as a many-authored manual of
how not to, and why, of heresy and truth.

Joyce, like Yeats, refused this relegation. Unlike Yeats, his rejection was the negative result of a positive affirmation. At the beginning of the twentieth century he completed the process begun by Petrarch in the fourteenth, the deification of man, ironically accomplished through the love of both for woman:

> --Heavenly joy! cried Stephen's soul in an outburst of profane joy. . . .

> Her image had passed into his soul for ever and no word had broken the holy silence of his ecstasy. Her eyes had called him and his soul had leaped at the call. To live, to err, to fall, to triumph, to recreate life out of life! A wild angel had appeared to him, the angel of mortal youth and beauty, an envoy from the fair courts of life, to throw open before him in an instant of ecstasy the gates of all the ways of error and glory.[36]

Such epiphanies serve at least a double artistic function: they reduce the spiritual revelation to poetic image, and equate the profane with the sacred. In his Stephen Hero fragment Joyce describes the epiphany as "a sudden spiritual manifestation, whether in the vulgarity of speech or of gesture or in a memorable phase of the mind itself."[37] The writer's duty is to record them. In noting that the epiphany is not peculiar to Joyce, Irene Hendry Chayes affirms its religious validity. Joyce, she asserts, simply systematized a common aesthetic experience that few writers have thought worth considering.[38] Eleven appear in Portrait. Others are elsewhere. But as Chayes further points out, all of Joyce's works are "a tissue of epiphanies, great and small, from fleeting images to whole books."[39]

Based on the earlier Stephen Hero, Portrait is divided into five chapters showing the progression of Stephen's artistic revelation, rather than self-containing action, the growth of his character more than external event. Frank O'Connor sees the book as "something new in literature," where "style ceases to be a relationship between an author and reader and becomes a relationship of a magical kind between author and object."[40]

According to O'Connor's hunch, the magic is achieved by the strategic use of words, about two hundred key terms "dropped in, like currants in a cake and a handful at a time, so that their presence would be felt

86

rather than identified."[41] But much of O'Connor's perspicacity is lost upon him because he cannot see much beyond the language which remains "insufferably self-conscious."[42] Nonetheless, the language is highly revealing of Joyce's technique in creating the implosive quality of his internal referents. The epiphany at the rivulet is described in language involving

1. The association of the physical;

   "girl," "slender bare legs," "flesh," "thighs," "hip," "fringe of her drawers," "slateblue skirts," "waits," "bosom," "breast," "long fine hair," "girlish" [twice], "mortal beauty of her face."

These evocations serve a decisively religious purpose when seen in the context of

2. The association of whiteness with purity;

   "bare legs," "pure" [legs], "ivory," "bared" [thighs], "white fringes of her drawers," "white down," "fair hair."

Joyce's intent is clear: the bared thigh of a bathing girl is equal in intensity of sublimity to the covered image of the Virgin.

The epiphanies are dialectical, working in a thetic and antithetic manner. In Chapter I Joyce begins a carefully orchestrated aesthetic and emotional framework for Stephen's ultimate rejection of Irish Catholicism. Stephen is at school. Simon Moonan has advised Stephen not to kick the ball again, as urged by a schoolmate. The latter turns to Simon and sneers. "--We all know why you speak. You are McGlade's suck." The following narrative plays upon "suck," "queer," "ugly," "lavatory," "dirty water," and "hole in the basin":

> Suck was a queer word. The fellow called Simon that name because Simon Moonan used to tie the prefect's false sleeves behind his back and the prefect used to let on to be angry. But the sound was ugly. Once he had washed his hands in the lavatory of the Wicklow Hotel and his father pulled the stopper by the chain and the dirty water went down through the hole in the basin. And when it had all gone down slowly the hole in the basin made a sound like that: suck. Only

louder.[43]

Then antithetically, the first line of the next paragraph employs "white" in a directly clashing way: "To remember that and not the white look of the lavatory made him feel cold and then not."[44]

At the end of Chapter I Stephen's hands have been beaten for his having broken his glasses in an accident. He is unable to see well enough to do his writing. Father Arnall had exempted him from punishment, but the sadistic Dolan called him a schemer, a "lazy idle little loafer!"[45] The narrative description of the swollen, reddened hands of the tearful Stephen is out of Dickens, but Joyce is not aiming at socio-economic causes of cruelty, but at the humiliating, brutal mortification of the body so much a part of Roman tradition.

Stephen is finally relieved by the Rector's concession to his impaired sight, his promise to prevent any further bruised palms and fingers. His schoolmates cheer. Once alone, he is happy again. But the ominous poignancy remains. He senses more tears to come:

> The fellows were practicing long shies
> and bowing lobs and slow twisters. In the
> soft grey silence he could hear the bump of
> the balls: and from here and from there
> through the quiet air the sound of the crick-
> et bats: pick, pock, puck: like drops of wa-
> ter in a fountain falling softly in the brim-
> ming bowl.[46]

Chapter II find Stephen committing fornication with a prostitute. In objective perspective the description of his awakening body--"His blood was in revolt"[47]--is little more than the normal expectable sexual hunger of budding young men, most often a matter of later fond, even humorous, reminiscence. For Stephen, of course, it is his first serious breach of the moral law. Thus, the narration of his inner struggle before capitulation reads like the prolegomenon of an Irish Inferno. Yet, its tenor, properly intense and implosive, readies him for the priestly damnation of Chapter III. His sense of guilt keeps pace with the frequence of his visits to the whores:

> He had sinned mortally not once but many
> times and he knew that, while he stood in
> danger of eternal damnation for the first
> sin alone, by every succeeding sin he mul-

88

tiplied his guilt.48

Within the drama of his imagination the Virgin Mary confronts the bawds:

> The glories of Mary held his soul captive . . .
> Her eyes seemed to regard him with mild pity;
> her holiness, a strange light glowing faintly
> upon her frail flesh, did not humiliate the
> sinner who approached her. If ever he was im-
> pelled to cast sin from him and repent, the im-
> pulse that moved him was the wish to be her
> knight.49

The Virgin's initial victory, however, does not bank
the fires of guilt and shame growing ever hotter. They
are stoked to unbearable degree at the retreat by the
most rabid hellfire-and-damnation sermons since Jonathan
Edwards across the Protestant sea. He is convinced
that he is totally depraved. At last he is brought
down abject. In a stupor of unrelenting terror he goes
to confession.

The climax to which Joyce skillfully contrives these
events places in glaring relief his central objection to
priestcraft. In its puerility and impotence, its hostility to the life-principle itself, it condemns Stephen's manhood as unfit for the holy. It is the sex
act itself, not mere whoring, that the priest damns:

> --You are very young, my child, he said
> [Stephen is sixteen], and let me implore you
> to give up that sin. It is a terrible sin.
> It kills the body and it kills the soul. It
> is the cause of many crimes and misfortunes.
> Give it up, my child, for God's sake. It is
> dishonorable and unmanly. You cannot know
> where that wretched habit will lead you or
> where it will come against you. As long as
> you commit that sin, my poor child, you will
> never be worth one farthing to God. Pray to
> our mother Mary to help you. She will help
> you, my child. Pray to Our Blessed Lady when
> that sin comes into your mind. I am sure you
> will do that, will you not? You repent of all
> those sins. I am sure you do. And you will
> never offend Him any more by that wicked sin.
> You will make that solemn promise to God, will
> you not?50

Now what some commentators, notably Roman Catholic,

grossly misunderstand is the way a novel functions as art, especially one whose devices of craft are so consciously employed as those of _Portrait_. On the other hand, Booth, a Mormon, objects to the lack of distance in the narrator from the story, making it ambiguous and uncertain. Booth is unhappy because he cannot surely tell the difference between Joyce as narrator, and Stephen as protagonist. He cites Caroline Gordon's contention that _Portrait_ is "the picture of a soul that is being damned for time and eternity caught in the act of forseeing and foreknowing its damnation."[51] Ms. Gordon arrives at this conclusion even as Stephen repudiates the whole canopy of Churchly sanctions. The one support for her manifestly unliterary conclusion is Stephen's concession to Cranly of the possibility of being wrong. Both Booth and Gordon impose normative presuppositions upon the work which question the validity of Joyce's vision, implicitly demanding that the author suit himself to their canons of purport, rather than his own. While pointing to Ms. Gordon's misreading of the author's intent as an example of the artistic flaw in Joyce's technique, Booth seeks to apply a critical standard inadequate alone to probe to the depth of the story. Where his Aristotelian quarrel strikes out at confusion of story and story-telling, the defect is not fatal. Indeed, the moving power of the novel is clear and compelling.

At the moment of Stephen's tremorous confession he has been systematically brainwashed by his Jesuit schoolmasters, deprived of individuality in its simplest meaning, and brutalized beyond endurance. These are but contrivances of an author whose quarrel is not with the categories of sin and vice, repentance and forgiveness--Joyce has never had any quarrel with them--but with the the smothering of the artistic instinct, the unconditional damnation of the very means by which the artist functions. Stephen is little more than an agent in ideation, and as such in the novel, he is not Joyce. To this extent Booth is right in insisting upon contextual reference, the protagonist as he is within the novel. Any other Stephen, as that of Ms. Gordon, is an invention of the reader. We can thus meet Booth's objection, as well as that of Ms. Gordon, by concentrating on the novel as it is, as the author has guided us throughout the telling by his devices of craft--chiefly Stephen's epiphanies. We need but accede to Joyce's story, and not try to write our own.[52]

At the beginning of Chapter IV, Stephen toys with the idea of becoming a priest. He has been found worthy by his priestly mentors. He has been brought by the author to that point in the artistic economy of the novel that churchly magic having redeemed him is supposed to transform him. In any Aristotelian terms the superimposed normative value demands development consistent with the reader's, not the author's, expectations. When it does not so occur, it becomes clear that the author has a purpose of his own. The epiphany at the rivulet halts the expectable cold. Though Stephen may appear confused and uncertain, his author is not. The beginning of Chapter V reveals the author's purport.

Again, Joyce supplies us with highly evocative words which spell out why the priest and the artist are eternally at loggerheads. The authorial device for this intent is Stephan's mental picture of the head and face of his friend, Cranly. The words evoking Stephen's image of the priest in Cranly are underlined:

> Even now against the grey curtain of the morn-
> ing he saw it before him like the phantom of a
> dream, the face of a severed head or death mask,
> crowned on the brows by its stiff black upright
> hair as by an iron crown. It was a priestlike
> face, priestlike in its pallor, in the wide-
> winged nose, in the shadowings below the eyes
> and along the jaws, priestlike in the lips that
> were long and bloodless and faintly smiling: and
> Stephen, remembering swiftly how he had told
> Cranly of all the tumults and unrest and longings
> of his soul, day by day and night by night, only
> to be answered by his friend's listening silence,
> would have told himself that it was the face of
> a guilty priest who heard confessions of those
> whom he had not power to absolve but that he felt
> again in memory the gaze of its dark womanish eyes.[53]

Further on, Stephen senses that "Cranly's dark eyes were watching him."[54] Noon finds the suggestion of homosexuality in Stephen's thought. The suggestion is more ominous than Noon implies. In the context of Cranly's "dark womanish eyes" of the quoted passage above, the "dark eyes" are directly referable to the priest, not to any like characteristic in Stephan. Nor, on the other hand, is Cranly himself of primary import. The charge is against the priesthood. Celibacy robs the priest of his manhood, and, of greater moment to Joyce, the creative impulse. The priesthood is fit only for men who have more woman in them than man. The point is clear in Stephen's contemplation of the girl with the "small ripe mouth":[55]

> To him she would unveil her soul's shy naked-
> ness, to one who has but schooled in the dis-
> charging of a formal rite than to him, a
> priest of eternai imagination, transmuting the
> daily bread of experience into the radiant body
> of everliving life.[56]

Booth has singled out Stephen's sensual villanelle
as an example of Joycean ambiguity. Those who interpret
the novel as ironic find the villanelle laughably adolescent. Readers who take it seriously see it as a
prime example of what Stephen calls "the phenomena of
artistic conception, artistic gestation and artistic re-
production," for which he seeks "a new terminology and
a new personal experience."[57] We cite both positions
here not to try to adjudicate the issue, but to point to
the consistency of authorial intent perceptible in the
thematic structure. The critical tools of Booth are
fashioned for the classical novel--The History of Tom
Jones--of settled value and artistic convention, and are
only partially suitable for the problems he finds in
confusion of author, narrator, and protagonist resulting
from Joyce's innovations of style. As the chief idea-
tional agent hidden beneath his narrator and protagonist,
Joyce as author systematically builds an idea and moves
it to its conclusion. Thus, reading the villanelle as
an artistic device, rather than as the discrete ecstatic
eruption of a silly boy, will immeasurably illumine its
significance. Before the villanelle the narrator tells
us that

> A glow of desire kindled again in his soul
> and fired and fulfilled all his body. Conscious
> of his desire she was waking from odorous sleep,
> the temptress of his villanelle. Her eyes, dark
> and with a look of languor, were opening to his
> eyes. Her nakedness yielded to him, radiant,
> warm, odorous and lavishlimbed, enfolded him like
> a shining cloud, enfolded him like water with a
> liquid life: and like a cloud of vapor or like
> waters circumfluent in space the liquid letters
> of speech, symbols of the element of mystery, flow-
> ed forth over his brain.

Stephan waxes passionate:

> *Are you not weary of ardent ways,*
> *Lure of the fallen seraphim?*
> *Tell no more of enchanted days.*
>
> *Your eyes have set man's heart ablaze*

And you have had your will of him.
Are you not weary of ardent ways?

Above the flame the smoke of praise
Goes up from ocean rim to rim.
Tell no more of enchanted days.

Our broken cries and mournful lays
Rise in one eucharistic hymn.
Are you not weary of ardent ways?

While sacrificing hands upraise
The chalice flowing to the brim,
Tell no more of enchanted days.

And still you hold our longing gaze
With languorous and lavish limb!
Are you not weary of ardent ways?
Tell no more of enchanted days.[58]

Booth admits that his querulousness about the villanelle is offset by his concession that the poem
should be experienced rather than dissected. He is
quick to preface, however, that "Hardly anyone has committed himself in public about the quality of this poem."[59] We may suggest that the reason lies in the currently popular ironic approach tending toward skepticism and elimination of significance. For us the poem
is strategic in our consideration of Joyce's art.

First, a villanelle is a fixed French form from the
Italian, originally associated with the pastoral. It
consists of nineteen lines divided into five tercets
and one quatrain. The first and third lines of the
first tercet are alternately repeated in each of the remaining four tercets as the last line, together becoming the last two lines of the final quatrain. With the
first line as A and the third line as A', which rhymes
with it, the rhyme scheme is AbA', abA, abA', abA, abA',
abAA'. The meter is basically iambic tetrameter in Stephen's poem.

This villanelle is a hymn, an invocation of the divine beauty of fleshly womanliness in direct contradis-
tinction to virginity. The four times we read the question "Are you not weary of ardent ways?" asked of that
"Lure of the fallen seraphim," create the impression of
inescapable attraction between feminine allure and its
male votaries, the resistless power of beauty over young
men. The repetition of "Tell no more of enchanted days"
advises the goddess that she alone can break the spell.

In imagery of the mass the poem suggests ritual sacrifice for the salvation of men by beauty, not from evil, but from the ugly. The "broken cries and mournful lays" which "Rise in one eucharistic hymn" suggest the need of constant invocation. She holds her suppliants with "longing gaze / With languorous look and lavish limb!" In wonder now, and plea, the poem closes with the AA' couplet.

What emerges from this youthful ardor is the clear distinction between the lure of feminine "beauty" and the plea for "love," the latter suggestive of a sexual element wholly absent from the villanelle. Where Stephen's revulsion at his whoring is quite real, his embrace of the creative principle inspired by the feminine form is equally compelling. Nowhere does the term "love" appear in any vital context. Revealed then, we have the essence of Joyce's idea: holiness in beauty may transcend itself without ever leaving its base in the sensual, a concept with which Tillich would heartily agree.

The final scenes of Stephen conversing with Cranly spell a dialectical, rather than eventful, climax working toward resolving the issue hanging fire since the first epiphany of Chapter 1. Much, of course, has been made of Stephen's flat--though often reported as declamatory--statment that he would not serve at Easter Mass, that he neither believed nor disbelieved in the Eucharist,[60] and of Cranly's observation that Stephen's mind is saturated with the religion he claims to disbelieve.[61] Upon such narrow logs wrenched out of the artistic structure of the novel hang most efforts to return Stephen against his will to Roman Catholicism. When Cranly further asks "You do not intend to become a Protestant?" Stephen replies, "I said I had lost my faith but not that I had lost my selfrespect." [sic][62] The critics who point to Stephen's adolescence as the basis for rejecting the validity of his mystical experience should be reminded that the title of the book contains <u>Young Man</u>, some indication of the emotional level at which Joyce deliberately pitched his story. No one familiar with the world out of which the novel grew can doubt its authenticity. The diction faithfully reflects the vivid, often purplish hyperbole of a highly imaginative, sensitive boy for whom the world contained limitlessly more than the stultifying, lower-middle-class life of the Church-bound Irish. In the dazzling and infernal world of his imagination he created his own self-peopled universe, the bright hues and shapes, the figures and associations unrestrained by sterile dogmas and emasculated minions. What keeps <u>Portrait</u> alive among young read-

ers, Noon even admits,[63] is its everlasting reach into
the experience of being young, and thus unspoiled or
uncorrupted by the leathery retaliation of the aged.
"Welcome, O life!" the young man exclaims. "I go to encounter for the millionth time the reality of experience
and to forge in the smithy of my soul the uncreated conscience of my race."[64]

That "conscience" has lain fallow, all but smothered, but its shoots valiantly persist, determined to re-
construct the image of the artist, both of himself and
the art-denying, self-hostile world around him. Whether Stephen's quest, like that of his namesake's son, is
to end in tragedy, is not determinative of the validity
of his quest. "Heroes" are often required to die so
that the principle might live. To this extent Stephen
Hero and Stephen Dedalus are one.

Here, like Yeats, Joyce illumines the unique role
of literary art, becoming a twin Irish pillar of the
temple of individual experience.

D. H. LAWRENCE: APOSTLE OF THE SEXUAL CHRIST

Our interest in D.H. Lawrence for this study centers on perhaps the most unique aspect of his literary significance, his doing what Joyce never dared do, or could never do: equate divinity with physical sexual fulfillment. Uncluttered by Roman Catholic moral schizophrenia, Lawrence not only sought purification in physical sex, but reduced spiritual pretensions to human proportions, while purporting undiminished belief in God. Not everyone, to be certain, appreciated Lawrence's approach.

For a man not formally trained in theological and Biblical disciplines he was remarkably accurate in his observations about the origins and compilations of the Holy Book and many of the doctrines stemming from it. His Christology, like all Christologies of course, was primarily a matter of personal conviction based upon evidence beyond the reach of scientific or rational proof. His major statements on Christianity, along with his novel, The Man Who Died, came late in life.

In his posthumously published essay, "On Being Religious," he wrote

> Now this isn't a deliberate piece of blasphemy. It's just one way of stating an everlasting truth: or pair of truths. First, there is always the Great God. Second, as regards man, He shifts His position in the cosmos. The Great God departs from the heaven where man has located Him, and plumps His throne down somewhere else. Man, being an ass, keeps going to the same door to beg for his carrot, even when the Master has gone away to another house. The ass keeps on going to the same spring to drink, even when the spring has dried up, and there's nothing but clay and hoofmarks. It doesn't occur to him to look round, to see where the water has broken out afresh, somewhere else out of some live rock. Habit! God has become a human habit, and Man expects the Almighty habitually to lend Himself to it. Whereas the Almighty--it's one of His characteristics--won't. He makes a move, and

97

laughs when Man goes on praying to the gap
in the Cosmos.[65]

This peripatetic God includes Jesus who cannot be
circumscribed by one revelation. Here, Lawrence echoes
Yeats who, as we have seen, also refused to believe
that revelation was a closed book. Lawrence further rejected the dogma that Jesus was the only Saviour sent
to man, declaring that other saviours have appeared in
other places with other revelations. He denied that
Jesus is the way and the life for modern man, and asserted that there is no Saviour for the modern era. But he
heard a "strange calling," and described his enthusiasm
as a "hound on the scent." He set out for "great fun,
God's own good fun." In a final comment he added, "My-
self, I believe in God. But I'm off on a different
road. *Adiós!* and if you like, *au revoir!*"[66]

The difference of that road is manifest in his
Apocalypse which sets out his religious philosophy and
launches an attack on the Book of Revelation. Whether
one can accept Lawrence's own theological constructions,
his critique on Revelation is highly defensible.

Perhaps the most difficult book of the Bible to
make sense of, Revelation was written circa 81-96 A.D.
during the reign of Domitian. As all books of the New
Testament, Revelation was prompted by a specific immediate occasion, this one of great significance to the
local Christian community. However much later Christians come to believe that the books sprang up miracu-
lously by God's own hand, the fact is that God's hand
used quite temporally limited mortal amanuenses. Although today it is extremely difficult to understand the
occult symbolism and allusions of Revelation, the author
had no intent to be vague. He took care to explain for
his original readers what they should already understand.[67] Unfortunately, the original Jewish apocalyse
upon which Revelation is based is lost, and with it the
key to a great portion of the author's sources.

Although the author's assigned name is John, we
have no way of knowing who or what John. The title,
"Divine," adds little, since the original Greek word
simple means "theologian." From internal evidence alone,
we can gather that unlike other canonical books--Isaiah
for example--Revelation was written by a single author.
He considers himself a servant of Jesus Christ concerned
only with the seven churches of Asia Minor. Nothing in
the book indicates that he was an apostle having dealt
directly with Jesus--he would be quite an old man in 81

A.D. Though he speaks of being a "prophet," nothing indicates that he had an official status of that rank, either.

Nevertheless, the author claims that while imprisoned on the Island of Patmos (as an enemy of Rome) he
received his visions. Of critical importance is the
fact that neither these visions, nor the style of the
writing indicates this John to be the same as the John
whose name designates the fourth synoptic Gospel. In
the first place, the vicious anti-semitic tone is miss-
ing--the John of the Apocalypse finds Romans, not Jews,
the enemy of the Christians. Secondly, there is little
evangelistic zealotry, and thirdly, he is not out to de-
fend the divinity of Christ. Instead, he seeks to warn
his fellow Christians of renewed persecution, but to
reassure them of the ultimate victory of Christ. Thus,
his message is entirely practical. What has drawn subsequent critical attack, in particular, Lawrence's, is
this John's consuming conviction that God's direct intervention was imminent. None of his predictions has
come to pass.[68]

In his "Introduction" to Lawrence's Apocalypse, addressed to Frieda Lawrence, Richard Aldington declares
the book more of a revelation of Lawrence, the man,
than of Patmos John. Lawrence casts aside Platonic-
Christian philosophy for Vitalism, the cosmos of the
"living thing."[69]

Vitalism argues the belief in a unique force char-
acterizing all living things, quite different from all
other forces operating in the universe. It directs and
controls all form and development. (Cf. Yeats' Anima
Mundi which is unrestricted.) E.W. Tedlock, Jr. observes that Lawrence tentatively identifies primitive
American Indian animism, which includes all objects ani-
mate and inanimate, in his Vitalist novel, The Plumed
Serpent.[70] Tedlock, of course, is dead wrong. Animism
should not be confused with Vitalism; the former in-
volves animal spirits; the latter is a mystical principle only. Animism was early advanced by Pythagoras
and Plato whom Lawrence explicitly rejected. But in
modern thought mechanistic and biochemical theories
have supplanted Vitalism. Yet for the mystic which Lawrence is essentially, Vitalism is crucially important
in understanding his radical religious approach.

Of decisive result, then, is the vitiation of the
Christian emphasis upon the depravity of man, the decay of life itself, and the ultimate destruction of the

99

world. What this is, certainly, is the culmination of
an artistic process in which Lawrence's Irish contemporaries, Yeats and Joyce, fit neatly like the parts of a
mosaic: the affirmation of humanly participant divinity.
Lawrence, however, reversed the historical Christian
process of regenerating flesh into a docetic spiritual
substance, and insisted upon the revivification of the
body and the passions themselves. In his essay, The
Risen Lord, Lawrence celebrates a Christ reborn fully
human:

> Christ is risen in the flesh! We must ac-
> cept the image completely, if we accept it at
> all. We must take the mystery in its fulness
> and in fact. It is only the image of our own
> experience. Christ rises, when He rises from
> the dead, in the flesh, not merely as spirit.
> He rises with hands and feet, as Thomas knew for
> certain: and if with hands and feet, then with
> lips and stomach and genitals of a man. Christ
> risen, and risen in the whole of His flesh, not
> with some left out.71

A Christ with genitals, therefore, is not a deity
without sexuality, nor as we discover in The Man Who
Died without sexual response to women. Where pagan religious ritual has often included sexual expression, it
usually is in placation of an irascible god. In Lawrence it is the ritual of revitalization.

Now to be sure, this tack is not without its pitfalls, chief of which is the elimination of the ancient
dualistic problem by eliminating spiritual supremacy
altogether. Joyce, of course, would blanch at that.

And Lawrence found it tough sledding. His fellow
man frequently proved vicious and vindictive. Keith
Sagar notes that in 1916, after completing Women in
Love, Lawrence became almost suicidally misanthropic.
For a number of years persecution and poverty followed
him.72 Aldington records that unable to share his
vision Lawrence represented his contemporaries in two
ways in his Apocalypse: in the "frustrated power lust"
of the "underdog dissenting sort of Christian," and in
their determined destruction of ancient pre-Christian
cosmogonies whose symbolisms they continued to use because their culture was saturated with them, and because they could not wholly invent others.73

In supreme disgust, Lawrence charged John of Patmos with like offense, distortion of the Jesus of the

100

synoptic Gospels. In these short narratives Jesus is invariably presented as intensely alone, meditative, preaching renunciation, knowledge, truth, forgiveness, morality and love. This is the religion of the individual, Lawrence argued, but it provides for only one side of the dual-natured human being. It is a religion for the "aristocrats of the spirit" who "find their fulfillment and self-realisation in service."[74] Nor is it restricted to Christians; spiritual aristocrats may be found in other religions such as Buddhism, and among philosophers such as Platonists.

The "collective person," the other side of human nature, is the one to which the Christ invented by John appeals. His Christ is a power symbol utterly opposed to the "suffering servant" of the Gospels. This power-broker appeals to the poor, the uneducated collier types whom Lawrence referred to as that "vast mass" of midling souls . . . who have no aristocratic singleness and aloneness."[75] Their hope, as John's, is to destroy the spiritual nobility and set up their vindictive figure instead. John had originally appropriated the idea of the Jewish elect and the triumph of the chosen seed. That notion had only been transmogrified, as

> you can hear any night from the Salvation Army
> or in any Bethel or Pentecostal Chapel. If it
> is not Gospel, it is Revelation. It is popular
> religion, as distinct from thoughtful religion.[76]

Especially irksome to Lawrence was the loss of the the cosmos, that "vast living body, of which we are still parts."[77] From the sun, the moon, and the planets emanate powers that move us, but even before the time of Jesus the loss had begun, because the cosmos had become a revealer of fate and destiny, a prison. The Christians escaped these constrictions by denying the reality of the body completely. The result has been a denial of life itself. Lawrence saw his quest as one to return the cosmic vitality to the lives of men. To this end he wrote until his death.

In the vise of fate and destiny religions had become obsessed with death rather than life, Lawrence charged, promising an after-reward for what they could not deliver on earth.. John, however, sought power then: "He was a shameless, power-worshipping pagan Jew, gnashing his teeth over the postponement of his grand destiny."[78] In some of the most virulent language in all apocalyptic criticism Lawrence lashed out:

101

But John of Patmos must have been a strange
Jew: violent, full of the Hebrew books of the
Old Testament, but also full of all kinds of pagan knowledge, anything that would contribute to
his passion, his unbearable passion for the Second Advent, the utter smiting of the Romans with
the great sword of Christ, the trampling of mankind in the winepress of God's anger till blood
mounted to the bridles of the horses, the triumph of the rider on a white horse, greater than
any Persian king: then the rule of martyrs for
one thousand years: and then, oh then the destruction of the entire universe, and the last
Judgment. "Come Lord Jesus, Come!"[79]

So consummately spiteful were these vengeful Christians that a Jesus to pull the supreme acts of malice
recorded in Revelation would of necessity be a Christ
too incredible to contemplate.[80] Lawrence tries to restore the pristine figure:

There is Jesus--but there is also John the
Divine. There is Christian love--and there is
Christian envy. The former would "save" the
world--the latter will never be satisfied till
it has destroyed the world. They are two sides
of the same medal.[81]

The Jesus of "Christian love," however, reflects a
love which must be construed in Lawrence's own iconoclasm. It is not ascetic, spiritualized, or docetic.
Where orthodoxy has been for all of its existence concerned to explain, justify, and empower the quite
tricky idea of perfect union of flesh and spirit, of
mortality and divinity in Jesus without a sexual aspect
--yet imperfectly achieved--Lawrence makes the daring
plunge in his novel, The Man Who Died.

Few studies seem to penetrate to the core of this
novel, perhaps because twenty centuries of programming
make extremely difficult the assimilation of a sexual
Christ figure. Lawrence confronts Christian culture
with an audacious corrective for its entrenched notion
that sexuality is intrinsically evil and can have no
part in the divine economy beyond the grave. When Biblical sanctions are sought against sexuality a point is
usually made of the Gospel accounts of Jesus' denying
marriage exists in the posthumous angelic status, and
of Paul's reluctant accession to sex only as a palliative against passion. Since all New Testament proscription is based on the eagerly awaited Second Coming,[82]

which unfortunately has been inordinately delayed, sexual paranoia seems increasingly indefensible. In most recent times, certainly, sexuality as at least a humanistically approvable source of self-fulfillment and inter-sexual communication on the profoundest of human levels—as distinct from unlimited procreation—is gaining increasing adherence in the West in spite of rock-ribbed official papal condemnation, and equally restrictive notions of comparable Protestant positions. The cleavage between orthodoxy and Lawrence lies in how each views man: the essentially depraved man in need of salvation, as opposed to the essentially good man however corrupted, but in an uncorrupted universe. According to Lawrence, man is corrupted by delusions of grandeur and baseness of purpose, rather than by an inherently evil heart and body. The scenario of The Man Who Died is an attempt to justify this claim.

Upon the Gospel narrative of the crucifixion and resurrection of Jesus, Lawrence constructs a story substituting affirmation of flesh for docetic failure, physical man for spiritual abstraction, and sexual intercourse for etherealized passion. He distinguishes sharply between human love and physical sex, and eliminates difference in love among men and women toward each other and toward their own sex. At the same time, he includes sexuality expressed in self-fulfillment in his concept of the holy..

Such "blasphemy, needless to say, does not go unchallenged. Graham Hough accuses Lawrence of "pantheistic animism,"[83] a charge we have refuted in the reception of Tedlock. Hough, in turn, has been attacked by Martin Jarrett-Kerr for "depreciation" of the Christian concept of sex.[84] Hough asserts, nonetheless, that "Lawrence's polemics do nothing and can do nothing, against real Christianity,"[85] which has little to do with human love, but with another kind of love "outside the natural order altogether, offered to humanity as grace, mediated by the Incarnation, by which all things become possible, even the subsistence of charity in the human heart."[86]

Hough's rationale is the commonest of orthodox explanation for anti-humanist divine "love," but his logic is less than pristine when he applies himself specifically to phenomenological concepts with which he is not at ease: "For Christianity," he says

> the life of the flesh receives its sanction and
> purpose from a life of the spirit which is eter-

nal and transcendent. For Lawrence the life
of the spirit has its justification in en-
riching and glorifying the life of the flesh
of which it is in any case an epiphenomenon.[87]

Now an epiphenomenon grows out of a phenomenon.
The phenomenon in this case is Hough's orthodox epistemology, the opposite of Lawrence's. Plotinian dualism is Hough's obvious root. Is he, therefore, imply-
ing that Lawrence argues that the flesh generates the
spirit as the orthodox maintain the reverse is true?
If so, he has not read Lawrence well. Would not Lawrence hold that spirit and flesh are phenomena, and
each the epiphenomenon of the other? Is he not seeking
an _artistic_ synthesis--a concept few theological critics
consider, much less understand--the quest of Western
artists since Plato was first misunderstood? The scandal lies in the demotion of docetism, not its elimination, in the inclusion of sexuality in the life of the
spirit, something we reiterate that Joyce would not
countenance. A reading of The Man Who Died in Hough's
homespun phenomenal-epiphenomenal grist, and in Jarrett-
Kerr's equally stingy dispensation succeeds only in
pumping new life into T.S. Eliot's tired charge that
Lawrence was "an ignorant man" who did not know how ignorant he was, and how "often ill-informed."[88]

The Man Who Died can refute its critics itself. In
Part One the protagonist is paired with a cock whose
freedom is restricted by a tether. This portion of the
novel had originally been entitled The Escaped Cock: A
Story of the Resurrection. In a letter to Earl Brews-
ster on May 3, 1927, Lawrence stated

> I wrote a story of the Resurrection, where
> Jesus gets up and feels very sick about every-
> thing, and can't stand the old crowd any more
> --so cuts out--and as he heals up, he begins to
> find what an astonishing place the phenomenal
> world is, far more marvellous than any salva-
> tion or heaven--and thanks his stars he needn't
> have a "mission" any more. . . . [89]

The expanded version under its present title was
not published in England until 1931 after Lawrence's
death the year before. The thesis remains pure vintage
Lawrence. Having been entombed on the mistaken notion
that he was wholly dead, The Man awakens, rises, and returns to the world, a world of flesh and things he had
not known in the barren spiritual world:[90]

> He felt the cool silkiness of the young wheat
> under his feet that had been dead, and the
> roughishness of its separate life was appar-
> ent to him. At the edges of the rocks he saw
> the silky, silvery-haired buds of the scarlet
> anemone bending downwards. And they too were
> in another world. In his own world he was
> alone. These things around him were in a
> world that had never died.[91]

Feeling "the great void nausea of utter disillusion,"[92] he contrasts his lot to that of the tethered
cock and is freshly aware of having "died" for nothing.
So, he concludes that his "mission" is over.[93].

Watching the peasant's wife, Madeleine, serve him
food, contemplating her swaying breasts, The Man is
aware of sexual desire, but is unable to respond. There
is no conflict in him however; his awareness of sexuality is unsuppressed, free of any sense of restriction
or condition: "Now he knew that he had risen for the woman, or women, who knew the greater life of the body,
not greedy to give, not greedy to take, and with whom
he could mingle his body."[94] He wants to live like the
cock responding to the lure of hens, while retaining
his aloofness.[95] Having bought the cock who had freed
itself in a mighty leap from the tether, the man enters
him in a cockfight at an inn. The bird wins and The Man
leaves him to reign among the hens.[96]

What Lawrence is quite consciously doing is casting
the Gospel accounts of Jesus into the mold of earthly
man without a suggestion of supernatural power. The
cock is symbolic of radiant masculine glory which the
tether would have destroyed. The Man perceives himself
to have been like restricted. Now, like the cock, he is
free to seek his destiny among the symbols of life, the
females.

The shock of so raw a blasphemy to Christians is
Lawrence's taking orthodox insistence upon the full humanity of Jesus--the Nicean Creed--to its ultimate conclusion. If they think at all about Jesus' having had
genitals, the organs were excretory only. If he were
capable of sexual arousal--as he must surely have been
to have been fully human--he had suppressed it, and
with it his capacity for artistic creativeness so integrally related to it. If Lawrence has chosen to remind
us of that fact, his blasphemy can only be what unpleasant fact usually is, in this case a rattling of bones
in the orthodox sepulchres of buried truth.

Part Two is concerned with The Man finding sexual compatibility with a priestess of the goddess Isis who is seeking the resurrection of the god Osiris. At twenty-seven the priestess is marble-like in her virginity, although many men have desired her charms, Caesar and Anthony among them. At last she finds her god in The Man Who Died.

To buttress his conception Lawrence contrasts Isis' attitude toward sex with that of slaves. A slave girl has ritually killed four pidgeons for food. This angers a slave boy who first beats her and then takes her carnally. Witnessing the scene the priestess is indifferent. "Slaves!" she thinks contemptuously. Her preserved virginity also stores the spiritual content she must invest in the sexual act. Carnality without spirituality is as abhorrent to her as spirituality without sexuality is to The Man.

This incident also corresponds to Lawrence's distinctions in Apocalypse between the aristocrats of the spirit and the coal-mine Christians.[97] The Man Who Died provides the priestess with that aristocratic spiritual height which makes of sexual intercourse with him a completion otherwise unattainable. Lawrence's point is strikingly illumined by a passage which reveals how strategically he differed from Joyce in artistic conception of woman in the spiritual completion of man. We recall that the girl at the rivulet is transformed into a fleshly replica of the docetic Virgin of Roman Catholicism. No physical act is contemplated. The villanelle is wholly fleshless. Now contrast The Man's goddess:

> The woman of Isis was lovely to him, not so
> much in form, as in the wonderful womanly glow
> of her. Suns beyond suns had dipped her in mys-
> terious fire, the mysterious fire of a potent
> woman, and to touch her was like touching the
> sun. Best of all was her tender desire for him,
> like sunshine, so soft and still.[98]

The Man contemplates the love he had offered his disciples, a corpse, particularly to Judas:

> "This is my body--take and eat--my corpse--"

> A vivid shame went through him. "After
> all," he thought, "I wanted them to love with
> dead bodies. If I had kissed Judas with live
> love, perhaps he would never have kissed me

106

with death. Perhaps he loved me in the flesh,
and I willed that he should love me bodyless-
ly, with the corpse of love--"[99]

With each sexual act with the priestess The Man
perceives more clearly the inextricable essence of sexuality in spiritual fulfillment. The slaves, however,
plot his destruction, those who cannot reach his exalted
level of true Christianity. He rows out to sea determined never to be betrayed again.

What Lawrence has ultimately achieved is more evident in modern secular humanism. He has compelled new
dialogue and re-thinking of the ancient war between body
and soul. The psychological sciences and advanced psychiatric thought are recognizing the critical importance
of a healthy, integrated, and open sexuality to a
healthy, integrated, and open spirituality. The more
enlightened branches of the Christian faith have also
begun to accept the sexual content of the spiritual nature of man, ever influencing, but without supplanting
or dominating it in the well adjusted individual. In
the literary vein, where he is at home, Lawrence sought
the whole, healed man secure in his humanity, blessed in
his sexuality, and abounding in his spirit. Keith Sagar has discovered a passage in Lawrence's essay Books
which definitively illumines Lawrence's convictions:

> I know the greatness of Christianity; it is
> a past greatness. I know that, but for those
> early Christians, we should never have emerged
> from the chaos and hopeless disaster of the Dark
> Ages. If I had lived in the year 400, pray God,
> I should have been a true and passionate Chris-
> tian. The adventurer.

> But now I live in 1924, and the Christian
> venture is done. The adventure is gone out of
> Christianity. We must start on a new venture
> towards God.[100]

EUGENE O'NEILL: THE TORMENTED AGONISTES

In Eugene O'Neill we have the dramatic prototype of the American literary reaction to currents affecting his English and Irish contemporaries. Like Joyce he was a renegade Roman Catholic at a time when being a Christian was less than of historic moment. He was, notwithstanding, unmistakably religious, a painfully limited agonistes wrestling with a dark angel. Like Jacob's less forbidding one, O'Neill's could not be thrown, but unlike Jacob's, O'Neill's celestial contender sought to ground him and bury an angelic heel in his mortal face. O'Neill's plays reflect the point at which his literary, philosophical, and religious motifs clashed irreconcilably.

A question arises as to his place in literary theory. Commentators tend to label him according to the play which impresses them most.[101] Glicksberg, for example, considers him a "thoroughgoing naturalist" with "a tragically split personality."[102] Sophus K. Winther can say that O'Neill is concerned with the "tragic end" of men's lives, which result from seeking more than life can give. But he denies that O'Neill fulfills the true purpose of tragedy, our purgation through sympathy with the hero's suffering.[103] It is literarily uncertain, then, how we should react to the helplessly crippled playwright unable to hold a pen, waiting for death in a bleak hotel room in Boston. It is clear that he cannot be a hero and a naturalist too. They are the opposites of each other.

At the heart of classical tragedy is predetermining resistless divine power wreaking havoc upon the utterly helpless mortal. The purgative drama lies in how the hero struggles, not in why. The inscrutability of why is the very reason for tragedy The hero's dignity, honor, and courage are measured by his reception of his destiny, by his stark hopelessness. As early as Homer the gods themselves could not alter fate. During the climactic battle of the Iliad those who went down to battle personally for the Trojans knew in advance that they would lose. In equally unremitting straits, Oedipus was compelled to ponder his eternal disposition determined before his birth. Without moral choice in the

toils of the most twisted of Greek irony, he personally
accepted an impersonally imposed primordial guilt more
vicariously demanded than that with which the Christians, with their equally impersonal concept of original sin, saddled the whole unsuspecting human race. Yet
at the heart of classical tragedy, as seen in Antigone,
a fundamental moral order is implicit, which, while it
discounted the individual, contained some primitive aspects of a humanly justifiable cosmogony. Fate was not
entirely irresponsible; it simply was not human. The
crux, therefore, of pure tragedy is the conflict between
the fateful and the human. What Greek tragedy could not
do, but what O'Neill wanted to do but did not know how,
was to humanize fate.

In the hands of Shakespeare classical tragedy was
modified into a means of returning cosmic order disturbed by the wilful acts of men. In Hamlet Claudius'
murder of the king set in motion a chain of events which
required Hamlet's death to right the things rotten in
the state of Denmark. This element of personal responsibility entered by way of Christian replacement of the
Greeks' impersonal fate with a humanly conceivable, but
not humanized, God. The Protestant Reformation would
personalize God in a sentimentalized individualism unrecognizable to any literary concept of tragedy. As
George Steiner argues, classical tragedy cannot exist
in a modern world where the outrages of inscrutably
hostile predeterminism have given way to the cry for
justice, a concept also wholly unknown to tragedy. Indeed, Steiner declares that tragedy died with Shakespeare. The debate is vigorous.[104]

But the Christians who expropriated a wrathful and
vengeful God from the Hebrews, a buffer for whom they
invented the mollifying, meek and submissive Son, did
not humanize him until intensifying anthropocentrism
compelled them to do so. What Christianity had purported was a cure for tragedy in ultimate redemption in another life; but not for worth or desert, but for God's
will, yet as inscrutably non-human as Greek fate. In
spite of the energetic humanistic enterprises of much
of organized religion, the orthodox sternly inveigh
against modernized doctrine. Salvation is limited.
All men are not saved. Salvation is a grace, not a
right. The noise level of the current re-proclamation
of this grim message across the United States rivals
the din of the Tower of Babel. The whipping boy of
this campaign is the monstrous Anti-Christ, "secular
humanism," so bizarre and incredible an evil as to
bear little discernible resemblance to the dogged march

of man toward greater knowledge and appreciation of himself, his creatureliness, and his place among other men
and the universe, which we have quite historically referred to in this study as humanism also, secular and
otherwise. What meanness can inhere in a literary use
of the term will become manifest when we reach T.S. Eliot. But to conclude that O'Neill's plays mark him as
a tragedian, or has having tragic aspirations is to misread the whole history of the concept in Western literature.

     Similarly, to think of O'Neill as a naturalist re-
quires more critical footwork than that supplied by
Glicksberg. As we have previously shown, naturalism is
a complex vision, with varying emphases depending upon
where one encounters it. The American naturalist is
basically an optimist, tracing the ills of mankind to
causes within his control. No optimism is detectable
in O'Neill that he does not ultimately repudiate--Days
Without End. Neither naturalist nor tragedian, he is
neither Christian. What he sought was the Greek spirit
as a pristine pre-Christian reflection of fundamental
human arch-types embodying primarily human values. Instead of focusing upon the mysterious will of God, he
concerned himself with man himself. Consequently, Leonard Chabrowe is right to take with some reservations Joseph Wood Krutch's report of a statement made by O'Neill:
"Most modern plays are concerned with the relation between man and man, but that does not interest me at all.
I am interested only in the relation between man and
God."105

     O'Neill's God was stripped of American Puritan par-
anoia and misanthropy, of Roman Catholic magic and mystery, and of promises of heavenly glory after the misery of earth. What God there remained eventually became whatever man found within himself, humanized from
within, with no cosmic relations, no power to determine
ultimate result. This, then, is a humanism which, by
concept and definition, is not impersonally directed nor
guided by personalized external control. There is neither fate nor primordial sin. What makes O'Neill's
approach mystical is his rejection of secular, scientific, or materialistic substitutes for God-consciousness which permeates himself and all of his plays. But
he was not always successful in dramatizing his obsession.

     Strange Interlude, first produced in 1926-27, has
been often cited for being anti-romantic,106 Freudian,107
naturalistic,108 and "tragic."109 The most often dis-

111

cussed passage in the play is Nina's Act-Two declaration
of alienation from the male image of God:

> The mistake began when God was created in a male
> image. Of course, women would see Him that way,
> but men should have been gentlemen enough, remem-
> bering their mothers, to make God a woman! But
> the God of Gods--the Boss--has always been a man.
> That makes life so perverted, and death so unnatur-
> al. We should have imagined life as created in
> the birth-pain of God the Mother. Then we should
> understand why we, Her children, have inherited
> pain, for we would know that our life's rhythm
> beats from Her great heart, torn with the agony
> of love and birth. And we would feel that death
> meant reunion with Her, a passing back into Her
> substance, blood of Her blood again, peace of Her
> peace! (*Marsden has been listening to her fascin-*
> *atedly. She gives a strange little laugh*) Now
> wouldn't that be more logical and satisfying than
> having God a male whose chest thunders with ego-
> tism and is too hard for tired heads and thorough-
> ly comfortless? Wouldn't it, Charlie?[110]

Only when she is carrying Ned's son, with whom she
intends to deceive her husband, Sam Evans, does she feel
a God relationship, but then only with God as mother.
In her soliloquy opening Act Five, she exclaims

> I am living a dream within the great dream of the
> tide . . . breathing in the tide I dream and
> breathe back my dream into the tide . . . suspend-
> ed in me . . . no whys matter . . . there is no
> why . . . I am a mother . . . God is a Mother . . .
> [Ellipses are the author's][111]

The precise point, obviously, is the desire to humanize God without a docetic virgin mother, as warmly
personal as foetal movement in the normally impregnated
woman. The depth of Nina's yearning was never reached
by the pietistic effort to personalize God because it
insisted upon the God of wrath whose demands remained
little less terrifying than those He made on Abraham
and then recanted. The utter inhumanity of the Divine
male vanity was wholly incompatible with a God to whom
Nina could relate in private meaningful experience.

Reflecting, of course, O'Neill's own artistic dilemma, Nina is a dramatic example of the contradictory
elements out of which the playwright carved his characters. The indifference of the Christian God, an early

tenant of American naturalism--see Stephen Crane's po-
etry--is nullified by Nina's insistent rejection of the
contours of faith in something other than the physical
which is absolutely required to give her drives the
meaning which she so fervently sought. Her wholly amoral attitudes toward limitless affairs, abortion, deception of her husband, and her son rob her image of God
as mother of any meaningful spiritual dimension. She
cries out for God but denies Him access. She yearns
for spiritual at-one-ment, but rejects its elements.
She is obsessed with men, but hates the male image of
God. She approaches the remainder of life as a void of
sense satiety and eternal lapse of meaning, but seeks
in sexually neutral Charles Marsden a surcease of the
inner warfare between the male and female components of
her sexuality. Thus, how do we literarily classify her?
Had she been a naturalistic heroine her dilemma would
point outward to external cause and cure. The mechanistic universe alone would determine that. But neither
Nina nor her creator was a mechanist. Had she been
clearly a product of her Freudian components her spiritual hunger would have dissipated into arch-symbols of
parental fixations, and the resolution of her fear of
male domination in something more Freudianly adequate
than Charlie. Had she been profoundly in search of the
religious experience as integrally spiritual as phenomenal, her gropings and experiments with life would point
to something more than the nothingness she accepts at
the end of the play.

     The answer lies, certainly, in O'Neill's unsure
grasp of his materials, particularly the theological.
At this stage of his career he knew what God was not,
not what God was. But every word he wrote was drenched
in God-consciousness, a matter which makes it, therefore, impossible to place O'Neill, himself, and his dramas in any neat literary category. He is <u>par excellence</u>
the example of Tillich's observation of what happens
when the secular and the religious worlds are separated,
and neither is complete without the other.[112] Nevertheless, the play was highly successful on the stage, the
audiences more compelled by its daring realism and dra-
maturgical psychology than by the inherent weakness of
theology.

     In <u>Dynamo</u> O'Neill's uncertainty is considerably
more pronounced in his further effort to weld Freudian
psychology to religious search. Nowhere in his plays
is it more evident that O'Neill cannot make the two
jell. But <u>Dynamo</u> seems motivated by O'Neill's general
theme of the death of the old God and failure of the

113

substitutes.   As originally conceived this play was to
be part of a trilogy which would include the subsequent
Days Without End and a never written sequel to be called
It Cannot Be Mad.113   As Travis Bogard notes. Dynamo
seems suggested by Chapter XXV, "The Dynamo and the Virgin," of The Education of Henry Adams.   There, Adams
described the dynamo as the life force of America, as
contrasted to that found in the earlier European worship of the Virgin woman.   It was not her beauty that
attracted followers: "She was goddess because of her
force; she was the animated dynamo; she was reproduc-
tion--the greatest and most mysterious of all energies;
all she needed was to be fecund."114   In O'Neill the
substitution of the dynamo itself for God worked no better than the repudiated Virgin cult.   The conflict between science and religion was not resolved in favor of
either.   Indeed, the mother-God symbolization of Strange
Interlude is carried to its most destructive ambivalence
in Dynamo.   The elements themselves of Dynamo are in irreconcilable conflict.   Note the following scenario:

The Reverend Hutchins Light is the Fundamentalist
Puritan whose God of wrath is the ugliest in all Chris-
tendom.   Ramsay Fife is the atheist who believes in the
generating power of the dynamo, the source of all life.
His wife, May, thinks of it as almost humanly intelligent.   Reuben, the son of Hutchins Light and Amelia
Light, rejects his father's awful religion and his
mother's jealousy of Ada, the daughter of Ramsay and
May.   He chooses the dynamo, only to shoot and kill Ada
over it, and to immolate himself on it.   The result is
a pastiche of Freudian Oedipal symbolism clearly inti-
mating incestuous desires, Virgin-mother religious
yearning, sexual guilt, and the spiritual need of a God
to replace the dead one.   It becomes impossible to determine whether Reuben kills Ada because of doctrinaire
Freudian imputation of sexual desire for his mother
which he has transferred to the dynamo in ritualized
symbolization; whether his self-destruction is an act of
insanity brought about by the rejection of his father's
repugnant religion--which then becomes a left-handed affirmation of the father's old God; or whether the play
is actually a nihilistic affirmation of nothingness.
The scene at the end of Reuben stretched against the dynamo as though on a cross can be either supreme mockery
or a shattering damnation of Christianity's chief symbol.
Or it could be the ultimate sacrifice of idiocy.   What,
for example, does Reuben actually mean as he prays to
the dynamo, building to the point of killing Ada?

Mother! . . . have mercy on me! . . . I hate her

114

now! [Ada] . . . as much as you hate her! . . .
give me one more chance! . . . what can I do
to get you to forgive me? . . . tell me! . . .
yes! . . . I hear you, Mother! . . . and then
you'll forgive me? . . . and I can come to you?
. . . [Ellipses are the playwright's][115]

If he has been searching for God-consciousness in the
play O'Neill's framing of the search in Freudian terms
renders it an absurdity. The very basis of Freudianism
is the non-existence of a spiritual God. Where Henry
Adams knew what he was about in his dynamo-Virgin concept, O'Neill was not so sure about his. Recognizing
this himself, the playwright called the play "a step
backward."[116] Produced in 1929, it was closed after its
required fifty subscription performances. During the
next five years O'Neill completely revised it, but it
has never been really finished.[117]

It remained for Days Without End to make some theological sense, this time in a capitulation to orthodoxy that O'Neill later repudiated in his own criticism
of the play. He reaffirmed the Nietzschean Dionysius,[118]
and at the approach of death refused a priest. So hard
did he fight against writing an orthodox ending that it
took seven drafts, including four complete versions, to
arrive at an ending of salvation. The play, then, cannot be taken as a revelation of spiritual progress, but
as theater designed to gain favor with the audience,
particularly the Roman Catholic, and with the Roman
Church hierarchy. He was not altogether successful.
When the miracle of faith and resurrection occur, after
earlier versions ending with realistic death, one just
does not believe it.

The drama concerns John Loving, an O'Neill version
of Faust, who is seen on stage as two selves, one simply
called John, played by an actor showing him handsome,
worldly, cynical; and the other called Loving, played
by another actor wearing a mask--supposing to be invisible to the other players--showing the ugly side, what
O'Neill's stage directions describe as *the death mask
of a* John *who has died with a sneer of scornful mockery
on his lips.*"[119]

As a boy John was devout. He even considered becoming a priest, that is, until both of his parents
died in the flu epidemic. In spite of his fervent prayers no miracle occurred. The effect was swift: "He saw
God as deaf and merciless--a Deity Who returned hate for
love and revenged Himself upon those who trusted Him!"[120]

115

Cursing God, he promised his soul to the Devil. Father
Matthew Baird, the orthodox foil, saw in John's rebellion the threat of the "isms"--atheism, socialism, anar-
chism, Marxism. John turned to Eastern religions, then
to Greek philosophy and numerology followed by mechanistic evolutionism. Finally, he found everything he
had been searching for in Elsa. Romantic love became
his spiritual panacea, and he was happy for the first
time since his parents' death.

But as Bogard well notes,[121] nearly three-fourths
of the play is taken up with John's vacillating spiritual condition. A thinly disguised autobiographical
novel which John is writing nearly destroys his new happiness, but it becomes the instrument by which he is returned to spiritual health. Through the plot of the
novel Elsa learns of a real adultery which John has committed with her friend, Lucy. In a pique she rushes
out into the rain. Pneumonia results along with a wish
to die. Dogged by his Mephistophelian alter-ego's
sneers, John is pursued by Father Baird quoting from
Francis Thompson's "Hound of Heaven." Desperate that
he is about to lose Elsa he turns helplessly to prayer.
And lo, the miracle comes. Elsa forgives him and recov-
ers.

In the last scene John is metamorphosed into a newly born saint full of thanksgiving and abounding grace
at the foot of a life-size Crucifix in an old church.
Loving goes down cursing God, but gasping out a final
prayer for forgiveness of his damned soul. John and
Father Baird celebrate the death of death, and the
deathlessness of love: "Life laughs with God's love
again!" John exults. "Life laughs with love!"[122]

If this be the closest O'Neill ever came to rapprochement with orthodoxy, his most successful religious
play from a literary standpoint was written earlier than
those just discussed. It stars that favorite Biblical
character of writers, Lazarus. The play, Lazarus Laugh-
ed, was produced only twice, but it succeeds because it
does not leave its realm of pure phantasy in which symbols dance pristinely about, unfettered by squalid
Freudianism. Nor does O'Neill attempt a lyrical return
to the one true faith. His Lazarus is radically different from that of Yeats, who, we recall, was angry because Jesus had disturbed his eternal surcease in death.
Yeats mocked the idea of a Jesus and a resurrection
which could bring no more than what D.H. Lawrence's
man who died discovered.

<u>Lazarus Laughed</u> is built upon the inevitability of
death, the exact reverse of traditional meaning. Death
is for the orthodox the end and the beginning, at once
the most dread of all certain fates and the promise of
a glory only hinted at in the most ecstatic argot of
apocalypses. Its awfulness for all is its inescapabil-
ity, its pervasive reality looming over the brightest
birth. Thus, the single most powerful promise of orthodoxy is resurrection of flesh, and the justice and desert so woefully absent from this life. The single most
powerful element of the human psyche is fear, that "conscience" of Hamlet's that "does make cowards of us all."
Without fear all punitive religions would collapse to-
morrow, particularly Christianity. Death would not only
lose its sting, but the whole rubric designed to keep
the faithful in line would disappear. Without fear, the
need to hate, to envy, to destroy would vanish, and the
whole of worldly power structures would crumble.

What would a truly revolutionary apocalyptic vision
see? How would it compare with, or contrast to, that of
Patmos John, D.H. Lawrence, W.B. Yeats? O'Neill endowed
his Lazarus, destined to die twice, with a vision which
robbed death of its doubled horror: laughter, and every
other quality the opposite of orthodoxy. There is no
God in wrath, no expiatory sacrifice, no insurmountable
pain, and of course, no fear of dying. Men are their
own miscreants, mete out their own fates, and in an inability to reach Lazarus' exaltation they insure their
own destruction by their own fear.

As Chabrowe ably discerns,[123] O'Neill's Lazarus is
fused of Dionysius, the Greek fertility god; Christ,
the Christian God, and Zarathustra, the Nietzschean superman. The fusion works. It spells out O'Neil's thesis: God is within man and cannot die as long as life is
ever recurrent in man, overcoming pain, suffering, and
death by dint of his own everlasting power of return.
In the first act, having been resurrected by Jesus to
delight in laughter at death, Lazarus is maliciously as-
sailed. To the frenzied shouts of the incited mob, Lazarus speaks, commanding deep silence:

> You forget! You forget the God in you! You wish
> to forget! Remembrance would imply the high duty
> to live as a son of God--generously!--with love!
> --with pride!--with laughter! This is too glori-
> ous a victory for you, too terrible a loneliness!
> Easier to forget, to become only a man, the son
> of a woman, to hide from life against her breast,
> to whimper your fear to her resigned heart and be

comforted by her resignation! To live by denying life! (*Then exhortingly*) Why are
your eyes always either fixed on the ground
in weariness of thought, or watching one another
in suspicion? Throw your gaze upward! To Eternal Life! To the fearless and the deathless! The
everlasting! To the stars! (*He stretches out his
arms to the sky--then suddenly points*) See! A
new star has appeared! It is the one that shone
over Bethlehem! (*His voice becomes a little
bitter and mocking*) The Master of Peace and Love
has departed this earth. Let all stars be for
you henceforth symbols of Saviors--Sons of God
who appeared on worlds like ours to tell the saving truth to ears like yours, inexorably deaf!
(*Then exaltedly*) But the greatness of Saviors is
that they may not save! The greatness of Man is
that no god can save him--until he becomes a god![124]

Had O'Neill consistently explored his Lazarus
theme, more remarkable than any others of his, his critics could have been more uniform in their estimate and
categorization of his work. Never quite able himself
to accept the optimism of Lazarus, O'Neill went on to
write the agonized plays of doubt and uncertainty, of
final resolution in the wait for death as a mere mortal,
Gordian-knotted in his spirit and in the lineaments of
his wracked and diseased body. His legacy, nonetheless,
is the power of the spirit over the mind. Even when it
cannot win, it does not lose.

DYLAN THOMAS: THE CHRISTIAN PAGAN

As we have seen, poetry is the art of evoking what otherwise may be incapable of expression, a means of communicating a reality for which words are inadequate. Thus, "A poem should be wordless," wrote Archibald Mac-Leish in _Ars Poetica_. Imagery, then, is the soul of poetry, something which sometimes has escaped as important a modern poet as W.H. Auden.[125] A "wordless" poem is one in which the senses are caught up so vividly that the words disappear in the image. Since the "modern" poet, as distinct from the traditional poet, experiences old significance in a radically new way, he may call upon the breadth of his knowledge to evoke it, creating sense patterns in image sequences and juxtapositions defiant of the expectable, the ordinary, the settled. What Dylan Thomas does with the imagerial structure and evocative intent of Milton's great ode of seventeenth-century religious experience, "On the Morning of Christ's Nativity," is exemplary. The first stanza of Thomas' poem "There Was a Savior" reads as follows:

> There was a saviour
> Rarer than radium
> Commoner than water, crueller than truth;
> Children kept from the sun
> Assembled at his tongue
> To hear the golden note turn in a groove,
> Prisoners of wishes locked in their eyes
> In the jails and studies of his keyless smiles.[126]

Milton wrote in the first stanza of his ode

> This is the Month, and this the happy morn
> Wherein the Son of Heav'ns eternal King
> Of wedded Maid, and Virgin Mother born,
> Our great redemption from above did bring;
> For so the holy sages once did sing,
> That he our deadly forfeit should release,
> And with his Father work us a perpetual peace.[127]

The contrast startled more than one contemporary. Dylan is too obscure, said Robert Graves and Vernon Watkins, the latter Thomas' friend and correspondence

119

editor. "It's nice work if you can get it," quipped Peter De Vries. "I don't get it." But Thomas also had his admirers. John L. Sweeney thought him an erudite scholar. Thomas coyly demurred.[128] Henry Treece and the other three "Apocalyptics," revolting from T.S. Eliot and W.H. Auden, placed Thomas among their top artistic choices. He showed little gratitude, dismissing the Apocalyptics as of little talent.[129] But Elder Olson's appraisal is incredible by its very unlikelihood. Thomas, he said, was a profound astrologist, a master of the zodiac. Olson set out a complete zodiacal chart by which to explicate in particular Thomas' religious sonnets.[130] As Tindall notes, such ascriptions to Thomas are nonsense. The poet probably learned his astrology as most people learn it, by reading charts on themselves and their friends.[131] In any event, reasonable estimates are available both on Thomas' obscurantism and brilliance. In his study of the religious sonnets. H. H. Kleinman[132] comments on the interpretations of Dame Edith Sitwell,[133] Sir Herbert Grierson,[134] Robert Lowell,[135] and Leslie Fiedler.[136]

When Henry Treece contrasted Thomas' lack of a "central image" to the poetry of Norman Cameron, Thomas replied in an often cited letter that it is "not my method to move concentrically round a central image. A poem by Cameron," he went on to say, "needs no more than one image; it moves around one idea, from one logical point to another, making a full circle." But

> A poem by myself needs a host of images because
> its centre is a host of images. I make one im-
> age--thqugh "make" is not the word, I let, per-
> haps, an image be "made" emotionally in me and
> then apply to it what intellectual and critical
> forces I possess--let it breed another, let that
> image contradict the first, make of the third im-
> age bred out of the dangling over the formal lim-
> its, and dragged the poem into another; the war-
> ring stream ran over the insecure barriers the
> fullstop armistice was pulled and twisted ragged-
> ly on into a conflicting series of dots and
> dashes. [sic] [137]

Thomas' letters are full of unintelligible dross, and it would require an editor of immense devotion to eliminate it for an edition of Thomas' thoughts we would treasure. What he meant in the above paragraph however, is a bit clearer several paragraphs later:

Each image holds within it, the seeds of its

> own destruction, and my dialectical method, as
> I understand it, is a constant building up and
> breaking down of the images that come out of
> the central seed, which is itself destructive
> at the same time.[138]

This theory is clearly demonstrated in "There Was a Saviour." It is a parody of Milton's ode, which Thomas described as "my austere poem in Milton measure."[139] The first four stanzas of Milton's ode are in iambic pentameter, with a rhyme scheme of AB ABB CC. The couplet at the end of each of the four stanzas adds a particular musical effect. Throughout the remainder of the poem, a "Hymn" of twenty-seven stanzas, Milton emphasizes the harmony which God brings to man, nature, and universe through a union of all three in the child.

Thomas' poem has no rhyme, relying upon assonance and alliteration, and no recognizable meter. His images are piled in contradiction upon each other in lines indented the reverse of Milton's. The saviour is "Rarer than radium," but "Commoner than water". Thomas is sneering. Babies born of virgins can be no commoner than radium, but the saviour's ubiquity in culture makes him "Commoner than water." He is crueller than truth" in purporting what he does not deliver, the "truth" being that he cannot deliver. In "Children kept from the sun / Assembled at his tongue" is a disjuncture of nature and the saviour. The sun is light and warmth. The "golden note" of the saviour is a sarcastic reference, evoking the mechanical sound produced from the "groove" of a recording, holding the children as "prisoners" who cannot escape "the jails and studies of his keyless smiles" to seek the "wishes locked in their eyes". The remainder of the poem mines a like poetic vein, in humanistic outrage like that in Yeats--whom Thomas regarded as his greatest contemporary--at divine inhumanity. Thomas could not accept the Calvinist depreciation of man upon which the genius of Milton is built. Tindall points to "There Was a Saviour" as proof that Thomas was no Christian, but an ex-believer who liked everybody but believers.[140]

However, the ten religious sonnets written in 1936, four years previous to "There Was a Saviour," raise the question which the latter poem dismisses. Indeed, Kleinman finds the last sonnet "a spiralling ascent of faith."[141] Even with his astrological impression Olson concludes that the sonnets are committed to a Christian interpretation.[142] What they are, certainly, depends upon the interpretive presuppositions of the reader.

Precisely because Thomas evokes "modern" religious experience, certainty of interpretation is impossible. What is affirmed, however, is the validity of individual experience. Uniformity of interpretation requires invariable poetic experience. Monolithic reality has not presented itself to the modern poet. Thomas insisted that his poetry was "the record of [his] individual struggle from darkness toward some measure of light."[143] To understand the religious sonnets, therefore, as to understand all of Thomas, is to understand the experience out of which they grew.

Very "un-British" in his eruptions of spirit and flesh, Thomas was born in Wales in 1914, soon to become a roustabout in waterfront bars and a pitcher of obscenities as quick and as compelling as his poetic flights.[144] Chubby and manic depressive as he grew older, he presented no somber O'Neill-like grappler with dark angels of fate. Instead, he overcompensated for his weakness in blustery defiance of the challenges of life. Constantine Fitzgibbon, his biographer, describes his heavy drinking as partly a means of hiding his excessive timidity, of enabling him to play the role demanded of him at the moment. It was also his elixir for a more kaleidoscopic vision of the world, in much the same way that laudanum had been the stimulant for Coleridge. He was also regressively infantile, unable to handle money, and the routine matters of daily life such as the laundry and the bureaucrat.[145] He was even thought to be a thief.[146] Such a man is not likely to find Milton's ascetic aesthetic evocative of his own spirituality. Obligated to many poets--Joyce, Yeats, Hopkins, even Eliot and Auden whose proper British intellectualism he disdained--his poetry reflected a man for whom orthodoxy was a "spent lie."[146] John Malcolm Brinnin reports that Thomas told him that his problems were "in praise of God's world by a man who doesn't believe in God."[148] In the total complex of Thomas' poetry "God" must be interpreted as restricted in meaning to Christian identification of Him as their "Saviour-Son-God amalgam. Thomas' own concept of a "God" involved a mystical power by which the poet sought to find his measure of light. Having read all of the poems of D.H. Lawrence, he was nevertheless unable to divest himself as cleanly, as Lawrence might have wished, of the trappings of an earlier lower-class form of Christianity. In spite of himself, he remained more religious than not. However, Stuart Holroyd presents him as a pantheist,[149] seeing Thomas' religious ideals as those of primitive man before moral concepts and religious experience became synonymous in pedestrian religiosity. Since pantheism has

122

little in common with the Christian God. Holroyd denies Thomas a "religion," restricting him to "the belief or feeling that all creation has a common identity because all things are manifestations of God."[150]

Of course, such a narrowed definition of religion flies in the face of our pains to validate religious experience as a phenomenon unlimited to the inexact science of descriptive labelling. What makes Thomas religious is his ultimate concern. "There Was a Saviour" castigates dead orthodoxy, and heralds the struggle toward a new experience of cosmic identity. Where Eliot had declared himself a royalist, classicist, and Anglo-Catholic,[151] Thomas proclaimed upon arrival in New York City in 1950 that "First, I am a Welshman. Second, I am a drunkard. Third, I am a heterosexual."[152] The latter declaration may have been inspired by the fact that among his contemporaries homosexuality was abundantly represented: W.H. Auden, whose homosexual doggerel would shame latrine walls; Christopher Isherwood, who has since published full disclosure of his sexual proclivities; Stephen Spender, who was a part of Isherwood's group; Benjamin Britten, whose music nevertheless testifies to his genius. Fitzgibbon states that Thomas' associated homosexuals with pretense, rather than talent; sobriety, curiously, rather than libertinism--the latter more to Thomas' poetic style and idea of the mode of talent; and ultra-conservative views rather than the free spirit. But to put a homosexual at ease, Fitzgibbon continues, Thomas could aver a homosexual encounter with a Member of Parliament, but most likely apocryphally.[153]

If in these attitudes the Christian God is in little evidence, the humanistic identification is distinct. They further explain to a large extent why Thomas' critics are in such disarray. Where Tindall summarizes the poetry as principally concerned with birth, life, and death on a cosmic, sexual, and aesthetic level,[154] Holroyd denies it metaphysical depth.[155] Disparity is dramatic in critical approach to the religious sonnets. The first question is whether the ten poems are sequential. Francis Scarfe, Olson, and Kleinman hold that they are. Marshall Stearns finds them discrete. Tindall opts for the single theme of Thomas himself, with all of his images referring to himself.[156] All may agree, however, that the poems resemble the traditional sonnet only in their length of fourteen lines each. The interpretive chaos can be illustrated by what Tindall, Kleinman, and Olson make of Sonnet I:

Altarwise by owl-light in the half-way house
The gentleman lay graveward with his furies;
Abaddon in the hangnail, cracked from Adam,
And, from his fork, a dog among the fairies,
The atlas-eater with a jaw for news,
Bit out the mandrake with to-morrow's scream.
Then, penny-eyed, that gentleman of wounds,
Old cock from nowheres and the heaven's egg,
With bones unbuttoned to the half-way winds,
Hatched from the windy salvage on one leg,
Scraped at my cradle in a walking word
That night of time under the Christward shelter:
I am the long world's gentleman, he said,
And share my bed with Capricorn and Cancer.[157]

Altarwise by owl-light

Tindall: The dim light in the place where an al-
           tar usually appears.

Kleinman: Suggesting a ritual offering and the
           position of the sacrificial victim at
           dusk, further suggesting imminence of
           a mysterious happening—based on a
           transformation of the Nativity story
           as recorded in Luke.

Olson: The sun moving southward at night to-
           ward the constellation Alta (hence
           "Altarwise").

half-way house

Tindall: Womb or half-way through life. Could
           also be the Eucharist or a housel.

Kleinman: Possibly an indefinite point in infin-
           ity where the descending world is
           poised half way between Heaven and
           earth. May also be the manger in
           which Christ was born, or the Incar-
           nation itself.

Olson: The autumnal equinox.

The gentleman lay graveward

Tindall: An unidentified gentleman in either a
           womb or a tomb. Possibly Thomas' fa-
           ther daring his fate by begetting a
           son or Thomas himself.

124

Kleinman: An unknown sacrificial victim--God?
              Christ? Abaddon? All three?

Olson: The Constellation Hercules declining
              in the west.

his furies

Tindall: Literal Greek mythology, sometimes
              confused by Thomas with the three
              fates.

Kleinman: Chthonic daughters of the night.

Olson: Scorpius (the Scorpion), Draco (the
              Dragon) and the Serpens Caput (Head
              of the Serpent in Ophiucus, the
              Snake Holder) following the Constel-
              lation Hercules in his westward de-
              cline.

Abaddon

Tindall: Abaddon, the Appolyon (destroyer), or
              angel of the abyss of Rev. 9:11.

Kleinman: A descendant of Adam brought into the
              world by Adam's sin.

Olson: Identified only as to his description
              in Rev.

the hangnail cracked from Adam

Tindall: A cross or phallus involving both Adam
              and the devil.

Kleinman: Genealogy and prophecy--Christ (the
              cuticle) descends from Adam (the fin-
              ger) to hang from the Cross. A typi-
              cal Thomas pun (echoing the phallic
              image seen by Tindall).

Olson: The mortalness of the constellation
              Hercules possessing Adam's destructive
              and perditious flesh.

his fork

Tindall: The gentleman's crotch.

Kleinman: Abaddon's loins, after the bifurcated

root of the mandrake.

Olson: Death biting out the "seed" of the
             world, figured in "fork" representing
             the loin, and the mandrake represent-
             ing the phallus.

a dog among fairies

Tindall: Dylan himself among his contemporar-
             ies.

Kleinman: To be understood in the context of the
             mandrake legend.

Olson: The dog is Cerberus; death is the only
             reality. Fairies represent our fan-
             cies.

The atlas-eater with a jaw for news,
Bit out the mandrake with to-morrow's scream.

Tindall: Thomas, himself, as a future reporter
             for his hometown paper with a "jaw for
             news" and tomorrow's story ("scream").
             Thomas is the "creative devil-dog-
             mandrake" who is born. With a son's
             birth being a father's death the
             young son (dog) bites out the father's
             job (mandrake) and takes over (re-
             ports the news).

Kleinman: The mandrake legend heralds the birth
             of Christ. The "scream" announces it.
             The forked root of the mandrake made
             it appear as though a small human
             form. In medieval times it was
             thought to promote fertility and to
             ease pain. When it was uprooted it
             emitted a scream fatal to anyone with-
             in hearing distance. Therefore, a dog
             was used to pull the mandrake from the
             ground, by tying him to the root and
             enticing him--at a safe distance--with
             a piece of food. As the dog lurched
             forward, pulling the mandrake free, it
             was killed by the mandrake's scream.
             These aspects of the legend symbolize
             the Nativity and the Crucifixion. The
             newspaper jargon is simply poetic fig-
             uration of the Christian events. (un-

126

like Tindall, Kleinman cannot decipher who the "fairies" are, wondering whether they are sexless creatures among Abaddon's group, and whether they bear a relationship to the furies.)

Olson: Cerberus, who guards Tartarus and symbolizes death, has three heads, one for each age of man. His biting out the mandrake symbolizes his biting out the seed from man's loins. Cerberus' "jaw for news" comes from his ability to smell out the seed. All of this is astronomically represented in Canis Major, the Greater Dog rising while the constellation Hercules and the head of Draco set.

penny-eyed, that gentleman of wounds

Tindall: An emasculated gentleman dead with pennies on his eyes, like the crucified Christ.

Kleinman: A conventional figure of death.

Olson: Hercules at dawn is dead, appearing as a ghost or dream of a ghost.

Old-cock from nowheres and the heaven's egg

Tindall: The wounded gentleman as the crucified Christ, and the father, are also the son conceived in an egg and hatched. The "Old cock from nowheres" is God, Jesus, father, and son, as well as D.H. Lawrence's escaped cock.

Kleinman: Grows out of an old legend about a cock which began crowing "Christus natus est" at the birth of Jesus. Thomas transforms the cock into a symbol of the descent of the Holy Spirit, usually symbolized by a dove. The "old cock from nowheres and the heaven's egg" is in Kleinman's words "a celestial hobo with a vague genealogy."

Olson: Hercules, the sun, mockingly put.

127

With bones unbuttoned to the half-way winds,
Hatched from the windy salvage on one leg,
Scraped at my cradle in a walking word
That night of time under the Christward shelter:

Tindall: "With bones unbuttoned" has phallic content to allow for the scraping at the cradle. The "half-way winds," taken with "on one leg," represents a weathercock and Christ on the Cross. The "walking word" is Christ as Word. and the poet himself. As God is one with Jesus, so the poet is one with his father whom he has killed and replaced. The "night of time" is the womb, and "Christward shelter" is the "half-way house" for the long (phallic) gentleman.

Kleinman: The "Disney-like molted old cock," writes Kleinman, transformed into the Holy Spirit, is that which stands on one leg at the cradle. It is Christmas Eve, the "Walking word" being the announcement of the cock's identity.

Olson: Hercules is dead, his "bones unbuttoned to the half-way winds." The bones are also at the mercy of the equinoctial gales. The position of the constellation Hercules explains "on one leg". The poet's hometown of Swansea, Wales figures in "Scraped at my cradle," as the constellations appear at this latitude. The "walking word" is Hercules in constellational motion speaking to the poet.

I am the long world's gentleman, he said,
And share my bed with Capricorn and Cancer.

Tindall: This gentleman is both father and son, as suggested by a pun on the sun. Consubstantiation of father and son in Heaven means consubstantiation of father and son on earth. On earth father and son create by the "Word" (poetry). A son is born, as Tindall puts it, "a long fellow to 'the fellow father'".

> Kleinman: The gentleman's identification with the sun and all the slain and resurrected gods, including Christ, who are buried in darkness and rise in light.
>
> Olson: Hercules identifying himself as the gentleman. As the sun he shares his bed with Capricorn and Cancer because these zones constitute the limits of his direct rays during the course of a year.[158]

From this melange we can conclude at least that Thomas' concept of Christianity is neither orthodox, liberal, nor recognizable. Unlike Yeats who wished to create new myth to replace a dead one, Thomas had little or no public consciousness. Nor is he like Eliot, rooted in the past. His sexual imagery, as distinct from that of Lawrence, is without a sacral aspect. But like all three poets, he was highly sensitive to the failure of non-humanist religion.

The esoteric charades played by Thomas' interpreters obscure his real significance. Sonnet I is a highly iconoclastic rendering of the Christian saviour myth, tinged both with the sneer of "There Was a Saviour" and Thomas' mockery of Milton. Its chief emotion is a religiosity desacralized, demythologized, and denatured, a salvation of sterility and ultimate death. If, as is most likely the case, the poem is primarily about the poet—the man himself—the obscure allusions should not offer insurmountable difficulty. Certainly, they should not present an occasion for wild flights of critical fancy. The very variety of dissimilar images piled on top of each other, drawn from clashing contexts, dramatically re-creates the world from which the poem was drawn. Older values no longer obtain. The Saviour of the old myth of godly impregnated virgins, of holy miracles and spiritual purity is little more than a joke. What God there is within man, consisting of real experience of the raw, unromanticized facts of life, from sexual intercourse—the required means of conception and birth—to the stars which bear directly upon the course of life. Indeed, the whole idea of Christian salvation is an utter illusion.

And in a very similar way the last sonnet of the ten sounds a note which does little to induce the giddy prognostication of Kleinman that Thomas soars upward in faith. Olson, certainly, is misled into claiming that the reappearance of the "rude, red tree" image of the

Cross signifies the Resurrection, while noting that the word "tree" in Thomas' poetry is always associated with "word, suffering, and knowledge," and is the last word of the last sonnet. He then advises that "tree" should be interpreted in the context of the first word of the first sonnet, "Altarwise." We think nothing so traditional, nor so optimistic. Between "Altarwise" and "tree," certainly, lies a hope, but in a transmutation of the Christian story, a blossoming within the poet's own private world denuded of the ancient expectations. The poet anticipates no Second Coming; he is his own. It is this we sense in Sonnet X:

> Let the tale's sailor from a Christian voyage
> Atlaswise hold half-way on the globe I balance:
> So shall winged harbours through the rockbirds' eyes
> Spot the blown word, and on the seas I image
> December's thorn screwed in a brow of holly.
> Let the first Peter from a rainbow's quayrail
> Ask the tall fish swept from the bible east,
> What rhubarb man peeled in her foam-blue channel
> Has sown a flying garden round that sea-ghost?
> Green as beginning, let the garden diving
> Soar, with its two bark towers, to that Day
> when the worm builds with the gold straws of venom
> My nest of mercies in the rude, red tree.[159]

NOTES: CHAPTER II

[1] *W.B. Yeats and Tradition* (London: Methuen, 1968), p. 21.

[2] *Cf.* Morton I. Seiden, *William Butler Yeats: The Poet as Myth Maker* (Michigan State University Press, 1962), pp. 237-38.

[3] Wilson, p. 19.

[4] Richard Elmann, *The Identity of Yeats* (London: Macmillan & Co., Ltd., 1954), p. 165.

[5] Peter Allt and Russell K. Alspach, eds., *The Variorum Edition of the Poems of W.B. Yeats* (New York: The MacMillan Co., 1957), pp. 318-19.

[6] "The fable for this poem ["The Dolls"] came into my head while I was giving some lectures in Dublin. I had noticed once again how all thought among us is frozen into 'something other than human life.' After I had made the poem, I looked up one day into the blue of the sky, and suddenly imagined, as if lost in the blue of the sky figures in procession. I remembered that they were the habitual image suggested by the blue sky, and looking for a second fable called them 'The Magi,' complementary forms of those enraged dolls." See *Variorum Edition*, p. 820.

[7] *A Reader's Guide to William Butler Yeats* (New York: Straus and Cudahy, 1962), p. 129.

[8] *Variorum Edition*, p. 625.

[9] W.B. Yeats, *A Vision: A Reissue with the Author's Final Revisions* (New York: The MacMillan Co.: Collier Books, 1966). See especially "Book V: Dove or Swan," pp. 276-300. See also Helen H. Vendler, *Yeats' "Vision" and the Later Plays* (Cambridge: Harvard University Press, 1963), pp. 61-70, where the author charges that Yeats was "radically inconsistent in his historical schemata."

[10] *A Vision*, pp. 140-45.

[11] See Unterecker, p. 286, and A. Norman Jeffares, *A Commentary on the Collected Poems of W.B. Yeats* (Stanford: Stanford University Press, 1968, p. 502.

[12] Jeffares, p. 502.

[13] *Essays and Introductions* (New York: Macmillan & Co., 1961), p. 114.

[14] *Autobiography: Consisting of Reveries over Childhood and Youth, Trembling of the Veil and Dramatis Personnae* (New York: Macmillan, 1953), pp. 70-71.

[15] *Ibid.*, 118.

[16] Quoted by Elmann, p. 250.

[17] *Variorum Edition*, pp. 824-25.

[18] See Jeffares, p. 242.

[19] *A Reader's Guide*, p. 165. Also p. 244, n. 21.

[20] According to Elmann, Yeats discovered the Japanese Noh plays in 1914 through the translation of Ezra Pound, a form he would use for most of his remaining plays: *The Identity of Yeats*, p. 183. Seiden defines "Noh" as "a drama in which aristocratic and religious themes are combined in a form which is evocative, yet simple, unadorned and restrained; while the actors, who wear masks, chant their speeches, dance ceremoniously, and enact their roles against a background of ritual music and a bare stage." See *Yeats*, p. 213.

[21] *Variorum Edition of the Plays*, p. 790.

[22] *Ibid.*

[23] *Yeats' "Vision,"* p. 173.

[24] A. Norman Jeffares and A.S. Knowland, *A Commentary on the Collected Plays of W.B. Yeats* (Stanford : Stanford University Press, 1965), pp. 168-69.

[25] *The Tragic Drama of William Butler Yeats: Figures in a Dance* (New York: Columbia University Press, 1965), p. 204.

[26] *Ibid.*

[27] In both versions of the *Variorum Edition*, the Egyptian of "The Adelphi" text and the Greek of the variant text perform similar roles, and for the ultimate outcome of the play their difference is insignificant.

[28] See J.L. Neve., *A History of Christian Thought* (Philadelphia: The Muhlenberg Press, 1946), II, 55.

[29] *"Portrait*: After Fifty Years," *James Joyce Today: Essays on the Major Works* (Bloomington: Indiana University Press, 1966), p. 80.

[30] "The Hours of James Joyce, Part II," trans. Lloyd C. Parks, *The Kenyon Review*, 25, No. 1 (Winter, 1963), 101.

[31] *Literature and Religion: A Study in Conflict* (Dallas: Southern Methodist University Press, 1960), p. 149.

[32] *"Portrait:* After Fifty Years," p. 81. See generally Kevin Sullivan, *Joyce among the Jesuits* (New York: Columbia University Press, 1967).

[33] *Literature and Religion*, p. 79.

[34] The Viking Critical Library, ed. Chester G. Anderson (New York: The Viking Press, 1968), p. 171.

[35] *Literature and Religion*, p. 215.

[36] Viking, pp. 171-72.

[37] *Ibid.*, p. 288.

[38] "Joyce's Epiphanies," The Viking Critical Library, p. 360.

[39] *Ibid.*, p. 366.

[40] "Joyce and Dissociated Metaphor," Viking Critical Library, p. 374.

[41] *Ibid.*, p. 373.

[42] *Ibid.*

[43] *Ibid.*, p. 11.

[44] *Ibid.*

[45] *Ibid.*, p. 50.

[46] *Ibid.*, p. 59.

[47] *Ibid.*, p. 99.

[48] *Ibid.*, p. 103.

[49] *Ibid.*, pp. 104-05.

[50] *Ibid.*, pp. 144-45.

[51] *The Rhetoric of Fiction* (Chicago: University of Chicago Press, 1961), pp. 327-28, quoting from Caroline Gordon, *How to Read a Novel* (New York: The Viking Press, 1957), p. 213.

[52] *Ibid.* An interesting question arises: where does criticism end and critical re-writing begin?

[53] Viking, p. 178.

[54] *Ibid.*, p. 194. See also Noon, p. 79.

[55] *Ibid.*, p. 220.

[56] *Ibid.*, p. 221.

[57] *Ibid.*, p. 209.

[58] *Ibid.*, pp. 223-24.

[59] *Rhetoric of Fiction*, p. 239.

[60] Viking, p. 329.

[61] *Ibid.*, p. 240.

[62]*Ibid.*, pp. 243-44.

[63]"*Portrait* after Fifty Years," pp. 55-56.

[64]Viking, p. 253.

[65]*Phoenix: The Posthumous Papers of* . . . , ed. Edward D. McDonald (New York: The Viking Press, 1936), p. 726.

[66]*Ibid.*, pp. 729-30.

[67]See for examples, Rev. 1:20, 4:5, 5:6. and 7:17.

[68]For brief accounts see Edgar J. Goodspeed, *An Introduction to the New Testament* (Chicago: University of Chicago Press, 1937), pp. 240-51, inclusive of bibliography; and Madeleine S. and J. Lane Miller, *Harper Bible Dictionary* (New York: Harper and Brothers, 1956), pp. 614-15.

[69](New York: The Viking Press, 1932), p. x.

[70]*D.H. Lawrence: Artist and Rebel: A Study of Lawrence's Fiction* (Albuquerque: University of New Mexico Press, 1963), p. 183.

[71]*Phoenix II: Uncollected, Unpublished, and Other Prose Works by* . . . eds. Warren Roberts and Harry T. Moore (New York: The Viking Press, 1968), p. 574.

[72]*The Art of D.H. Lawrence* (Cambridge: Cambridge University Press, 1975), p. 103.

[73]"Introduction" to *Apocalypse*, p. xxix.

[74]*Ibid.*, p. 23.

[75]*Ibid.*, pp. 26-27.

[76]*Ibid.*, p. 13.

[77]*Ibid.*, p. 45.

[78]*Ibid.*, p. 59.

[79] *Ibid.*, pp. 54-55.

[80] *Apocalypse*, p. 187.

[81] *Ibid.*, p. 189.

[82] Matt. 22:25-33; Mark 12:20-27; Luke 20:29-39; 1 Cor. 25:39; 1 Tim. 5:11-16.

[83] *The Dark Sun: A Study of D.H. Lawrence* (New York: The Macmillan Co., 1957), p. 254.

[84] *D.H. Lawrence and Human Existence* (New York: Booksellers & Publishers, 1971), p. 16.

[85] *The Dark Sun*, p. 254.

[86] *Ibid.*, p. 255.

[87] *Ibid.*, p. 253.

[88] "Foreword," *D.H. Lawrence and Human Existence*, p. 10.

[89] As quoted by Ronald P. Draper, *D.H. Lawrence* (New York: Twayne Publishers, 1964).

[90] Lawrence's difficulties with censors are legendary. One needs not hope that he escaped them with his version of the Resurrection. It was in Volterra, Italy that Earl Brewster called Lawrence's attention to an Easter egg showing a cockerel emerging from the shell. According to Brewster, the picture suggested the title of Lawrence's story, *The Escaped Cock--A Story of the Resurrection*. While many letters-to-the-editor were provoked by its publication, no effort was made to suppress it. But no English periodical would dare print it. The later addition of "Part Two" was not calculated to assuage the ruffled piety of the offended. See Richard Aldington, *Portrait of a Genius . . .: The Life of D. H. Lawrence, 1885-1930* (Melbourne: William Heinemann Ltd., 1950), p. 323, and p. 331.

[91] *The Man Who Died* (New York: Vintage Books, 1953), p. 168.

[92] *Ibid.*

[93] *Ibid.*, p. 174.

[94] *Ibid.*, p. 178.

[95] *Ibid.*, p. 182.

[96] *Ibid.*, p. 183.

[97] *Apocalypse*, pp. 24-26. The aristocrats are always threatened by this class.

[98] *The Man Who Died* (New York: Vintage-Random House, 1953), p. 201.

[99] *Ibid.*, p. 205.

[100] *The Art of D.H. Lawrence*, p. 67.

[101] On reading *Mourning Becomes Electra*, Kenneth Burke charged O'Neill with threatening "to dissolve drama into behaviorism." See *A Grammar of Motives and A Rhetoric of Motives* (Cleveland: Meridian Books-The World Publishing Co., 1962), p. 247.

[102] *Literature and Religion*, p. 155.

[103] *Eugene O'Neill: A Critical Study* (New York: Random House, 1936), p. 21, quoting Arthur Hobson Quinn, O'Neill's good friend. See also p. 12.

[104] See Steiner's *The Death of Tragedy* (New York: Hill and Wang, 1961), pp. 2-10. Whatever position one takes, it is clear that Ancient Greek tragedy is distinct from modern adaptation. St. Paul early supplied an antidote to unyielding Greek fate in the newly resurrected God. Thus Rheinhold Niebuhr can deny that there is tragedy for Christians. See his *Beyond Tragedy: Essays on the Christian Interpretation of History* (New York: Charles Scribner's Sons, 1937), pp. 153-69. But see Roger L. Cox who declares that there is a viable genre of Christian tragedy, in *Between Earth and Heaven: Shakespeare, Dostoevsky, and the Meaning of Christian Tragedy* (New York: Holt, Rinehart and Winston, 1969), pp. 215-38. See discussion on the "hero," pp. 188-90, *infra*.

[105] "Introduction," *Nine Plays by Eugene O'Neill* (New York: The Modern Library, 1932), p. xvii, as commented upon by Leonard Chabrowe, *Ritual and Pathos--The theatre of O'Neill* (Lewisburg,

Pa.: Bucknell University Press, 1976), pp. 102-02.

[106] Winther, pp. 32-38.

[107] Chabrowe, pp. 134-39.

[108] Glicksberg, *Literature and Religion*, pp. 74-79.

[109] Doris Falk, *Eugene O'Neill and the Tragic Tension: An Interpretative Study of the Plays* (New Brunswick: Rutgers University Press, 1958), pp. 121-26.

[110] Eugene O'Neill, *The Plays of* . . . (New York: Random House, 1947), I, 42-43.

[111] *Ibid.*, pp. 91-92.

[112] *Supra*, p. 43.

[113] See O'Neill's letter to George Jean Nathan describing *Dynamo* as "A symbolical and factual biography of what is happening in the American (and not only American) soul right now." Quoted by Chabrowe, p. 61.

[114] As quoted by Travis Bogard, *Contour in Time: The Plays of Eugene O'Neill* (New York: Oxford University Press, 1972), p. 319.

[115] Act Three, Scene Three, *Plays*, 3, 487.

[116] See Bogard, p. 317.

[117] *Ibid.*

[118] Chabrowe, pp. 53-66.

[119] Act One, *Plays*, *3, 493-94.*

[120] *Ibid.*, p. 511.

[121] *Contour in Time*, p. 327.

[122] Act Four, Scene Two, *Plays*, 3, 565.

[123]For an excellent discussion see *Ritual and Pathos*, pp. 34-58.

[124]*Plays*, pp. 289-90.

[125]Much of Auden's poetry is a poetry of statement, rather than a poetry of image.

[126]*Collective Poems, 1934-1952* (London: J.M. Dent & Sons, Ltd., 1964), p. 125.

[127]John Milton, *The Complete Poems of . . . Excluding His Translation of Psalms 80-88*, ed. John Shawcross (Garden City: Doubleday & Co., 1963), p. 40.

[128]William Y. Tindall, *A Reader's Guide to Dylan Thomas* (New York: Farrar, Straus and Cudahy, 1962), pp. 11-12.

[129]H.H. Kleinman, *The Religious Sonnets of Dylan Thomas: A Study in Imagery and Meaning* (Berkeley: University of California Press, 1953), pp. 1-2. Members of the Apocalypse included Henry Treece, Nicholas Moore, S.F. Hendry, G.S. Fraser, and Tom Scott. The artists they espoused, among whom they placed Thomas, included James Joyce, Frank Kafka, Vincent Van Gogh, and Pablo Picasso. See Thomas' letter to Henry Treece, 31 December 1938 in which he stated a refusal to sign the Apocalyptic Manifesto of Treece and his friends: *Selected Letters of Dylan Thomas*, ed. Constantine Fitzgibbon (London: J.M. Dent & Sons, 1966), p. 219. The group was short-lived. Each of its members soon went his own way.

[130]*The Poetry of Dylan Thomas* (Chicago: The University of Chicago Press, 1954), p. 67.

[131]Tindall, p. 12.

[132]*The Religious Sonnets*, pp. 3-4.

[133]"Four New Poets," *London Mercury*, 33)Feb. 1936), 386.

[134]And J.C. Smith, *A Critical History of English Poetry* (New York: Oxford University Press, 1946), p. 566.

[135]"Thomas, Bishop, and Williams," *Sewanee Review*, LV, No. 3 (Summer 1947), 493-96.

[136]"The Latest Dylan Thomas," *Western Review,* XI, No. 2 (Winter 1947), 103-06.

[137]Fitzgibbon, *Selected Letters,* p. 190.

[138]*Ibid.,* p. 191.

[139]See Tindall, p. 216.

[140]*Ibid.,* 217.

[141]*The Religious Sonnets,* p. 11.

[142]*The Poetry of Dylan Thomas,* p. 66.

[143]As quoted by Louis Untermeyer, *Lives of the Poets: The Story of One Thousand Years of English and American Poetry* (New York: Simon and Schuster, 1963), p. 719.

[144]*Ibid.,* pp. 718-19.

[145]*The Life of Dylan Thomas* (London: J.M. Dent & Sons, Ltd., 1965), pp. 146-50, p. 259.

[146]*Ibid.,* p. 300.

[147]See Stuart Holroyd, *Emergence from Chaos* (London: Victor Gollancz Ltd., 1957), p. 88.

[148]*Dylan Thomas in America: An Intimate Journal* (Boston: Little, Brown & Co., 1955), p. 128.

[149]
There is little in Thomas to indicate that he was an articulated or conscious pantheist as Holroyd tends to suggest. Anything but a systematic or abstract thinker, Thomas was viscerally and emotionally involved in his poetic evocations too much to have distance enough to formulate the kind of theory, for example, in Yeats. While denying the incarnation of God in Jesus Christ, he nevertheless maintained corporal imagery of the spirit, as provocative of himself and his spiritual relationship to himself, other men, and the powers of the universe, whatever they may be.

[150]*Emergence from Chaos,* p. 82.

[151] See "Preface" to Eliot's essay, "For Lancelot Andrewes."

[152] Tindall, p. 4.

[153] *The Life of Dylan Thomas*, pp. 96-98.

[154] *A Reader's Guide*, p. 15.

[155] *Emergence from Chaos*, p. 86.

[156] For Scarfe through Stearn see Kleinman, pp. 9-10.

[157] *Collected Poems*, p. 71.

[158] See Tindall, pp. 128-30, Kleinman, pp. 12-22; Olson, pp. 63-69.

[159] *Collected Poems*, p. 76.

CHAPTER III: THE SOCIAL HUMANISTS

GEORGE BERNARD SHAW: THE CROSS OF "CROSSTIANITY"

The distinguishing feature of the social humanist writer is his disavowal of any phenomenon which cannot be rationally apprehended. While he does not deny spirituality, purposiveness, directedness, nor ultimate valus, his paramount belief is in man as the ultimate achievement of the universe. At one end he dedicates himself to the reconstruction of the human enterprise in a dignity of at-one-ment within a meaningful universe. At the other end he seeks to rehabilitate the human spirit after its near destruction by the failure of traditional approaches. His literary method depends upon his degree of desperation. If he is a George Bernard Shaw he is fundamentally an optimist, a believer in himself primarily perceived upon a religious respect for truth as rational, a universal religion of "naturalistic mysticism" purged of orthodox superstition and reliance upon magic. This "mysticism" is not one of incarnate spirit, but one in which the Vital Force of the universe is ultimately to consume flesh into itself and exist as pure thought. Its distinguishing mark is its origin in the mind, thus not being a true other-dimensional reality with its own distinct structural elements penetrating the human. As Eric Bentley points out, Shaw has been attacked by almost everyone, as he sought no berth among the complacent be they churched or unchurched, Socialist or Marxist, free-thinkers, Darwinians, or anti-Darwinians.[1]

What is most striking about the Shavian mentality, existing as much as legend as fact, is its attempt to extract from the venerable, as well as the obsolete, the best of man's attempts to explain his relationship to the universe of which man is inextricably a part. While unwilling to reject the Christian claim outrightly, Shaw was equally unwilling to accept its creation of a new religion out of those already existent. Neither would he accept a mechanical, amoral, and brutal selective process which he abundantly attributed to Charles Darwin. Mind could indeed control the evolutionary process, Shaw insisted, but within its own understanding and constant growth, evolving as the universe itself evolved, with God Himself, an incomplete process in constant evolution.

143

Between 1916, when he wrote the "Preface" to Androcles and the Lion, and 1932, when the "Preface" to
his story, The Adventures of the Black Girl in Her
Search for God, appeared, his religious views remained
remarkably consistent. However, the prefaces, some
thirty-seven in all, bear little relationship to the
plays and novels to which they are attached. They
serve as a forum for Shavian thought. Because of his
self-acknowledged status as an outsider, his theater
became chiefly his instrument of social involvement.
In the Preface of his first novel, Immaturity, he wrote
"I was outside society, outside politics, outside sport,
outside the Church. If the term had been invented then
I should have been called The Complete Outsider."[2] Colin Wilson points to Shaw as the paradigmatic outsider:
"There is no place in society for the extraordinary in-
dividuals, and neither should there be; all their power
and importance lies in their being outside society."[3]

The idea of the outsider is crucial in grasping
Shaw's apprehension of Jesus as opposed to Paul, of
Christ as opposed to Christianity. Shaw labelled the
Jesus of the synoptic gospels Communistic and Social-
istic, the opposite of materialistic, capitalistic, and
acquisitive. It should be added, however, that Shaw's
construction of these descriptions did not remotely
resemble the modern ruthless totalitarian state appro-
priating these terms. With typical Shavian wit he sub-
titled the first segment of his Preface to Androcles
and the Lion, "Why Not Give Christianity a Trial?"
The principles which Jesus preached, he asserted, had
never been tried. Instead, Barrabas was triumphant,
whom Shaw identified with violence and insurrection.
Shaw's prime interest was in the Sermon on the Mount
which he extracted from supernatural aura and millen-
nial eschatology, and emphasized this life in this
world. He argued that Jesus preached conduct rather
than baptism and vows, the family of mankind instead of
the closed nuclear group, all under the Fatherhood of
God; that Jesus renounced revenge and punishment, urging that good be done for evil, that one is his brother's keeper and should love his neighbor as himself.
The results would be a better world now, not merit
points for personal reward in Heaven.

However, Shaw saw little that was meek and submissive in Jesus the man. The imputed saviour showed
great courage in undergoing crucifixion, when he might
have exerted his boasted powers in his own behalf. But
literally believing in his claim to divinity, Jesus was
rightly charged with blasphemy by the high priests. To-

day, said Shaw, such a claim would merit a diagnosis of madness and sentence to an asylum. While millions accept Jesus' delusions as inerrant truth, salvation for them is more economic than spiritual. Divine attention was originally meant for those who could afford it, Shaw continued, requiring endless expensive sacrifices and offerings. Jesus' coming as a ransom for all provided the cheapest route for all. His Second Coming will be the reward for those who patiently bear the oppressions and dispossessions of this world. Hell awaits those who cause strife and insurrection. This, the bedrock dogma of orthodox Christianity, Shaw called "Crosstianity."

World War I was in progress as Shaw was writing. He was convinced that salvationism could not save civilization; indeed, its very denigration of the world contributed to the plight of man. The hope in Crosstianity put an end to the principles of the Sermon on the Mount, Shaw maintained, and replaced them with tragicomedy such as the English clergy of his day. In Samuel Butler's The Way of All Flesh he saw the prototypal perversions of Jesus' original message. He then scathingly denounced the disciples as anti-Semites, as vindictive superficial showmen using their gift of miraculous powers to entertain, and to cancel Jesus' mission to redeem man from folly and error. Exploiting John the Baptist's magic formula required no enlightenment, no perception of truth from error. Shaw reserved his sharpest contempt for Stephen. "A tactless and conceited bore," Stephen was rightfully stoned to death.

One may, of course, quarrel with such iconoclasm as much as with Lawrence's equal hostility to Patmos John, realizing, however, that our concern here is the artist's vision as grounded in his experience of the world about him. Shaw worked within the reality of the living organism beset with limitations of time and chance, while his spirit sought a universal reality of the mind.

His distinction between the religions of Jesus and Paul, therefore, rests upon firm critical grounds. Relying almost entirely upon internal evidence, Shaw outlined the sharp differences between the two men. Paul was pathological, consumed by two terrors: sin and death, otherwise identifiable as sex and life. On the other hand, Jesus was healthier, free of manic depression. Shaw's ratiocination of what happened to Paul on the road to Damascus is one of the most remarkable extant. Said Shaw, Paul was both fascinated and horrified by Je-

145

sus' fearlessness in the face of death:

> The fascination accounts for the strangest of
> his fancies: the fancy for attaching the name
> of Jesus Christ to the great idea which flash-
> ed upon him on the road to Damascus, the idea
> that he could not only make a religion of his
> two terrors, but that the movements started by
> Jesus offered him the nucleus of his new church.
> It was a monstrous idea: and the shock of it, as
> he afterwards declared, struck him blind for
> three days. He heard Jesus calling him from the
> clouds, "Why persecute me?"[4] His natural hatred
> of the teacher for whom Sin and Death had no ter-
> rors turned him into a wild personal worship of
> him which has the ghastliness of a beautiful
> thing seen in a false light.[5]

What so profoundly offended Shaw was Paul's blanket
removal of responsibility for one's sins and imputing
them to a vicarious condition invented as Original Sin,
an absurdity removed by the sacrificial death of Jesus.
Nothing in the utterances of Jesus, Shaw insisted, hinted at this intent. In his outrage Shaw revealed a fundamentally unaffected puritan character, an aristocracy
of spirit, and an unremitting sense of sin:

> The notion that he was shedding his blood in or-
> der that every petty cheat and adulterator and
> libertine might wallow in it and come out whiter
> than snow, cannot be imputed to him on his own
> authority. "I come as an infallible patent for
> bad consciences" is not one of the sayings in
> the gospels.[6]

Thus, a "violently anti-Christian system of criminal law and stern morality" resulted which, aided by the
police and Church, suppressed the religion of Jesus
while Paulinism ran rampant.

Shaw can appear contradictory and inconsistent.
While believing that men are essentially good, with
minds free to choose courses determined by their wills,
he found them endemically enthralled by the chicanery,
deceit, and unworthiness of Butler's Pontifexes in The
Way of All Flesh, that however good man may be essentially, his choice of the worst in his nature cannot be
laid at the foot of Jesus to be absolved. The hope
that ultimate responsibility can be escaped, Shaw declared, is a superstition which Jesus denied, but which
Paul resurrected.[7]

146

Shaw wrote only a few plays or stories which can
be properly called religious, however much his religious
compulsion peppers most of his work.[8] Archibald Henderson, his authorized biographer, finds Shaw's religious
position essentially stated in the third act of Man and
Superman. Here, Shaw "reveals himself in prophetic,
Messianic character."[9] The third act of this play has
seldom been staged, being little more than a lengthy dialogical aside. The play identifies Shaw's Vital Force
personified in a woman. His John Tanner of the play is
his updated British version of Don Juan. Instead of being the pursuer, Tanner is the pursued. Instead of
serving as a horrible seventeenth-century example of
damnation transplanted in the beginning of the twentieth-
century, Tanner is both a Nietzschean superman and a morally impeccable paradigm. In characteristic Shavian
fashion he defies traditions rather than morals. However, by consenting to marry Ann Whitefield, his design-
ing ward, he is defeated by woman and thus loses his
moral superiority. The significant scene of Act III is
Tanner's dream in which he becomes Don Juan, but a man
of moral passion; Ann becomes Dona de Ullola, the eternal maternal female; and Roebuck Ramsden, the co-guard-
ian of Ana, is Don Gonzalo, the leader of the bandits.
The Devil plays himself.

Don Juan scoffs at virtue. What is it, he demands
of Ana, "but the Trade Unionism of the married?" Since,
therefore, "The Life Force respects marriage only because marriage is a contrivance of its own to secure the
greatest number of children and the closest care of
them," it is indifferent to "honor, chastity and all the
rest of your moral figments." Thus "Marriage is the
most licentious of human institutions--"

Ana, of course, is duly shocked. Don Gonzalo, her
father--the statue--is astounded. Don Juan continues
undeterred:

> I say the most licentious of human institu-
> tions: that is the secret of its popularity.
> And a woman seeking a husband is the most unscru-
> pulous of all the beasts of prey. The confusion
> of marriage with morality has done more to de-
> stroy the conscience of the human race than any
> other single error.

He scathingly derides Don Gonzalo for having been the
minion of traditional morality whose towering hypocrisy
is its most readily discernible characteristic. His
legendary advances toward women, he insists, were not

147

for breeding honorably or unhonorably, but for the meeting of minds, of intellectual stimulation, and constant
growth in reason and understanding. To the Devil's
blandishment of having these things, Don Juan makes his
oft-quoted reply:

> On the contrary, here I have everything
> that disappointed me without anything that I
> have not already tried and found wanting. I
> tell you that as long as I can conceive some-
> thing better than myself I cannot be easy un-
> less I am striving to bring it into existence
> or clearing the way for it. That is the law
> of my life. That is the working within me of
> Life's incessant aspiration to higher organi-
> zation, wider, deeper, intenser self-conscious-
> ness, and clearer self-understanding. It was
> the supremacy of this purpose that reduced
> love for me to the mere schooling of my facul-
> ties, religion for me to a mere excuse for la-
> ziness since it had set up a God who looked
> at the world and saw that it was good, against
> the instinct in me that looked through my eyes
> at the world and saw that it could be improved.
> I tell you that in the pursuit of my own pleas-
> ure, my own health, my own fortune, I have nev-
> er known happiness. It was not love for Woman
> that delivered me into her hands: it was fatigue,
> exhaustion.

Henderson insists that such views make Shaw "a
confirmed mystic."[10] As we have restricted the term,
"mystic," in this study, Shaw is less a true mystic than
a confirmed rationalist. Mysticism, we reiterate once
more, must admit of guidance by a force or power beyond
the mind, from a supra-rationalistic dimension which informs the rational. Nowhere does Shaw concede such a
force or power, or any idea greater than his own ultimate force, power, or idea. Superman means precisely
that. Don Juan surrendered to Woman and her conspiracy
with the Life Force to destroy him. This loss of self-
hood is the lot of men who are not "super" in their
"manhood," modelled after Nietzsche's übermensch. Pure
thought, Shaw's final stage of development, is inherent
in the universe itself, not something added to it. In
this sense only is "God" meaningful, a metaphor for the
best in man. In a lecture at Kensington Town Hall, Shaw
advised his audience that

> When you are asked "Where is God? Who is God?"
> stand up and say "I am God, and here is God,"

148

> not as yet completed, but still advancing to-
> wards completion, just in so much as I am work-
> ing for the purpose of the universe, working
> for the good of the whole society and the whole
> world, instead of merely looking after my per-
> sonal ends.[11]

He had previously urged a Cambridge society called The
Heretics to get a God they could understand.[12] Little
mysticism would inhere in such a God. In "The Revolutionist's Handbook," appended to Man and Superman, he
declared that "Every genuine religious person is a heretic and therefore a revolutionist."[13] Most revealing
is his quip that with the demand that one be born again,
should come the demand that he be born differently.[14]

Consequently, to interpret Shaw's religious significance is to separate him from docetic or Manichaeis-
tic dualism which is inescapable in the Christian dichotomy of spirit and flesh. But in stark contrast to
Lawrence, he found woman a deadly menace to man's moral
ascendence. Much of Shaw's revolt can be traced to his
having been a Protestant Irishman born in Dublin, called
by Bentley "the most fanatically Catholic city in the
world."[15] In a lecture on "Modern Religion" Shaw asserted that both the Roman Catholic Church and the
Church of England were obsolete, that indeed the latter
was a "contradiction in terms."[16] The true Protestant
had neither a "Church" nor a priest. He believed in direct communion with the spirit that rules the universe.
A religion to fit the times, Shaw stated, must rid itself of useless doctrines such as Apostolic Succession
and make room for every religious person, mystic, prophet, and priest. Crosstianity, therefore, had been a
longtime conspiracy to destroy the dignity and promise
of man the creature. At one with Lawrence on one point,
he scorned the dogma of the Second Coming, tracing its
invention to Patmos John whose Revelation he called
"the vision of a drug addict."[17]

His most trenchant ideation is the slim story. The
Adventures of the Black Girl in Her Search for God,
written in 1932, in which he depicts the evolution of
God from "the monster Bogey Man to the Father; then to
the spirit without body parts, nor passion; and finally
to the definition of that spirit in the words God is
Love."[18]

The story of a Bantu girl, introduced to Christianity by a uniquely demythologized Shavian missionary,
and her encounters with a series of strange white men

149

in the jungle have offended, as well as puzzled, many. His purpose was to dramatize the creative aspect of evolution, to give the literary lie to what he perceived to be mindless Darwinism. He met the problem of evil as Voltaire dealt with it in Candide, removal to a garden spot in which to work, to contemplate. Because God is not yet complete, evil has its sway.

Although critical commentary is sparse, a chief cause of reader outrage is the marriage of the black girl to an Irishman. Together they produce a slew of mulatto children. Shaw admits that the adventures of the black girl could not have happened to a white girl "steeped from her birth in the pseudo-Christianity of the Churches."[19] Charles H. Maxwell promptly responded with Adventures of the White Girl in Her Search for God, a fundamentalist rebuttal. Maxwell roundly ridiculed Shaw as the Irishman who had married the black girl. A dramatist (Shaw) stands on his head to condemn the burning of Joan at the stake. The white girl asks him whether he were uncomfortable. "What else can I do if I am not to starve?" the dramatist responds.[20] He explains how much money he makes by making an ass of himself. Maxwell is parodying the sculptor in Shaw's Black Girl, who carves crucifixes for pay from a live model lying on a cross flat on the ground. Through similar ridicule the white girl leads the dramatist to the true Cross where she finds God. The dramatist scoffs at "that vulgarity," and in ringing tones, the white girl proclaims the empty tomb and the new life she is going to live.[21]

In Shaw's story, of course, the black girl has the wit and discernment of her creator. The missionary, who had taken such delight in six successive broken engagements to clergymen, had tried to teach the black girl the ecstasy of the Cross so triumphantly exalted by the white girl. However,

> the black girl hated the cross and thought it
> a great pity that Jesus had not died peaceful-
> ly and painlessly and naturally, full of years
> and wisdom, protecting his granddaughters (her
> imagination always completed the picture with
> at least twenty promising black granddaughters)
> against the selfishness and violence of their
> parents.[22]

Her enounters in her search correspond to stages of development in Shaw's theology. The first man she meets has flowing hair and beard. While killing an obeisant

150

mamba he claims to be God and demands bloody human and animal sacrifices. This God, of course, is the most primitive of Christianity, the one who had invited Abraham to kill Isaac to satisfy the divine caprice. The black girl fearlessly attacks him with her knobkerrie, at which he disappears.

The second old man she meets has silver hair and is dressed in a nightshirt. He is seated at a writer's table. Kinder than the former, he gives an egg to the rattlesnake who had brought the black girl to him. This God wants the girl to dispute with him. She promptly demands to know why he had done so badly in making the world. Delighted with such impudence, he castigates an old servant, Job, who was too "stupid" to complain without all manner of unprovoked disaster. The girl refuses to argue and swings her knobkerrie at him also. He likewise disappears.

Her third encounter is with Ecclesiastes, the Preacher of the Old Testament. He has a Stoic philosophy and the Ancient Hebraic concept of an endlessly cyclical universe. Decidedly non-linear, as is Christian time, Ecclesiastical time is going nowhere, with no change to come. To the girl's question concerning God's whereabouts, he denied knowing, and advised her instead to learn Greek, "the language of wisdom."

The fourth man is stark naked except for sandles, and makes odd shouting noises. The girl, now with a cowardly lion, approaches him. He calls himself Micah the Morasthite, who is the Old Testament prophet deploring blood sacrifice. "[W]hat does the Lord require of you," he asks, "but to do justice, and to love kindness, and to walk humbly with your God?" At that, Micah lets out so horrible a scream in denouncing the old God of wrath and blood that both the girl and the sissy lion run in opposite directions.

The fifth claimant is a short-sighted old man in spectacles, the scientific God whom the girl scoffingly out-maneuvers and rejects. As would be expected, she is put off by his mechanistic convictions which further permit Shaw to get in a blow against vivisection, a common scientific practice of his times.

A sixth man at a well is an obvious symbol. He offers the girl water in remembrance of him. Also a conjurer and a magician, he makes the cup disappear. He tells the girl that God is within her, "our father." Having unpleasant memories of being beaten by her father

151

since she was a child, with his having once tried to sell her to a white man, she refuses to call God her father. "Grandfather," she will accept. The conjurer wishes her well in her search, but admonishes her that to find God she must come by way of the conjurer's magic. He too then disappears.

The seventh man is an ancient fisherman with a huge cathedral on his back. Fearful lest he break his back, the girl rushes to help. He reassures her: "I am the rock upon which the church is built." He is soon joined by others carrying paper churches "much uglier" than the fisherman's. They begin to deny the validity of each other's church, and to throw badly aimed stones at each other. The girl flees. She would find no God to her taste among the contentious churches.

In direct contrast, the eighth man is the wandering Jew waiting for the Messiah to come. He hopes the Messiah will come before men have totally destroyed each other. The girl doubts that such a coming will change men. "You will wait forever," she says. He simply spits at her and totters away.

The ninth encounter is with "The Caravan of the Curious," a supercilious group of Englishmen on safari exhibiting every obnoxious trait attributed to the white man in the land of the "white man's burden." Here, Shaw takes the opportunity to deride colonialism and racism. An Arab joins a man at the well, and together with the sculptor of crucifixes discuss the contrasts, foibles, and pretensions of men, of Christianity, and Islam. In about as chauvinistic a manner as Shaw was capable, his disputants scoff at the importance of women. They agree that God must be a father, as only a father could assert primacy. A mother, they aver, would put herself before God. The blatant sexual bias drives the black girl away.

Her tenth man is a wizened old gardener who introduces her to the eleventh, the Irishman whom she marries. Having found many Gods instead of the One she sought, she despairs. The Irishman, however, affirms his belief that God is yet in process, an inner and outward dynamic:

> Sure God can search for me if he wants me. My
> own belief is that he's not all that he sets up
> to be. He's not properly made and finished yet.
> There's somethin in us that's dhrivin at him, and
> somethin out of us that's dhrivin at him: that's

152

certain; and the only other thin that's
certain is that somethin makes plenty of
mistakes in thryin to get there.[23]

What the black girl learns finally with her white
husband and half-caste children is modesty, a scaled-
down self-importance. God must indeed have more important things to do than attend to her salvation. Right
now she would raise her children and tend to her husband. Once the children are grown and her husband has
become an unconscious part of her, she would think
again on these matters. More than likely, she will have
grown herself enough to put aside her knobkerrie, and
find a little fun in chasing away those pretending more
than they can deliver.

Thus, for all of his irreverence and cheek, Shaw
was unmistakably a religious man, a strong admirer of
Jesus, the man stripped of Crosstianity. While thrust-
ing toward secular humanism, Shaw nevertheless responded to the deepest call of his spirit to attach itself
to something intelligent enough to set up the universe,
and to put within him the proof of its slow, but certain
teleological evidence. While he gave fits to the orthodox, laughter to the skeptics, and challenge to the
theater audience, he brilliantly illumined his profound
religious commitment.

153

ARCHIBALD MACLEISH: LIFE, THE TRAGIC CONDITION

Few living American men of letters are more distinguished than Archibald MacLeish. His career as poet, literary theorist, playwright, and public servant spans most of the twentieth century. He is modern man <u>par excellence</u>. He started out as an imitator of the late nineteenth-century romantics, but has settled on dialectical ideation and symbolization of the abstract, a fact which Signi Lenea Falk notes as the characteristic which clearly distinguishes "modern" from the earlier romantic.[24] MacLeish has conducted a poetic love affair with the human race, but has never been quite able to take the Kierkegaardian leap into faith. Unlike T.S. Eliot or Graham Greene, he has not been able to resolve in what Tillich calls the divine abyss his doubts about the fate of man. In 1926 he wrote MAN!

> *FREE*
>> To the World
>>> *THE PATENT PROPAGATIVE,*
> The Cause of Causes in the Handy Case,
> Tomorrow in Tubes, Eternity in Cartons,
> One hundred billion lives in each Container,
> Cities, Nations, Continents, even, Planets,
> New Hopes, New hungers, New despairs, New Christs,
> Ages, Eras, Centuries, Ends, Beginnings,
>> *LIFE*
>>> *LIFE* in the vial, with the Safety Catch,
>>>> *LIFE* in the Perpendicular Decanter,
> The insulated, thermo-static, safe
> In every clime and climate, weather-proofed,
> Perfected, folding Holder decorated
> With fancy hair and finished in the likeness
> Of the Inventor. His face on every package.
> None genuine without the photograph,
> Free! Death's cure, Grace's simple, Time's elixir,
> The drug for darkness, Night's mandragora--
>> *FREE*
>>> To the World
>>> For nothing . . . .[25]

Twenty-five years later in 1951 he wrote "What Riddle Asked the Sphinx" in memory of André Gide:

In my stone eyes I see
The saint upon his knee
Delve in the desert for eternity.

In my stone ears I hear
The night-lost traveller
Cry *When?* to the earth's shadow: *When: Oh Where?*

Stone deaf and blind
I ponder in my mind
The bone that seeks, the flesh that cannot find.

Stone blind I see
The saint's eternity
Deep in the earth he digs in. Cannot he?

Stone deaf I hear
The night say *Then!* say *There!*
When cries the traveller still to the night air?

The one is not content
With silence the day spend;
With earth the other. More, they think, was meant.

Stone that I am, can stone
Perceive what flesh and bone
Are blind and deaf to?

                    Or has hermit known,

Has traveller divined,
Some question there behind
I cannot come to, being stone and blind?

To all who ken or can
I ask, since time began,
What riddle is it has for answer, Man?[26]

In 1957 MacLeish eulogized Yeats in an address at the University of New Hampshire in terms which reveal his own poetic vision:

> To believe in man as men of our generation must
> believe is not to glorify man or put him in
> place of God or otherwise to blind ourselves to
> the realities of human life. Yeats never at-
> tempted to conceal from himself the fact that
> human life is, in its condition, tragic. In-
> deed he early came to the conclusion that men
> only begin to live when they have come to un-
> derstand how wholly tragic their lives are.[27]

The element of the tragic in MacLeish is authentic, a rare purity of concept among modern writers. He attaches no primordial guilt to man, finds no defect in man's nature which supernatural intervention can remove, and seeks to come to terms with the religious aspect inhering at the deepest levels of human experience. He reinterprets the arch myths of Christianity to reflect his human commitment, and to that extent becomes a notable heretic in a pervasive pessimism. A notable example is his twenty-eight lyrical sequences, "Songs for Eve," composed in 1954. Those miscreants of orthodoxy, those arch sinners of Milton's Paradise Lost become in "Songs for Eve" the progenitors of a true homo sapiens awakened from a state of animal somnolence by the taste of the forbidden fruit. Thus, Eve becomes an instrument of Adam's growth, not the cause of his downfall.

In the first of the twenty-eight poems Eve becomes aware of being alive in time and space:

> But Oh! I heard the whole of time
> And all of space give ringing rhyme
> And ring and ring and chime and chime
> When I reached out to touch and climb
> In spite of space, in spite of time.

In the second sequence Eve recites the limits of human life:

> Eve said:
> From tree to tree
> Will journey be;
> The one, she said,
> Alive and green,
> The other dead,
> Eve said,
> Our lives mean.
>
> Eve said:
> With tree began
> That traveller man;
> With tree, she said,
> Will journey end.
> That tree, though dead,
> Its leaves will spend,
> Eve said,
> World without end.
>
> Eve said:
> The first is his
> Whose world this is:

157

The last, she said,
Blossomed and blown
Though would be dead,
Is mine, my own.
Eve said:
O my son! O my son!

Both knowledge and death are symbolized by the
trees, one "Alive and green" and the other "though
dead, / Its leaves will spend . . . World without end."
The death of Eve's son, Abel, at the hands of his brother, Cain, is evoked in the last line above. This construction of the first tragedy foretells a life of unremitting tragedy for man, prepared in advance. Certainly, remaining in a state of lethargic innocence
would have prevented Adam's knowledge of his state without changing it, but it would have also prevented conscience, thought, imagination, ideals, all of the qualities which distinguish men from animals. That God had
intended the first couple to remain for eternity in dumb
innocence in the Garden of Eden is incredible to the humanist. However, the ineluctable alternative, as Mac-
Leish sees it, is little better.

In "What Riddle Asked the Sphinx" MacLeish echoes
the centuries of questioning, with no sign of answer:
"In my stone ears I hear / The night-lost traveller /
Cry *When? Oh where?*" The hope for more than "the
saint's eternity / Deep in the earth he digs in" is futile. Yet, as with Yeats, MacLeish wills to believe in
the digging, in the state of awareness of knowledge not
had.

This sense is intensified in the fourth poem of
the Eve sequence where the green tree observes that
"Our exile is our eyes that see. / Hawk and fish have
eyes but we / Behold what they can only be." The serpent is a cynical duper, reversing the role it plays in
the orthodox reading of Genesis. In the twenty-second
poem the serpent muses:

You are the children of Eve by the apple.
By the pip of the apple she came to conceive.
Adam, that cuckold, never begot you.
You are the children of Eve
By the apple.

Adam was hot
In the heat of the day,
And he lay in her lap
And she gave him his way,

158

But the pip of the apple
I taught her to eat
(Tart?--sweet!)
Was quick in her womb.
When Adam came knocking
The inn had no room.

Said the king to the cock:
When the day comes to bloom
Be quiet for once!
I must sleep in the tomb.
Said the king to the huntsman:
Quiet your horn!
Let the day begin dumb:
There is sleep to be born.
But the pip of the apple
Was quick in his blood:
Eve's children can sleep
But not well--not for good.

Instead of enticing Eve to disobey God, the serpent is making fun of her, taunting and reviling her to
her children. Note the reptilian malice of "When Adam
came knocking / The inn had no room." The seed of the
apple had already closed Eve's womb to Adam.

However, Eve is not to take such sneering lightly.
"Who teaches child that snivelling guilt . . . ?" she
demands. What she had done was to liberate Adam and all
his progency from everything deceitful that the serpent
represented. She had made man, man forever, as opposed
to the lower order to which the serpent, the lion, and
the cattle belonged, and to which they would remain:

Had I not, in wonder's awe,
Disobeyed the lion's law,
Voice and hand were shriek and paw.

Had I not, for wonder's sake,
Broken law no leaf may break,
Lids were closed that now awake.

Only when I disobeyed
Was the bliss of Eden stayed--
Bliss of sleep in that thick shade.

Was it shame and was it sin,
Shameful out and shameless in,
So in waking to begin?

How else can heavenly thunder shake

159

The heart but if the heart awake?

Eve's triumphant defiance of the stupid order to remain an animal, however, did not diminish the tragic consequence of life. In raising man to self-consciousness she also awakened him to his finitude, the finality of death. In the last of the sequences the wind reminds the water of this fact, to which the water replies (in italics):

Man, like any creature
Dies where two days meet:
Dead, by time eaten.

Sea worm leaves behind
Shell for wave to find:
Man, the shell of mind.

Like any creature, man
Lives by luck and vanishes:
The chance wind takes the candle.

No creature leaves behind
Huck or shell or rind
Obdurate as the mind.

Life is luck, death random.

Tell me, what is man
That immortal order can?

Where the New Critics, Allen Tate and Cleanth Brooks, charge MacLeish with little systematic principle and depth, John Ciardi complains that MacLeish's poetry from 1917 to 1952 contains opposite theories of poetic responsibility.[28] We are tempted now to launch into a discussion of poetic theory in which MacLeish has been a vigorous participant, especially in the nature of poetry as defined in the celebrated close of "Ars Poetica": "A poem should not mean / But be."[29] However exciting, it would carry us too far afield of our purpose. Most critics, nonetheless, admit that MacLeish is a superb craftsman.

MacLeish early demonstrated such skill in "The End of the World" where he unites disparate form and content to evoke a unique poetical experience achievable in few other ways:

Quite unexpectedly as Vasserot
The Armless ambidextrian was lighting

160

A match between his great and second toe
And Ralph the lion was engaged in biting
The neck of Madame Sossman while the drum
Pointed, and Teeny was about to cough
In waltz-time swinging Jocko by the thumb--
Quite unexpectedly the top blew off:

And there, there overhead, there, there hung over
Those thousands of white faces, those dazed eyes,
There in the starless dark the poise, the hover,
There with vast wings across the canceled skies,
There in the sudden blackness the black pall
Of nothing, nothing, nothing--nothing at all.

Into the sonnet form, the loveliest of all poetic
media, MacLeish has poured the content of total anni-
hilation. Some time later, having brilliantly analyzed
the Shakespearean sonnet, particularly Sonnet 116, Mac-
Leish concluded that Shakespeare's technique was built
upon the harmonizing of irreconcilable opposites, and
that the language of the Shakespearean sonnet is the
characteristic language of poetry:

> [T]hat language is founded on a very curious
> paradox: a marriage of strictly regulated sound
> with illimitably liberated sense--sound more
> strictly regulated than it is in any other use
> of words--senses more largely liberated than by
> any other verbal means. The language of poetry
> is a language composed of words arranged in a
> certain relationship, and the characteristic of
> that relationship is that it combines these con-
> trary elements.[30]

Thus, the "propositions" arising from the poem
would not arise from orderly statement in assertive discourse. But we may quickly note that what Shakespeare
was doing in the sonnet with contrariety of language is
the very opposite of what MacLeish is doing. The propositions of the Shakespearean sonnet are of love simply, in its multifarious manifestations, in its elations,
devastations, inspirations, and anguish. They are, in
short, the poetry of affirmation. The rhyme scheme, the
meter, the number of lines, and the divisions of quatrain, sextets, octaves and summation couplets all lend
themselves to the production of an expertly cut poetic
gem whose many faceted images conduce to ultimate confirmation of beauty, order, stability, and intelligible
direction in the universe. MacLeish's sonnet, on the
contrary, blows the top off of that universe. The sonnet form for him becomes a means of caching the experi-

161

ence of a generation whose world was anything but that of Shakespeare.

Appearing in 1926 "The End of the World" expresses the disillusion and alienation, the loss of God of the era of Pound, Eliot, Hemingway, O'Neill. MacLeish conceives of an image in the poem which we meet years later in J.B., the world as a huge circus tent in which an audience is being entertained by freaks, clowns, and performing animals. The cataclysmic explosion suggests the destruction of received ideas, values, and controlled destiny. The effect is heightened by the repeated "there" and "nothing" within a calculated prosodic destruction of the traditional lyricism of the sonnet. Amos Wilder, who writes from a committedly Christian point of view, describes "The End of the World" as an example of "modern man's acute sense of the 'abyss'" which "without even animal faith, as a consequence of his overrationalism, he peers down the precipices of the mind, and is seized with giddiness and horror . . . ."[31]

Wilder's choice of words is ironic. It was that unreasoning "animal faith" from which Eve boasted in the twenty-third sequence of the Eve poems of saving Adam. A reasoning creature, for better or worse, MacLeish is unable to make the absurd reasonable. He remains committed to THE PATENT PROPAGATIVE. The Kierkegaardian leap will not span the abyss.

MacLeish's religious stance is perhaps best established in his play, J.B. Based on the Biblical Book of Job, the play is a contemporized adaptation of the ancient demand to know the why of divine caprice. Orthodoxy has developed an extensive vocabulary to deal with the enigmas of Job, terms such as "divine justice," "the sovereignty of God," "the inscrutable will of God," "man's creatureliness," and "unquestioning faith" among others which do not improve the bitter taste.

The Book of Job attempts to answer the question of whether one gets his just deserts on earth, i.e., whether the wicked are punished and the righteous rewarded. It should be remembered, however, that the book was written before the Christian era with its new dispensation of reward in Heaven later on. It is not, therefore, a Christian document; it is an expropriation both out of context, time, and original purport. Robert H. Pfeiffer puts the composition of the book at about 600 B.C., most probably by an Edomite wise man.[32] This author was an extraordinarily gifted poet, possessed of an incredibly extensive vocabulary for his time. He confronts Job,

the faithful servant of God, with undeserved suffering.
Job refuses to accept the received view that God is just,
but he refuses to revolt against Him.

The problem of evil, never quite understood, much
less solved by any epistemological system in Western history, preoccupies Job in his struggle to discover some
rational cause for his problem. He sees three kinds of
evil: physical, moral, and mental. Man's lot under these
conditions is physical pain, penury, illness and death.
If man's conduct is responsible for his suffering, the
question of God's justice does not arise. When one is
blameless the problem is formidable. With little alternative Job concludes that no causal relationship exists
between conduct and fate, between deed and result. The
first existentialist, Job declared life to be hopelessly
evil. While man is at war with himself and his fellow
man, nature is at war with man. The idea of man's in--
nate depravity gets a real boost, as Job sees sin and
evil as concomitants of the natural universe itself.
The later Christian idea of discrete sin resulting from
equally discrete causes within the will of man--aside
from the vicarious inheritance from Adam--is wholly alien
to Job's experience. Therefore, because God is the supreme cause of man's misery, only death offers surcease.
The distance between man and God, then, is absolute. In
no sense can the two ever meet on common ground. The
Christian concept of an incarnate God would have left
Job in utter stupefaction.

Yet Job will trust God, neither because of sentiment, nor hope for those later twin Christian concepts
of "love and compassion." He has no sense of possible
"union" with God whatsoever. It is simply accept, or
take his wife's advice to "Curse God and die." (2:9)
Job's solution is not very palatable to modern humanistic tastes. His absolute abjection before a God who tor-
ments men as senselessly as a wanton boy dismembers a
helpless fly is not the model of other-directed men.
First, Job's faith is the affirmation of hopelessness
for men who will not accept his miraculous return to
health and wealth--a postscript they believe to be apocryphal. Second, it is the utter denial of man's direct
power to control himself, his environment, and his future. Third, it is the implicit assertion of an innate-
ly hostile universe indifferently bent on man's ultimate
destruction. Fourth, it sets up a primitive God little
beyond the sacrifice-demanding blood deities of savages.

In _J.B._ MacLeish provides an interpretation consistent with his thesis that quite the reverse is the case:

163

Instead of capriciously ruling the affairs of men, God
is helpless. He is not dead: He is impotent. In a
guest sermon delivered on the Book of Job at the Sunday
service of the First Church of Christ, Farmington, Con-
necticut on 8 May 1955, MacLeish made this remarkable
comment:

> If one were to write an argument to go at the
> head of the Book of Job in some private note-
> book of one's own, it might well be written in
> these words: Satan, who is denial of life, who
> is the kingdom of death, cannot be overcome by
> God who is his opposite, who is the kingdom of
> life, except by man's persistence in the love
> of God in spite of every reason to withhold his
> love . . . .
>
> Man depends on God for all things: God depends
> on man for one. Without man's love God does
> not exist as God, only as Creator, and love is
> the one thing no one, not even God Himself, com-
> mands. It is a free gift or it is nothing. And
> it is most itself, most free, when it is offered
> in spite of suffering, of injustice, and of
> death.[33]

This concept of God, it goes without saying, is un-
abashedly romantic of the most sentimental variety. The
equation of human love and divine need gives Job a stature not even Shaw would contemplate for his _übermensch_:

> Which means that in the conflict between
> God and Satan, in the struggle between good
> and evil, God stakes His supremacy as God up-
> on man's fortitude and love. Which means,
> again, that where the nature of man is in
> question--and it is precisely, you will note,
> the nature of man which Satan has brought in-
> to question with his sneering challenge--where
> the nature of man is in question _God has need
> of man_.[34]

Which is where Biblical Job becomes decisive:

> Only Job can prove that Job is capable
> of the love of God, not as a quid pro quo but
> for the love's sake, for God's sake, in spite
> of everything . . . in spite even of injustice,
> even God's injustice. Only man can prove that
> man loves God.[35]

This should not be taken as a version of free will, that dogma of grace freely offered to men with unrestricted option to accept or reject. It is the inability of the King of Heaven to alter the course of His own creation, his powerlessness to be a complete God without the suffering obeisance of his creature. And when complete with the love of man God does not return a like sentiment, just the reassertion of His arbitrary nature, His utterly incomprehensible arrogance. For man it is a one-way street, an upward spiral of devotion while evil reigns unchallengeably supreme around him. In further elucidation MacLeish states that

> The justification of the injustice of the universe is not our blind acceptance of God's inexplicable will, nor our trust in God's love, His dark and incomprehensible love, for us, but our human love, notwithstanding anything, for Him. 36

To this arrangement MacLeish adds an equally sentimentalized emollient taken, as Andrew MacLeish suggests, from the opposite side of the Old Testament-New Testament amalgam of orthodoxy:37 that mercy, that plenary forgiveness proclaimed by the gospel writers as an exclusive downward flow from God to miscreant become the agents of mollification in the attitudes of men toward each other. The principle is reversed: Job forgives God.

J,B. was successfully staged in spite of much carping among critics as to the difficulties of staging verse drama, dialectic rather than action, and of attempting to portray God and Satan.38 The play is structured around five arguments. The first is a running commentary between two old broken-down characters, Mr. Zuss and Nickles, who sell balloons and popcorn respectively. They assume the masks of God and Satan; Zuss applauds Job, and Nickles ridicules his trust in an untrustworthy God. The second discussion takes place between J.B. and his wife, Sarah, on J.B.'s proper attitude toward his prosperity and his disasters. Sarah maintains that God had justly rewarded J.B. for his virtues, but she is unable to assimilate calamity without just cause. Loss of their five children in swift unspeakable disasters undoes Sarah--David lost in the war (WWII), Jonathan and Mary killed in a car crash, Rebecca raped and murdered, and Ruth lost in a bombing attack. The bombs also destroy J.B.'s bank and factory. Reduced to blubbering incoherence, but insisting on God's right to pummel him, J.B. loses Sarah's remaining shreds of patience. She leaves him.

165

The third encounter consists of J.B. and three "comforters:" Bildad, Eliphaz, and Zophar, characters out of the Book of Job, appearing in the play as a Marxist reformer, a psychiatrist, and an orthodox priest. Rejecting their alternatives, J.B. is convinced that God has deserted him. He wishes only to die.

The fourth discussion is between God and J.B. To his miserable plea for enlightenment and a chance to prove his steadfastness, J.B. hears God's distant voice proclaiming his omnipotence, and his ire at the impudence of men questioning Him.

The final argument occurs between J.B. and Nickles, who counsels J.B. to reject any God as monstrous as the one J.B. has faith in. But Sarah returns and the reconciliation with her restores J.B.'s determination to begin living again. They need only each other's love. Certainly, institutionalized religion is of no use to them, nor do they need "justice" as they thought it should be. To deny God under such circumstances is also useless. In the last scene Sarah has brought with her a twig she found growing in the ashes. She is looking up and down at J.B.:

Sarah: You wanted justice, didn't you?
            There isn't any. There's the world...

She begins to rock on the doorsill, the little branch in her arms.

            Cry for justice and the stars
            Will stare until your eyes sting. Weep,
            Enormous winds will thrash the water,
            Cry in sleep for your lost children,
            Snow wil fall...

J.B.:   Why did you leave me alone?

Sarah: I loved you.
            I couldn't help you any more.
            You wanted justice and there was none--
            Only love.

J.B.:   He does not love. He
            Is.

Sarah: But we do. That's the wonder.

J.B.:   Yet you left me.

166

Sarah: Yes, I left you.
         I thought there was a way away...

              Water under bridges opens
              Closing and the companion stars
              Still float there afterwards. I thought the
                 door
              Opened into the closing water.

J.B.:   Sarah!

She turns, pulls his head down between her hands and
kisses him.

Sarah: Then blow on the coal of the heart, my darling.

J.B.:   The coal of the heart...

Sarah: It's all the light now.

Sarah comes forward into the dim room, J.B. behind her.
She lifts a fallen chair, sets it straight.

              Blow on the coal of the heart.
              The candles in churches are out.
              The lights have gone out in the sky.
              Blow on the coal of the heart
              And we'll see by and by...

J.B. has joined her, lifting and straightening the chairs.

                         We'll see where we are.
              The wit won't burn and the wet soul smoulders.
              Blow on the coal of the heart and we'll know...
              We'll know...

The light increases, plain white daylight from the door,
as they work.

Curtain[39]

What has thus become of man is the ultimate synthesis of humanism in a God-helpless universe, the classical condition of tragedy. Man is a pawn, not a shaper.
Marion Montgomery criticizes J.B. for not being bigger-
than-life in dramatic tension on stage.[40] Montgomery
misses the point. Where indeed the tragic hero of Ancient Greece was usually a godling or mortal of similar
stature, whose fate at the hands of the capricious gods
carried national significance, the crux of the tragic
was in the hero's direct relationship with the divine.

167

But Montgomery complains that instead of being moved to pity and horror at J.B.'s plight, as we should be, we are aroused in anger at his blameless fall. The fact is that culpability is not a requirement, but only a condition of pre-ordained destiny. Pity and horror result from helplessness, not from hamartia (αμαρτία). What happens to J.B. is what happened, for example, to Oedipus. The Theban king's rash act at the crossroads had been planned by fate before Oedipus was born. What happened to J.B. was equally out of his hands. The destiny of both results from divine meddling into the affairs of men, both compulsively acting, one to struggle out of his noose, the other to accept its strictures. No choice is presented either. The Oedipan dilemma had consequences for the whole state; J.B.'s tragedy portends the fate of all mankind. Tragedy, then, as MacLeish spelled it out in his lecture on Yeats, lies in man's inescapable plight. The hero is he who, in his complete humanity, attains moral stature by his struggle, not by absolution of his faults. Both Oedipus and J.B. knew that divinity cannot ultimately control fate, or has any discernible intention of trying to control it. We are purged in the dramas of both in realizing this ineluctable conclusion, flushed of any sense of removal from or being unaffected by the catastrophes of other men. J.B.'s heroic stature, therefore, is as pristine as any in the authentic classical mode.

On the other hand, it is Biblical Job who, in no sense, is a hero, nor in any conjecture tragic. That his God can deliver him from his God's own outrageous behaviour denies Job all basis of a claim of stature--reward goes to him who can wait for it. He and J.B. have little in common, representing instead the polar dimensions of the modern religious experience. In Job God is glorified at man's expense; in J.B. man achieves dignity, the ultimate compliment the social humanist can pay him.

WILLIAM FAULKNER: THE ARCHETYPAL BEAR

The chief religious significance of William Faulkner lies in his implicit concept of a natural covenant between God, man, and the land, revealed chiefly in his final version of The Bear. The religious significance of much of his other fiction lies in the central issues of reality and phantasy, and of truth and myth. When the like terms of these pairs are placed together, phantasy and myth become the carriers of a reality and truth which are revealed in The Bear as the corruption by man of his divinely intended relationship with the land. What is peculiarly Faulknerian in this vision is the elevation of the natural relationship to the highest spiritual level, with the hope of an ultimate restoration of the pristine covenant.

While many critics would agree that little room exists in Faulkner for a spirituality much beyond this point, they present a variety of emphases which reflect what appears to be Faulkner's ultimate affirmation of secular humanism. George M. O'Donnell believes that with the exception of As I lay Dying all of Faulkner's novels are variations of a single theme: the conflict between the decadent Old South and the brash New South, between the Sartoris clan and the Snopes interlopers. Where the Sartorises act with a moral sense, the Snopeses act without one. Consequently, the Snopeses destroy the world of the Sartorises. Thus, the myth explored is the rise and fall of the Southern Cavalier tradition, or the struggle between humanism and animalism.[41]

On the other hand, Irving Howe sees the Faulknerian myth as "the fate of a ruined homeland." Provoked into a war which it lost, the South fought with a gallantry which made of defeat almost a vindication. But from defeat came misery and squalor, and most of all, the rise of "white trash" who fell upon the prostrate aristocrats and played havoc with their anachronistic code of honor.[42]

Peter Swiggart takes the point of view that Faulkner was involved with "social myth" on much more of a universal plane than Howe suggests. What Faulkner wrote about, Swiggart states, is "the collapse of so-

ciety and the dehumanization of mankind."[43] To this end
Faulkner's characters are prototypal.

When we turn to Malcolm Cowley we have a reassertion of regional particularism in Faulkner as compared
with Hawthorne's attitude toward New England. "The
North and the South were two distinct nations in opinions and habits," Hawthorne wrote, "and had better not
try to live under the same institutions."[44] Although
as different from each other as night is from day, both
authors, according to Cowley, committed themselves to
"moral fables and legends" which existed solitarily within their hearts. Faulkner was much less a novelist than
"an epic or bardic poet in prose, a creator," Cowley
concludes, "of myths that he weaves together into a legend of the South."[45]

Hyatt H. Waggoner speaks of a "mythological method" as characteristic of Faulkner's writings, an expression borrowed from T.S. Eliot's description of the
technique of James Joyce. Faulkner imitated both Joyce
and Eliot, Waggoner claims, expanding images into symbols. But Faulkner was able to transcend his regional-
ism to express "eternal and timeless truth."[46]

Olga W. Vickery discusses myth in Faulkner as invention, particularly with reference to Joe Christmas
of Light in August, whose disastrous mixture of white
and black genes determines his character. In this
sense myth becomes something to analyze, to expose,
rather than to illumine or delineate.[47]

But little of this discussion lends overwhelming
light on Faulkner's most mysterious novel, A Fable, one
which critics uniformly disparage. Unlike his Yoknapa-
tawpha saga, whose natural spiritual quest is discernible, A Fable is a thinly disguised parody of the life
of Jesus told as the account of a corporal in a French
regiment during World War I. With eleven others of his
squad--abruptly becoming twelve--he spreads behind the
lines ideas about peace and good will, and induce the
regiment not to attack. When the Germans in the opposite trenches also refuse to fight, the generals on
both sides are required to find a means of resuming the
war. The stubborn resistance of the troops causes rage
and fear everywhere. Death has a free ride in all manner of grisly ways: suicide, shootings, and immolation.
The corporal is discovered to be the illegitimate son
of the French marshal, and is finally executed between
two murderers. Although his body vanishes from its
grave after heavy shellfire, it is ultimately placed in

the tomb of the unknown soldier under the <u>Arc de Tri-</u><u>omphe</u>. Other correspondences between the corporal and Jesus are numerous:

1. The corporal was born in a stable; there was no room at the inn.

2. His father was a French nobleman of god-like bearing who becomes the supreme commander of the Allied Armies in France.

3. His two half-sisters are named Marthe and Marya (the actual number of Jesus' sisters is not given in the synoptic gospels: Matt. 13:56; Luke 6:3.)

4 His wife was a prostitute (Jesus had no wife but showed concern for a prostitute.)

5. He gathers a band of disciples. One is named Paul; another, Pierre, and a third, Polchek. Pierre denies him, tries to give Marthe and Marya thirty pieces of silver, and is believed to have died by hanging.

6. After being shot he falls into a coil of barbed wire and lacerates his head.

In this bizarre story Faulkner intends no ideation of the Christian myth. His focus is man, his bestiality, his outrageous destructiveness, and his lack of charity to the world. R.W.B. Lewis is one of the few commentators who have taken the story seriously enough to discuss its implications at length. Using a Yeatsian distinction, Lewis find the corporal to be

> a rhetorical figure, the product of Faulkner's quarrel with others; not a poetic figure, the product of Faulkner's quarrel with himself. It is a rhetoric that nearly drowns any protest against it in the warmth and beauty of its torrential flow. But through it all we feel a particular presence orating in endless fury against the majestic imbecilities of the modern world. The quarrel is outward, not inward; and the corporal is its instrument.[48]

This outward flow of Faulknerian wrath is unlike that of Graham Greene, for example, who is equally disgusted with man's depravity. But Greene finds its source principally in man's defection from God, and directs his anger inward to the unregenerate heart. Faulkner finds man less in need of reaffirmation of his divine author than in need of giving up his evil ways and returning to his natural covenant with God, in which his basic goodness is affirmed, and by which he is held accountable. This thesis, while underlying A Fable, is central in The Bear. To extract it, however, presents a formidable task.

More than one reader has thrown up his hands in exasperation after futilely trying to sort out the entangled skeins of Faulkner's fiction. In The Bear the overlapping flashbacks, indistinguishable mergers of narration and dialogue, the interminable and unrecognizable sentence structure, and the seemingly unrelated story lines make deciphering the story seem an exercise in the perverse.

What the reader becomes aware of is the crucial fact that Faulkner is not simply telling a tale, with the conventional beginning, middle, and end, whose purpose is merely to titillate the reader's fancy. He aims at no less than the re-creation of the whole spiritual quest of man. He founded his thesis on the Old Testament conviction that man is a tenant of the earth, not its proprietor, and that because man has corrupted his tenancy the land is cursed, as are all who lay claim to it.

This damnation is not the kind which carries the personally discrete punishment of those who break the law of Christ; it is vicarious and undifferentiated. Nor is it the inherited liability of Adam and Eve. It derives from man's direct participation in the natural economy and absolute dependency upon the land as the only means of natural survival. This decisive aspect of The Bear places emphasis upon the care and preservation of this world as man's chief legacy from God. Man's punishment for failing to carry out his charge is his own demise as a natural consequence, not as the result of divine interruption.

The story did not first appear in all of its five parts. The first to appear was "The Deer Hunt" in The Saturday Evening Post in 1934. Ike McCaslin, later the principal character, is only minor here. in 1935 "Lion" appeared in Harper's, a first-person narrative of an abortive chase of Old Ben, the bear, by Ike McCaslin, Major de Spain, and Boon Hogganbeck. Another story appeared in The Saturday Evening Post in 1942 called "The Bear." A boy much like Ike McCaslin in his youth learns

the key lessons about his relation to the primeval land.
In 1942 Faulkner also published the present conflation
greatly revised and expanded, entitling it <u>Go Down Mo-
ses</u>. In 1955 he published a book about the wilderness
call <u>Big Woods</u> which included "The Bear," but without
the long fourth section dealing with miscegenation
among the McCaslins.

The result of leaving out the section on the blacks
is a tightening of the central theme of man's relation
to the land, but the spiritual power of that theme is
greatly diminished. If even the bear hunt itself were
considered the central story, the relationship of the
characters to the bear and the woods would remain primary. The fourth section insures, however laboredly,
that the author's intent is not obscured. At the same
time. it adds the more profound aspect of man's relationship to himself and other men--white, black, red--as determined by his relationship to the land and primeval
nature as symbolized by Old Ben.

The first three sections of the present version
deal with the hunt for Old Ben whom nobody really wants
to kill, but who is tracked yearly in a ritual of ancient challenge of the untamed wilderness. So monolithic is Faulkner that chronology and sequence are mere
tools to illumine and develop his idea. At the beginning of the first section Ike McCaslin is sixteen, but
for only a few pages. Almost immediately Faulkner
launches into a lengthy flashback. On p. 331 of the
Dell edition Ike is ten. The remainder of the section
carries him back to the age of sixteen. The third section is concerned principally with Old Ben's death which
occurs during Ike's sixteenth year. We are thus brought
back to the point at which the story began in the first
section.

Ike is twenty-one as the fourth section opens, but
is carried back to his early childhood during Carothers
McCaslin's philandering with slave women. Then, Faulkner ranges Ike's years all the way to his old age, in-
serting observations and commentary, whether the time
and circumstances have anything to do with the context
of the moment. Indeed, the fourth section brings the
story to the point at which most of the McCaslins are
gone. But in section five we are taken again to the
wilderness where Boon sits in helpless defiance at the
base of a tree, beating his broken rifle, waiting for
the inevitable death of the last wilderness being relentlessly trampled by civilization. Then, once more,
Faulkner reviews Ike's life from boyhood to the moment.

173

Such an erratic style, of course, is not designed
for the casual reader. We are frequently uninformed as
to whom it is that Faulkner is referring. For example,
the elder McCaslin--or someone else--will speak of Tom-
ey's son as "Turl." The narrator, however, will refer
to him as "Terrel." The reader must figure out for himself that the spelling is phonetic in the one instance
and actual in the other for the same name.

In like manner, many readers become frustrated when
attempting to decipher which of the two McCaslins is
speaking in the lengthy colloquies between Ike and his
cousin. The problem is acute in section four which contains one of the longest sentences in American fiction.
Cowley counts eighteen hundred words in it, countable
by the reader on pp. 388-93 of the Dell edition. On
p. 408 Ike has just delivered a long monolgue on God's
primal intent with the land which man has perverted:

> [Ike] "So He turned once more to this land which
> He still intended to save because He had
> done so much for it--"
>
> [Ike's cousin] "What?" and he [Ike]
>
> "To these people He was still committed to
> because they were his creations--" and
> McCaslin [Ike's cousin]
>
> "Turned back to us? His face to us?"
> and he [Ike]
>
> "--whose wives and daughters at least made
> soups and jellies for them when they were
> sick [slaves] . . . ."

The purpose of the style is to suspend a whole concept between a capital letter and a period, so that the
words convey a facet of an unfolding spiritual reality
of ultimate purposiveness behind creation. The dialogue
is dialectic, theses and antitheses from whose syntheses ever higher syntheses are developed. Individuality
is obscured because the idea enveloping it is more important.

And that idea is powerful, that in subjugating the
black man, and in vanquishing the red man, the white man
corrupted the interdependence of them all. The chain
of natural relation binds the wilderness, the wild life
(as typified by Old Ben), the Indian, the white man, and
the black slave. The destruction of any link can be

174

traced back to the defilement of the land. Consequently, the destruction of any link portends the destruction of every other link. As Old Ben dies, Sam Fathers—half Indian, half black—also dies. Ike ultimately becomes an old bachelor living in one room. The slaves and their descendents inured to the curse of the polluted land manage to endure, as by an irony, Ike notes, aping the white man's vices.

Ike finally concludes that white men, having been sent by God to redeem the land, have corrupted it worse than those who possessed it before them; that slavery and the Civil War have permanently corrupted the land; and that he has no choice but to make what amends he can to his half-black relatives, and to reject his inheritance.

In section five Faulkner recapitulates his thesis. "Progress" having inevitably come to the woods, with a lumber company removing the trees, and a train waiting to haul them away, those like Boon who depended upon the wilderness must await their own demise.

To carry the spiritual symbolism of this vision Faulkner devised the following cast which we meet in the first three sections:

Old Ben: The bear. Symbol of the free wilderness in conflict with encroaching man.

Boon Hogganbeck: Symbol of the lost white purity.

Sam Fathers: Half Indian, half black, the pristine primeval man in perfect harmony with the uncorrupted wilderness.

Lion: The wild dog whose untamed courage, together with Boon's, proves equal to Ben's.

Ike McCaslin: The principal bearer of the author's values.

Cousin McCaslin: Ike's alter ego and intellectual antithesis.

Major de Spain
General Compson   } White members of the hunt.
Walter Ewell
Bayard Sartoris

```
Tennie's Jim  ⎫
Uncle Ash     ⎬  Blacks of the hunt.
```

The difficult fourth section sets out the white
and black branches of Ike's genealogical tree, and the
ancestry of Sam Fathers:

The Indians

Issetibbeha: Father of Ikkemotubbe, whose ances-
    tors were first given the land.

Ikkemotubbe: Son of Issetibbeha, Chief of the
    Chickasaw Indians, father of Sam Fathers,
    and from whom Carothers McCaslin bought the
    land over which Ike agonizes.

Sam Father's mother: A slave woman whom Ikkemo-
    tubbe traded to Carothers McCaslin for a trot-
    ting gelding.

The white McCaslins

Carothers: Ike's grandfather, the founder of the
    clan.

Amodeus (Uncle Buddy): One of Carothers' twin
    sons, father of Ike's cousin.

Theophilus (Uncle Buck): Carothers' second twin
    son, Ike's father.

Ike: Principal character and heir.

Cousin McCaslin: The remaining heir.

The black McCaslins

Ike discovers in the old family ledger the record
of Carothers' offspring by a slave girl, assigned the
ostensible parentage of a slave father.

Tomasina: The first daughter of Eunice, but fa-
    thered by Carothers, who dies in childbirth
    at twenty-three.

Terrel (Turl): The second child of Eunice, who
    manages to survive.

Tennie Beauchamp: Won by Amodeus (Uncle Buddy)

176

from Ike's godfather, Hubert Beauchamp, in a
poker game; marries Terrel. Their first three
children die.

James Thucydides Beauchamp: The last name is taken
from his mother; the first child of Terrel and
Tennie to live.

Miss Sophonsiba (Fonsiba): The second child of
Terrel and Tennie to live; marries the "uppi-
ty" Northern-educated Negro preacher who has
no interest in the land.

Lucas Quintus Carothers McCaslin Beauchamp: The
symbol of the entire clan; the last of the
mixed McCaslins to survive.

Percival Brownless: Described as "tragic and mis-
cast," the slave who is utterly unfit for
slave labor. He is almost humorously depicted. The efforts to sell him are futile. His
emancipation costs two hundred and sixty-five
dollars which, of course, he cannot pay. He
leaves with the federal troops, finally ending
up as the keeper of "a select New Orleans
brothel."

Eunice: The slave mistress of Carothers, who committed suicide to the consternation of the
McCaslins who are unable to understand why a
"darky" would do such a thing. It is she who
begins the line of black McCaslins.

With such a cast Faulkner has probed, as few writers have, the nature of Southern miscegenation, the
forced one-sided sexual liaison of white master and
black slave woman--to be certain, it did not happen in
the reverse; sure torture and death awaited the slave
"buck" who eyed a white woman. Ike freely concedes the
blacks to be a part of his family and defends them
against his cousin's charges of "Promiscuity. Violence.
Instability and lack of control." He counters with
"Endurance, and pity, and tolerance and forbearance and
fidelity and love of children."

But it is the exchange between Ike and Fonsiba's
husband that the sharpest cleavage is revealed. The
guilt-ridden Ike is confronting the poverty-stricken,
but studious black with the anomaly of his condition,
blaming it on the cursed land:

177

"Don't you see?" he cried. "Don't you see?
This whole land, the whole South, is cursed, and
all of us who derive from it, whom it ever suckled,
white and black both lie under the curse? Granted
that my people brought their curse onto the land;
maybe for that reason their descendants alone cannot resist it, not combat it--maybe just endure
and outlast it until the curse is lifted. Then
your people's turn will come because we have for-
feited ours. But not now. Not yet. Don't you
see?"

The black preacher is unconvinced:

"You're wrong. The curse you whites brought
into this land has been lifted. It has been void-
ed and discharged. We are seeing a new era, an
era dedicated, as our founders intended it, to
freedom, liberty and equality for all, to which
this country will be the new Canaan--"

But Ike is unable to assimilate this new sense of
freedom and dignity out of what to him is yet unmistakable evidence of the violation of the natural covenant
with God. Unwilling to accept book learning as an adequate substitute for re-establishment of mutual dependency with the land, Ike is contemptuous:

"Freedom from what? From work? Canaan?
He jerked his arm, comprehensive, almost violent:
whereupon it all seemed to stand there about
them, intact and complete and visible in the
drafty, damp, heatless, Negro-rank room--"

Blacks have frequently accused Faulkner of pater-
nalism, of a wish to return them to the plough. However justified the suspicion, Faulkner's approach is
fundamentally sacramental, perceiving man's fate as inextricably rooted in the destiny of the land. Fonsiba's
husband represents a new profaneness, a fresh violation
of the ancient covenant. The curse can be lifted, Faulkner thinks, but only after purgation. Ike's purge of
himself is complete. He sees the black preacher's dream
of a new Canaan as an attempt to escape the penalty
equally upon him. Yet, Faulkner knew as he wrote that
the black attitude was inevitable. Boon and Lion, as
well as Sam Fathers and Ike, are obsolete. Their
deaths leave Ike alone to bear their collective guilt
and to expiate their guilt.

By the time he received the Nobel Prize for literature in Stockholm on 10 December 1950, Faulkner's pessimism had mellowed, his sacramental attitude toward the land dissolved into an exaltation of the human spirit. He is ready to chide the young writer for forgetting "the problems of the human heart in conflict," and to urge him back to "the old universal truths" of "love and honor and pity and compassion and sacrifice." Above all, the Faulkner of the Nobel Prize Address refutes his own conclusion in _The Bear_. "I decline," he declares, "to accept the end of man." Man will prevail, in spite of himself. Alone among animals with a soul and spirit he is, for this reason, immortal. The writer's job is to remind him of his heritage and duty."

Ultimately, Faulkner embraced the most fervent faith in man of which humanism is capable, now affirmed entirely within the precincts of man's own inner divinity. Where God is a direct, if silent, partner in _The Bear_, He is undiscernible in the Nobel Prize Address. It remains unclear, nevertheless, whether Faulkner contemplated in the speech that covenant he so passionately spelled out in _The Bear_. It is more certain that Christianity itself is of minor importance in both. Spiritual dimensions are abundant, but in concern for man the creature. Whatever our final estimate of Faulkner, yet inconclusive at this writing, _The Bear_ remains his most profound effort to bridge the human and the divine.

ERNEST HEMINGWAY: GOD DAMNS YOU

Ernest Hemingway's chief underlying theme is alienation from God, man cast adrift without reliable means to chart his course, or any course to chart. This darkened vision is established in his first novel, <u>The Sun Also Rises</u>, in which Jake Barnes is emasculated in World War I, as a result of which he is emptied of the capacity for meaningful prayer. The irrelevance of the Roman Catholic Church, his only known medium for reaching God, is total. Yet filled with religious consciousness, he can in no way find a means for spiritual communication. The spiritual vacuum is filled by alcohol and the physical sensations of the fiesta and bullfight. Even Lady Brett Ashley, whom Glicksberg says is one of the first American fictional women without remorse for amorality (*cf.* Sister Carrie), is aware of the loss of God. When she leavs Romero for his sake she substitutes her resultant good feeling for a sense of God.[49] Symbolizing the spiritual emasculation of a whole generation by World War I, Jake, who cannot have any sex, and Brett, who wants little else, reflect also Gertrude Stein's characterization of them as "a lost generation."

Stylistically, Hemingway is to modern American literature what Stephen Crane is to the naturalist movement. Between the two of them what is distinctly the American novel was fashioned. Robert Penn Warren has observed that Hemingway has been for twentieth-century prose what Wordsworth was for nineteenth-century poetry.[50] His lean, tough, direct prose would shape American style for decades. At heart, however, he remained a romantic, searching in spite of himself for ultimate meaning. He yearned for deeper purpose and final resolution which would defy all of the skeptics in whose ranks he was so pre-eminent. But he was not to find such meaning. He would die by his own hand, accidentally, some say; deliberately, others say, with his hunting rifle aimed at his head. It would not be, nevertheless, until the midsixties that the Hemingway mystique would give way to another compelling artistic vision, in particular, that of Saul Bellow.

We focus here on his second novel, <u>A Farewell to Arms</u>, which is as fresh and provocative as it was when

first published in 1929. Its total denial of meaningful
destiny, however, has been challenged by new writers,
chiefly Bellow. The story is principally concerned with
the transformation of Frederic Henry, an American ambu-
lance driver, and Catherine Barkley, an English nurse,
both serving as volunteers with the Italian forces in
Italy during World War I. What seems like a tender romance of little more significance than a private disaster is, in reality, a damnation of the whole human
enterprise. The universe emerges as a cold mechanism
with neither purpose nor plan. The very thought of a
God, a Heaven, or benign forces somewhere "out there"
to help preserve men becomes sheerest mockery.

The novel is divided into forty-one chapters, most
of which are short, deceptively simple scenes grouped
into four "books." These divisions are not made on a
set of actions or events, but correspond to stages in
the emotional development of Frederic and Catherine.
It is decisively important to note this fact, as the
lovers are transformed from spiritual war casualties
to helpless pawns of cosmic hostility. In many respects A Farewell to Arms is the first genuinely existential novel, a little more than a decade before the
shattering effects of World War II produced the existentialist movement in France. Its nihilism is complete. The major difference between Hemingway and
the writers of World War II is his romantic sentience
and their naturalist rejection of sense. Where Hemingway tied his novels to those crippled in some vital way
by war, Camus, for example, saw war as only the symptom,
not the cause of, spiritual malaise. Camus' characters
reflect a societal illness turned vengeful against the
innocent (Meursault of *L'Étranger*). In Hemingway the
disease is specific and induced, the cause generalized
and undirected, where loss is measured in personal grief
instead of cosmic significance. Where Meursault was
average, normal, and in no way at war with his society,
Frederic and Catherine increasingly reject their war-
ravaged world and all of the values associated with the
fighting--country, honor, patriotism, sacredness, glory.

In Chapter XXVII when it seems as though the Germans are winning, Frederic muses:

> I was always embarrassed by the words sacred,
> glorious, and sacrifice and the expression in
> vain...and I had seen nothing sacred, and the
> things that were glorious had no glory and the
> sacrifices were like the stockyards at Chicago
> if nothing was done with the meat except to bury

it . . . . Abstract words such as glory, honor
courage, or hallow were obscene beside the concrete names of villages, the number of roads,
the names of rivers, the numbers of regiments
and the dates.[51]

His and Catherine's protest is not against the destruction of societal innocence; theirs is a demand for
meaning and fulfillment based on their psychic and physical needs. When they discover no rights above the demands of war, they brand those demands as false, a cruel
delusion, or as Catherine succinctly put it as she lies
dying "a dirty trick."[52]

In such deception the priest is an object of impotence and gentle ridicule. In Chapter XXV Rinaldi
makes fun of St. Paul who demanded chastity. Accusing
Paul of having been a "rounder and a chaser," Rinaldi
complains that "When he was finished he made the rules
for us who are still hot." Drunk, Rinaldi continues to
bait the priest. His eyes mirror inner anguish. "To
hell with you, priest!" he mutters again and again.
"To hell with the whole damned business."

The priest understands. "It's all right, Rinaldi.
It's all right."

But when Frederic agrees that the whole business
should be damned, Rinaldi cries, "You can't do it. I
say you can't do it. You're dry and you're empty and
there's nothing else. There's nothing else I tell you.
Not a damned thing. I know when I stop working." There
follows the grisly jab about the priest's eating meat on
Friday. The priest asserts that it is Thursday. Too
drunk to care, Rinaldi denies it. "It's a lie. It's
Friday. You're eating the body of our Lord. It's God-
meat. I know. It's dead Austrian. That's what you're
eating."[53]

In the following chapter, only four pages long, a
simple conversation between Frederic and the priest
points up the poignancy of the priest's uselessness,
the nearly total bankruptcy of the church. Its empty
spiritual gestures are no match for the reality of violence, cruelty, and futility. Rinaldi has discovered
what Jake Barnes and Brett Ashley know, that only in
physical sensation is there reality, that when it stops,
life ceases, and nothing remains. The pointlessness of
the war, its unspeakable stupidity, and the degradation
of all human impulses reach him in a shattering crescen-
do. At the end of Chapter XXXII he is prepared to de-

> I was not made to think. I was made to eat.
> My God, yes. Eat and drink and sleep with Cath-
> erine. To-night maybe. No that was impossible.
> But to-morrow night, and a good meal and sheets
> and never going away again except together. Prob-
> ably have to go damned quickly. She would go. I
> knew she would go. When would we go? That was
> something to think about. It was getting dark.
> I lay and thought where we would go. There were
> many places.[54]

Much construction of this declaration is simply romantic, a man turning his back on his obligations and
commitments for the woman he loves. The flight of the
two, Catherine's pregnancy, and their idyllic hideaways
all conduce to a surface impression of the heroism of
love against the world. Nowhere in modern literature
has the tenderness between two people, the dulcet epi-
thets by which they know each other, and their whole
absorption in themselves been more beautifully depicted.
But Hemingway's sure artistic hand is far more sinister.
Convinced that the rules and regulations of society gov-
erning personal conduct, and the institutional structures set up to proscribe and delimit--whose preservation motivated both sides in the war--were designed
chiefly to thwart individual self-fulfillment, he fashioned his lovers as a missile hurled at the system and
its presumed divine sanction.

Delivery of Catherine's child should have been a
routine matter. She was a healthy, normal young woman
in every sense. Nevertheless, her baby was stillborn,
its lifeline curled about its neck, choking off its
breath. When Catherine hemorrhaged, Frederic knew that
his loss would be double. He collapsed into incoherent
prayer to a God who was not listening:

> Don't let her die. Oh, God, please don't let
> her die. I'll do anything for you if you don't
> let her die. Please, please, dear God, don't
> let her die. Dear God, don't let her die.
> Please, please, please don't let her die. God
> please make her not die. I'll do anything you
> say if you don't let her die. You took the ba-
> by but don't let her die. That was all right
> but don't let her die. Please, please, dear
> God, don't let her die.[55]

The physician scoffed. He was sure that she would

live. It is now, as Frederic is ordered out of the room, that Catherine impudently challenges the powers of death: "Don't worry, darling, I'm not a bit afraid. It's just a dirty trick."[56]

What would have been soap opera-like immersion of the reader in depthless personal poignancy becomes, instead, a shattering revulsion. The absolute indifference of a God who ignores the terrified, child-like plea of a helpless man is perhaps here more piercingly illustrative of Hemingway's lifelong attitude than at any other place in his fiction: God damns you.

Into the rain, the tears of the world, Frederic went. There were no howls of execration for him, just a broken heart, the vulnerable Hemingway behind the tough masculine front.

Among theological critics Hemingway is a favorite. They see much in his writings that Christians can learn. Glicksberg, at least, stresses the point that Hemingway tried to make clear that clerical vows and religious sanctions have nothing to do with the spiritual validity of Frederic's and Catherine's personal quest.[57] In the absence of God the necessities of war dictate that they grab what happiness they can. John Killinger discerns that the lovers are not concerned to become Nietzschean supermen. They want only to be human. Killinger lauds Hemingway for writing honestly about the obsolete God and killing him off:

> The God he has slain is only a God who has de-
> served to be slain. The honesty with which he
> faced the contemporary religious situation is
> --or should be--a welcome curative to an unfor-
> tunate kind of supernaturalism quite popular in
> any age, whose God just floats around in the
> wild blue yonder without really seeming to be in
> touch with things.[58]

But Killinger gets carried away. What would have been a credible thesis becomes unsupportable speculation when he sees in Hemingway's handling of The Old Man and the Sea a reuniting of "certain important symbols of the Christian faith or of almost any faith--the sea, the fish, the cross--with their primeval sources, reviving in power and eloquence figures which had to some extent become arid and dumb."[59]

To speak of symbols in Hemingway is dangerous business. It implies a new Hemingway abandoning his intense-

ly private and wholly personal world for the larger, socially significant protagonist. Indeed as Killinger
would have it, the sea may prefigure "the mysterious
cradle of life"; the fish may represent "primitive forms
of life"; and the Old Man's bearing the mast up the hill,
with hands lacerated from the struggle with the marlin,
may suggest the cross. But to propose that Hemingway
has imbued the story with a profound Christian consciousness is to misread it entirely, to have it say
what the commentator wishes it to say rather than what
it does say.

What is more surprising in a critic who so often
strikes at the crux, Glickesberg would have us believe
that in Santiago's struggle against the sharks for the
eighteen-foot marlin which he ultimately loses Hemingway "found God."[60]

The fact is that Hemingway has not supplied a God
for the one he has killed, nor has he evinced any suggestion of religious conversion. His theme remains consistent: the dignity and courage of individual man
struggling against impossible odds without cosmic help
or concern. Santiago is mellowed, patient, full of the
wisdom of years, and determined, but he does not differ
generically from his younger compatriots in the Hemingway world. He is the apotheosis of Hemingway's unvary-
ing thesis that it is the struggle that counts, not the
victory, for that is denied man. To give up struggle is
to give up life. Thus, Santiago goes back to sea, as he
must. In that alone does he justify his dignity, his
manhood.

If Hemingway's disaffection were without sentiment
just below the surface, it would compare with that of
the nihilists for whom struggle itself is as meaningless as the purposeless universe. But Hemingway remained God-conscious, never forgiving God, in whatever way
encountered, for deserting him. The shadow of the
crippled Jake Barnes, made impotent in the service of
an ideal, hovered over Hemingway's pen. Hemingway's
vision manifested a quarrel with God, rather than a rejection, a fear stained into his being that God did not
care. The cool dispassionate prose, the syntax of the
simple sentence, and the terse image veiled the deepest
yearning for contact with Jake Barnes' God to whom Jake
earnestly wished to pray, but could not. Here, it
seems, is the core of Hemingway's religious dilemma: the
ineluctable accession to a broken dream, but the refusal
to give up, even in the face of unyielding damnation by
a God who yet refused to let him go.

186

SAUL BELLOW: PHOENIX RISING

Saul Bellow is persistently asked whether he considers himself a "Jewish" writer. The soft-spoken, shy author denies any special Jewishness in his works. Although many of his characters have Jewish backgrounds, he finds nothing unique in their experiences. When he was nine his parents emigrated from Montreal to Chicago. Russian in origin, the family became thoroughly Yiddish. Young Saul became fluent in the dialect. Whatever his artistic intent, Bellow personally maintains his Jewish heritage.

His first novel appeared in 1944, at a time the Allies were beginning to win the war against Germany and Japan, but various existentialisms were about to become the post-war literary modes. Entitled Dangling Man, the novel foreshadowed Bellow's career-long concern with urban disaffection and the struggle to overcome. The decisive aspect was Bellow's casting the struggle in terms of the human spirit, rather than in the predominating naturalist tradition.

During the fifties American writers such as J.D. Salinger were concerned to expose the sham of middle-class value structure, as interpreted, for example, by Holden Caulfield, the somewhat askew teenager of The Catcher in the Rye. In 1953, two years after Catcher appeared, Bellow published The Adventures of Augie March. Although a Jewish lad, Augie is the first cousin of Holden and all of Bellow's subsequent characters in their youth. Indeed, except for his wealth, Henderson of The Rain King could be Augie grown-up.

Augie March won for Bellow his first National Book Award. This novel established his style which employed the comic as well as the serious. Augie is clearly the ethnically Jewish young man, but his quest for understanding in the world of his life knows no ethnic or religious bounds. Like Holden Caulfield, Augie is no young hero; he may even be described as picaresque. As the Rain King Henderson becomes almost ridiculously picaresque. Bellow's point is clear: the anti-hero "stranger" is dead along with the pristine Aristotelian hero. In the places of both a new modern man is rising from his own ashes.

Bellow's achievement is all the more remarkable when one considers that although Aristotle's concept of the hero no longer prevails, with widely scattered exceptions such as Graham Greene's whiskey priest in The Power and the Glory, a caricature does: the young, handsome, preferably Nordic, male; the shaggy, chest-bared sex symbol. Herzog, Bellow's sixth novel, assuredly contains none. The protagonist's full name is Moses Elkanah Herzog. He is middle-aged, a university professor with a Ph.D. degree, and cuckolded by his best friend. Furthermore, he is Jewish. Neither Aristotle nor the Christian version has contemplated Jews as heroes.

Scarred by holocaust and catastrophe the modern Jewish experience has been explored in several directions. We have already noted J.D. Salinger's gentle ridicule of pretension, but from the vantage of the boy out of step with the hypocrisy surrounding him. There is Bernard Malamud's suffering Jew in alien lands, and Philip Roth's horrible contemporary realities. It remained for Bellow to cast his protagonists in roles which showed the impossibility of heroes, the yearning for which lies implicit in much of the literature of disaster. Bellow would seek among his characters for full self-affirmation in the common man who can lose his commoness, if not his existential entrapment. To understand why it is not likely that an Aristotelian hero will emerge in the resurgence of re-affirmation, we might simply glance at the requirements as a modern novelist would view them:

Modern pluralized society does not present the required conditions for the heroic model. Competing socio-economic and religious groups poise themselves against older, entrenched political and economic ruling groups, whoever they may be at whatever given moment. Racial and cultural minorities ever gaining vocal and political influence insure that such a model cannot rise. If, for example, a novelist wished to lend heroic stature to a fictionalized John F. Kennedy and Martin Luther King, Jr., he would have these criteria to consider:

1. The hero must be fully human in abilities, attitudes, and limitations. However high his social, economic, or political status he cannot be above the national law or a god.

   In the case of King an appeal to a "higher law" might

188

*be made, considering how the Civil Rights leader relied
upon it to validate his breaking of the national law.
The model is* Antigone. *With Kennedy the national law
would suffice. Both men were pre-eminently human, perhaps the strongest point under this criterion.*

2. The hero must be "a man like ourselves," neither too good or too bad, making mistakes and
   being subject to fate--or God.

   *The question here, obviously, is whose fate, whose God?
   Kennedy was a nominal Roman Catholic; King was a Southern Baptist. Herzog was a Jew. The argument that all
   have the same God is in heroic terms absurd when one
   glances over the irreconcilable claims made by them all.
   This flaw is fatal for the Aristotelian concept.*

3. The hero is faced with a dilemma which requires
   him to act decisively. He can neither escape
   nor shirk the challenge. He may be required
   to die or suffer grave deprivation. His death
   or deprivation is not punitive; it is simply
   decreed by inscrutable fate--or God.

   *With this requirement we run headlong into an impassable
   wall. The hero purports to be acting in concert with
   fate--or God--for the good of the nation. There is no
   such literary animal as the private hero rising to do-
   mestic height. The absolute essential is homogeneity
   of people, God, and goal, a situation achieved only
   once in the Judeo-Christian world: at its birth during
   the epoch of the Ancient Hebrews called by Yahweh--or
   Elohim to be "a holy people" set aside for His special
   purpose. This election of Israel provides the only
   historical reason for the existence of the Jewish religion at all. The Christians shattered this reason by
   expropriating the Jewish Scriptures for themselves and
   declaring an ultimate meaning for them that would outrage their authors. From its inception Christianity
   made virtually impossible the survival of Aristotelian
   principles; indeed, tragedy, the essential milieu of the
   hero, has no place in Pauline theology.*

4. For all intents and purposes the hero is a cosmic pawn.

   *The ultimate result of heroic action is a restoration of
   cosmic or divine order, balance, or stability; the human is only incidental. The offense in which the hero
   is involved, culpably or merely instrumentally, is
   against the heavens, not the mere human. Heroism is the*

189

substance of the human actions demanded to satisfy the divine rancor. Neither Kennedy nor King could meet this criterion in a heterogeneous society,

5. God--or fate--is the supreme consideration and ultimate significance. The hero is tragic because he is the reminder of that fact, the means by which the nation may purge itself of its sloth and be reminded of its utter subjection to divine caprice.

As the bulk of our study indicates, the gradual shift in Western literature has been from theocentrism to anthropocentrism. With the dialectics of literary genre moving from romanticism into realism, naturalism, and ultimately into nihilism, the key role of God or fate was dissipated, thus removing the foundation of heroism. Without God, therefore, there can be no heroic stature. Misfortune can be no more than misfortune. What under the aegis of divine sanction is tragedy becomes without it only disaster or catastrophe--private calamity such as early death of a loved one, or a three-car accident. A novelist would have a difficult time convincing the literary cognoscenti that God or fate was classically central in the significance of the death of Kennedy or King. However private and public were the disasters occasioned by their assassination, neither could be made literarily recognizable as heroes.

As we have seen, the writer reflecting the loss of heroic qualities most influentially was Hemingway. In him the compatible elements of the genres coalesced producing the dominant American artistic vision until the aftermath of World War II.

With fresh insight pointing a way back from the ashes of burned out human aspiration, Bellow possesses both the peculiar elements of ethnic origin and religious consciousness combined with the literary genius to rise from Hemingway and the cult of hopelessness. The death of the hero does not leave us only the alternative of nihilism. We see this best in Herzog.

But first a word about the structure of the novel. If form is mimetic, with an Aristotelian beginning, middle and end, then Herzog is formless. Further, if form relates to a set of actions in which a group of characters moves and comes to some conclusions growing out of these actions, then Herzog is poorly constructed. And if there is a world-of-the-novel, as opposed to the real world, where the one is merely an illusion of the

other, then Herzog defies the distinction. It is a
novel superbly of the human spirit, an adventure of the
soul in search of itself, as itself, in the circumstances of itself. It is the odyssey of a man falling back
upon the essence within himself in the manifest failure
of essence external to himself. We move not from scene
to scene, nor from action to action, nor are the characters necessarily related to each other. We move from
the nucleus of Herzog's inner being outward, ever widening concentrically until we have been engulfed in Herzog's consciousness, until the distinction between author and reader, between Herzog's world and our own has
vanished.

Bellow's intent is to establish an identity of reality between Herzog and us, so that the stages of
spiritual growth in the profoundly disturbed Herzog of
the early part of the novel become our own in ever-in-
creasing intensity.

In classically disputatious style Herzog builds his
way through four major areas of his life: sex, love,
faith, reason. To achieve spontaneity and contempora-
neity, the author uses nearly all of the literary techniques at his command: the flashback, the interior mono-
logue, the narrative interpolation, and the episodic
fragment relayed from the depth of Herzog's mind chiefly though letters, sundry missives to everyone, living
and dead. The epistolary technique affords Bellow an
unmatched method to illumine and discuss the complex
issues of history, culture, religion, and philosophy
which in the hands of any less skilled author would
have proved disastrous. No one was more surprised than
Bellow when Herzog not only became a best seller, but
won the National Book Award for fiction in 1965. For
whatever reason the ordinary reader purchased a book
about a university professor's intellectual and spiritual crisis written on a Ph.D. level of concept, Herzog
remains a literary turning point.

Herzog first sought fulfillment in sex, but little
came of his relationship with his first wife, Daisy.
She bore his ponderous intellectualism "with heavy neu-
trality, recording her objections each time." A simple
girl, she was hardly his intellectual equal.

With Madeleine, his second wife, he achieved intellectual parity, but hardly improved his sex life. Writing a doctoral dissertation on Russian religious history, she brings her dusty volumes to bed. To Herzog's
complaint, the supremely disorderd Madeleine, who has a

stint at conversion from Judaism to Roman Catholicism, "jumped at him with her fists, not pummeling him woman-like, but swinging like a street fighter with her knuckles." In discussing the incident with Gersbach, his best friend and rival for her sexual favors, he mentions her outrageously unhygienic habits and unpredictable behavior. That night before the abrupt attack she had consented to sexual intercourse, "but as soon as it was over she turned on the light, picked up one of those dusty Russian folios, put it on her chest and started to read away." If that were not enough, Herzog adds, "As I was leaving her body, she was reaching for the book. Not a kiss. Not a last touch. Only her nose twitching." Though enraged, she once submitted on the bathroom tiles.

Then there were Ramona and Sono. The warmth of the little Japanese, Sono, who stayed with him against her parents' wishes, contrasted comfortingly to Madeleine's cold rapacity. Ramona wanted to replace the castrating bitch wife, "wanted to add riches to his life and give him what he pursued in the wrong places." He hoped eagerly that she was right, that he could renew the spirit through the flesh. But women were not the route. There was nothing Lawrentian or Joycean about Herzog. Indeed, he could not find a spiritual source in any woman. He was trapped between the monstrous Madeleine and the extremely feminine Ramona and Sono.

In matters of love without a sexual content Herzog was equally stymied. Gersbach, who swore his undying love of Herzog and Madeleine both, made a mockery of love and a prize fool of Herzog by bedding the willing Madeleine. Family love attached too much duty, tedia, burden, sterility.

Religion certainly offered him little solace. A free-thinker at sixteen, he had been revolted by Oswald Spengler's estimate of the fate of the West. From that "sinister kraut" he recalled learning

> That I, a Jew, was born Magian and that we Mag-
> ians had already had our great age, forever
> past. No matter how hard I tried, I would never
> grasp the Christian and Faustian world idea, for-
> ever alien to me. Disraeli *thought* he could un-
> derstand and lead the British, but he was totally
> mistaken. I had better resign myself to Destiny.
> A Jew, a relic as lizards are relics of the great
> age of reptiles, I might prosper in a false way
> by swindling the *goy*, the laboring cattle of civil-

ization dwindled and done for. Anyway, it was
an age of spiritual exhaustion--all the old
dreams were dreamed out. I was angry; I burned
like that furnace; reading more, sick with rage.61

He was equally outraged at the notion of *"Creative
suffering"* said by a Professor Hocking in his latest
book to be *"At the core of Christian belief."*62 What
Herzog determined he wanted was justice, the justice
that billions of mankind had never had. That justice,
Herzog concluded while looking at his lathered face in
the bathroom mirror, was the granting of his humanity.

Almost paralyzed with horror, he sat in a courtroom
listening to testimony of child abuse ending in death.
In total frustration at the child's inability to be toi-
let trained, and at his constant crying, the mother had
hurled him against the wall while her boyfriend lay in
bed, smoking. Close to vomiting, Herzog left with a
feeling of impotence. In what way was suffering "creative?" How should he act in the overwhelming presence
of helplessness?

> Herzog experienced nothing but his own *human
> feelings*, in which he found nothing of use.
> What if he felt moved to cry? Or pray? He
> pressed hand to hand. And what did he feel?
> Why he felt himself--his own trembling hands,
> and eyes that stung. And what was there in mod-
> ern . . . post-Christian America to pray for?
> Justice--justice and mercy? And pray away the
> monstrousness of life, the wicked dream it was?
> He opened his mouth to relieve the pressure he
> felt. He was wrung, and wrung again, and wrung
> again, again.63

His disordered thoughts began to reach a lucidity
that had eluded him. Intellectualism had not prepared
him for the reality of the heart, for suffering as the
universal common denominator. Before, he had complained
about being trapped in pain, at a time he was discovering no answers among his girlfriends:

> I fall upon the thorns of life, I bleed. And
> then? I fall upon the thorns of life, I bleed.
> And what next? I get laid, I take a short holi-
> day, but very soon after I fall upon those same
> thorns with gratification in pain, or suffering
> in joy, who knows what the mixture is! What good,
> what lasting good is there in me? Is there noth-
> ing else between birth and death but what I can

193

get out of this perversity--only a favorable
balance of disorderly emotions? No freedom?
Only impulses? And what about all the good I
have in my heart--doesn't it mean anything? Is
it simply a joke? A false hope that makes a
man feel the illusion of worth? And so he goes
on with his struggles. But this good is no pho-
ny. I know it isn't. I swear it.[64]

Now he was ready to accede, to embrace the reality
of the moment in all of its horrors and its joys. He
had touched bottom, but he would not settle there. Nor
could he soar up from it. But he was not a Camus-like
stranger, nor a faceless Kafkan K. He was instead at
last on the route to self-affirmation, becoming imbued
with the majesty of nature, with the sheer fact of just
being alive. There is no Eliot-like recantations, no
casting himself up on the shoals of Mother Judaism. He
has had, notwithstanding, a genuine religious experience
in his intense battle with non-being within the phenomenological encounter with the ground of his being. True
existential man, as Tillich has observed, is alone as
every essentially motivated man is, who begins to rely
upon manifest self-evidence, the knowledge that ultimate concern transforms finite concern, the everyday te-
dium and frustration into the dynamic reality of the
here and now.

Taking that first step as he walked from the court
house, he began to realize that he was not responsible
for man's cruelty, his ignorance, selfishness, and greed
either by primitive code, heavenly decree, or by vicarious liability. Being not condemned to his fellow man
he need not be bound by him. The universe is a free
agent, and he within that freedom was free to choose
and embrace himself. He was no hero; neither was he
a tragedy:

> I look at myself and see cheek, thighs, feet--
> a head. This strange organization, I know it
> will die. And inside--something, something,
> happiness . . . "Thou movest me." That leaves
> no choice. Something produces intensity, a ho-
> ly feeling, as oranges produce orange, as grass
> green, presumably. Does it signify anything?
> There are those who say this product of hearts
> is knowledge . . . . "Thou movest me." "But
> what do you want, Herzog?" But that's just it--
> not a solitary thing. I am pretty well satis
> fied to be just as it is willed, and for as long
> as I may remain in occupancy.[65]

194

NOTES: CHAPTER III

[1]*Bernard Shaw* (London: Methuen & Co., 1967), pp. x-xvi.

[2]*Prefaces by Bernard Shaw* (London: Constable and Co., 1934), p. 648.

[3]*Religion and the Rebel* (Westport, Con.: Greenwood Press, 1957), p. 253.

[4]Acts 9:4.

[5]*Prefaces*, p. 566.

[6]*Ibid.*, p. 568.

[7]See Shaw's discussion of the obsolescence of the Roman Catholic and Protestant churches in *Platform and Pulpit*, ed. Dan H. Laurence (New York: Hill and Wang, 1961).

[8]Religion defined as ultimate concern beyond human self-sufficiency.

[9]*Bernard Shaw: Playboy and Prophet* (New York: D. Appleton and Co., 1932), p. 517.

[10]*Ibid.*, p. 519.

[11]*Ibid.*, p. 521 n.

[12]*Ibid.*, 520 n.

[13]*Prefaces*, p. 167.

[14]*Ibid.*, p. 168.

[15]*Bernard Shaw*, p. 134.

[16]*Platform and Pulpit*, p. 113. Delivered on 13 November 1919.

[17]*The Adventures of the Black Girl in Her search for God* (London: Constable & Co., 1932), p. 73.

[18]*Ibid.*, p. 74.

[19]*Ibid.*

[20]*Adventures of the White Girl in Her search for God* (Milwaukee: Morehouse Publishing Co., 1933), p. 9.

[21]*Ibid.*, pp. 29-30.

[22]*The Adventures of the Black Girl*, pp. 24-25.

[23]*Ibid.*, p. 55.

[24]*Archibald MacLeish* (New York: Twayne Publishers, 1965), p. 19.

[25]*The Collected Poems of Archibald MacLeish* (Boston: Houghton Mifflin Co., 1962), p. 48.

[26]*Ibid.*, pp. 165-66.

[27]*Yeats and the Belief in Life* (University of New Hampshire, 1958), p. 13.

[28]See Allen Tate, *Reactionary Essays on Poetry and Ideas* (New York: Charles Scribner's Sons, 1936), pp. 202-09; Cleanth Brooks, *Modern Poetry and the Tradition* (Chapel Hill: University of North Carolina Press, 1939), pp. 116-25; John Ciardi, "The Poetry of Archibald MacLeish," *The Atlantic Monthly*, 191, No. 5 (May 1953), 67.

[29]See Archibald MacLeish, *Poetry and Experience* (Boston: Houghton Mifflin Co., 1954).

[30]"The Prose of Poetry," *The Saturday Review*, 5 Mar. 1955, pp. 47-48.

[31]*The Spiritual Aspects of the New Poetry* (New York: Harper & Brothers, 1940), p. 98.

[32]*The Books of the Old Testament* (New York: Harper & Brothers,

[33](Farmington, Conn.: First Church of Christ [Congregational: 1652], 1955), p. 8.

[34]*Ibid.*

[35]*Ibid.*

[36]*Ibid.*

[37]"The Poet's Three Comforters: *J.B.* and the Critics," *Modern Drama*, 2, No. 3 (December 1959), 228.

[38]*Ibid.*, pp. 224-30; Marion Montgomery, "On First Looking into MacLeish's Play in Verse, *J.B.*, pp. 231-42; Falk, pp. 149-50.

[39]*J.B., A Play in Verse* (Boston: Houghton Mifflin Co., 1958), pp. 151-53.

[40]"On First Looking into MacLeish's Verse Play." p. 240.

[41]"Faulkner's Mythology," *Faulkner: A Collection of Critical Essays*, ed. Robert Penn Warren (Englewood Cliffs: Prentice Hall, 1960), pp. 24-25.

[42]*William Faulkner: A Critical Study* (New York: Vintage Books 1951), pp. 27-28.

[43]*The Art of Faulkner's Novels* (Austin: University of Texas Press, 1946), pp. 27.

[44]Quoted by Malcolm Cowley, intro. and ed., *The Portable Faulkner* (New York: The Viking Press, 1966), p. xxix.

[45]*Ibid.*, p. xxx.

[46]*William Faulkner: From Jefferson to the World* (Lexington: University of Kentucky Press, 1966), p. 14.

[47]*The Novels of William Faulkner: A Critical Interpretation* (Louisiana State University Press, 1964), pp. 84-102.

[48]*The Picaresque Saint: Representative Figures in Contemporary Fiction* (New York: J.B. Lippincott Co., 1959), p. 213.

[49]*The Sexual Revolution in Modern American Literature* (The Hague: Matinus Nijhoff, 1971), p. 83.

[50]Cited by John Killinger, "Hemingway and 'Our Essential Worldliness'," *Forms of Extremity in the Modern Novel*, ed. Nathan A. Scott, Jr. (Richmond, Va.: John Knox Press, 1965), p. 36.

[51]New York: Charles Scribner's Sons, 1929), pp. 184-85.

[52]*Ibid.*, p. 331.

[53]*Ibid.*, p. 174.

[54]*Ibid.*, p. 233.

[55]*Ibid.*, p. 330.

[56]*Ibid.*, p. 331.

[57]*The Sexual Revolution*, p. 87, and p. 91.

[58]"Hemingway and 'Our Essential Worldiness'," p. 51.

[59]*Ibid.*

[60]*Modern Literature and the Death of God*, p. 145.

[61]*Herzog* (New York: The Viking Press, 1964, p. 234.

[62]*Ibid.*, p. 219.

[63]*Ibid.*, p. 240.

[64]*Ibid.*, pp. 206-07.

[65]*Ibid.*, p. 340.

CHAPTER IV: THE NIHILISTS

ROBINSON JEFFERS: THE HUMAN INHUMANIST

In the first part of our study we were at some labor to delineate the course of humanistic development
in Western literature, showing the gradual shift from a
theocentric to anthropocentric emphasis. After the literary pessimism of the first half of the twentieth century, the cry of Bellow's Herzog in his rise from the
slough of despair to the plain of self-embrace was the
initial triumph of a man who had battled inhumanity,
the forces arrayed against his recognition and affirmation of his dignity and participation in the universe.
Such a pattern of ascent presupposes a worth inherent
in the human enterprise, frequently abused, suppressed,
exploited, but never fully smothered. Those self-evi-
dent truths which the Age of Reason provided Jefferson
in the writing of the Declaration of Independence, those
goals of life, liberty, and the pursuit of happiness
now at least theoretically affirmed by every major socio-political structure in the world today, have supplanted the literary disillusion resulting from the two
world wars which so shattered Robinson Jeffers, as well
as a great many of his contemporaries. Traditional
Christianity has not made a significant literary come-
back beyond a few major writers, but the reassertion of
human worth by writers resisting traditional faith is
the first step toward rapprochement. If this trend be
growing in modern literature, then what Jeffers termed
"inhumanism" is a decided anomaly. In purport it is a
complete denial of human worth, the inversion of the
Calvinism he fled at an early age. For those encounter-
ing Jeffers for the first time it will be difficult to
assimilate the horrors which he depicts human beings in-
flicting upon each other, without at least the passing
thought that his omission of the opposite manifestations
of the human character results in deliberate distortion
of the totality of the human proposition.

It is no suprise, then, that opposition against him
clamored. He was compelled to explain what he meant by
"inhumanism." In the Preface of his long poem, <u>Double
Axe</u>, he wrote that it was

> a shifting of emphasis and significance from
> man to not-man; the rejection of human solip-

sism and recognition of the transhuman magnificence. It seems that our race began to
think as an adult does, rather than like an
egocentric baby or insane person. This manner of thought and feeling is neither misanthropic nor pessimistic, though two or three
people have said so and may again. It in-
volves no falsehoods, and is a means of main-
taining sanity in slippery times; it has objective truth and human value. It offers a
reasonable detachment as rule of conduct, instead of love, hate and envy. It neutralizes
fanaticism for the religious instinct, and
satisfies our need to admire greatness and
rejoice in beauty.[1]

We should take care to discern the distinction between inhumanity and inhumanism. Inhumanity is the violation of men by other men, the abuse, denial, and destruction of the rights, privileges, and opportunities
due them all. Inhumanity is the reduction of men from
an a priori status of something higher than other animals, but less than godhood, and from that uniqueness
in the universal hierarchy worthy of preservation, respect and affection.

Inhumanism is a radical change of focus and direction from the fulfillment of the individual to rejection of his claim to be something special in the universe. The scientific development of the nineteenth
century, notably Darwinism, spurred Jeffers' acceptance
of the mechanistic evolutionary principle, while inspir-
ing his rejection of the romantic notion of discrete
human consciousness and feeling. He turned to physics
and astronomy, impressed by the discovery that the neb-
ulae in the Milky Way were really distant galaxies,
rather than as supposed cosmic specks in its tail. In
such an almost inconceivably vast universe the pretensions of earthlings were utterly ridiculous.

Nevertheless, Jeffers' prime motivation was the inhumanity around him, the commonplace cruelty and bestiality of the vainglorious creature who would claim a place
equal to the stars. Where Herzog, faint from the shock
of a child murder by a crazed mother, became abject in
claiming his humanity, Jeffers could only turn away in
disgust. The magnificence of nature was his alternative,
not in some Wordsworthian sense, but in its vast compos-
ite of timelessness, imperviousness to men, and utter
reliability of cosmic reality.[2]

200

Christianity fared little better, lumped into the malevolence of humanity. Yet nowhere is the power of the historical Jesus upon artistic consciousness more starkly illustrated. And perhaps as much as any literary rebel of the twentieth century--including Lawrence--he has been subjected to virulent attack. His dramatic poem--some say passion play--Dear Judas, with its companion, The Loving Shepherdess, explores the concept of Jesus within the inhumanist context. It is, to say the least, astounding. Dear Judas caused a critical explosion, the most damning of which came from Yvor Winters: "Mr. Jeffers' mouthpiece and hero, Jesus," Winters declared, "is little short of revolting as he whips reflexively from didactic passion to malice, self-justification, and vengeance."3 Jeffers' reputation never fully recovered from the assault. Robert J. Brophy recorded the uproar caused when the poem was adapted for the stage in the late 1940's by Eric Vaugn. It was to be premiered in Oakland, California. The local Roman Catholic bishop was so incensed that he threatened excommunication of the two principal players and the choreographer. The play was then moved to Boston where Bach chorales and interpretive dancing were included.4 Predictably, as Melba B. Bennett writes, churchmen were so outraged that both the mayor and the local censor publicly condemned it. Moved on to Ogunquit, Maine, the play finally opened in spite of continued opposition. The audience was small and unenthusiastic, Ms. Bennett says, but persisting, its producer, Michael Meyerberg, took the play to New York City. He induced Jeffers to write an explanation of the play, hoping to clarify some of the gross misinterpretation of its intent. On 6 October 1947, a lengthy apologetic appeared in the drama section of The New York Times. In it Jeffers denied that his play was written to disturb anyone's religious faith:

It was written, like other poems of mine, because the great passions that produced some significant event came visibly into my mind and sought expression. But these were the passions of Jesus, of Mary, of Judas; I was fool enough to think that I could succeed where Milton nobly failed . . . .

To anyone who reads the gospels attentively--as I was required to do under the stern eye of the Presbyterian clergyman, my father--it soon becomes apparent that, though the deeds and sayings are of a beautiful simplicity, the minds of some of the persons are very far from simple. Peter's mind was

simple, no doubt, faithful, impulsive, bewilder-
ed, very human. The mind of Jesus is shown to
us as if unintentional, in wonderful glimpses,
through the objective narrative. It is deep,
powerful and beautiful; and strangely complex,
not wholly integrated. He is the Prince of
Peace, and yet He came "not to bring peace but
a sword." He is gentle and loving yet He drives
men with whips from the temple, He calls down destruction on Jerusalem. His curse kills an innocent fig tree.

This is not the mind of mere incarnation of
love, as the sentimentalists represent him, but
of a man of genius, a poet and a leader, a man
of such great quality that He has been regarded
as God--literally God--by successive millions of
people for eighteen centuries (and some future
ones) of the greatest age in human history. That
is why there is no attempt in my play to represent
this mind directly; but only through its ghost,
its haunting echo of after-flame.

Again, the mind of Judas, as represented in
the gospels, is obscured and sick and divided.
It may be reptilian, according to the motive that
drives him; but surely the motive was not mere
lust for money. He was a man who had been accepted
among Christ's disciples; his despair at the end
was so deep that he threw back the silver to those
from whom he had received it, and went and hanged
himself. One is left free to imagine his mind,
provided only that it tallies with his acts; and I
have imagined it as skeptical, humanitarian, pessimistic and sick with pity.[5]

However sincere Jeffers' words ring, the play ran
only two weeks.

Like many of Yeats' plays, Dear Judas shows the influence of the Japanese Noh plays in which the scenes,
rather than the players, are central. Its action is
slow, ritualistic, filled with chants to drum and flute,
and carried to establish a mood more than a pattern of
causation. Three divisions within the continuous action
are discernible: the dreams of Judas, Jesus, and Mary
determined by the change of point of view.

The play opens with Judas' betrayal of Jesus, and
then takes Judas back in a dream flashback to his first
meeting with the "Master." Upon pity for a dog struck

202

by a butcher with a meat cleaver, Jesus advises Judas from the heart of Jeffers' inhumanist concept: "To other men I say *Be merciful* / To you alone / *Be cruel.* Life is not lived without some balance." To this counsel Judas replies, "I knew that you had no power to save me."

It is, of course, such lines that so greatly offended the churchmen. Although Jesus insists that he is doing God's will, Judas is unable to assimilate the idea that Jesus' true mission is to eliminate life itself as the greatest obstacle to man's merger with God. The advice to be cruel, however, is aimed at eliminating any respect for the utterly pointless strife of baneful existence, at clearing the way for the conscious to lose itself in the timelessness of the unencumbered universe.

Jesus explains the lateness of his mission--why he waited until his thirtieth year--by blaming his mother for having kept him in ignorance of his true identity, which he did not discover until John the Baptist informed him. Judas is warned by a woman claiming to be both "Night" and his mother against Jesus' delusions of grandeur. Fearing that Jesus will deliver the people to "sudden bloody destruction," Judas betrays him to prevent it.

In the next division we learn of Jesus' dream. When informed by his mother of Judas' intent to betray him, Jesus boasts of power over men. Either he is the son of God, as she claims, or a bastard. To save him from manifest folly in persisting in his role as saviour, Mary denies that he is either. His father, she mutters, is "The great stone on the road to Nazareth." Refusing to believe her, Jesus insists on his Godly origin.

A long statement follows in characteristic Jeffers style. Jesus denounces the Jews for swallowing "Absurd marvels / Without winking . . . ." He accuses them of loving terror, for making pain "almost the God / Of doubtful men, who tremble expecting to endure it."

However insulted were the bishops and laity of the established religion, Jeffers makes some kind of sense within the consistency of his vision. No one, least of all his mother, understands what salvation is. There is little doubt, nonetheless, that the historic Jesus conceived of his mission as Messiah exactly opposite of Jewish expectation. He was indeed dangerous to the existing religious order. To urge renunciation for its own sake, to seek oblivion in the repudiation of human struggle, and to insist upon scorn of the hopes of men to improve their earthly lot understandably brought the wrath of the establishment down upon him. When in Jeffers' play Jesus is surrounded and taken, the beleaguered poet is at least historically accurate.

We now enter upon Mary's dream, a flashback to what she had thought would be her son's triumph, in spite of her trepidation. What may have shocked churchmen most was her calling her conception her "secret sin." In a prayer to God she exclaims "How marvelously thou hast made my secret sin the glory of the world. I saw his triumph in his eyes / Before they told me. Without my sin he'd not have been born, not yet without my falsehood have triumphed . . . ." But when Lazarus announces to her that Jesus has been hanged, Mary curses Judas as the cause of her son's downfall. Lazarus, however, understands. The crucifixion is a triumph, not a defeat. Jesus has conquered humanity, what we term humanism. There is no resurrection, of course, as that would mean capitulation to what Jesus has vanquished. Thus Judas need not be mourned in his self-destruction. His death complements the crucifixion. Lazarus proclaims it:

> Let him go. He has done all he was made for;
>   the rest's his own. Let him and the other
>   at the poles of the wood
> Their pain drawn up to burning points and cut
>   off, praise God after the monstrous manner
>   of mankind.
> While the white moon glides from this garden'
>   the glory of darkness returns a moment, on
>   the cliffs of dawn.[6]

Jesus has consistently praised Judas, calling him a faithful friend who is unable to understand the nature of Jesus' mission. He fears that Judas will die or torture himself in remorse. Yet, Jesus does indeed catch a glimpse of what his crucifixion has meant down through the ages, although in a decidedly different set of contexts. Upon explaining why he he has refused to submit, even mildly, to the clamor against him, Jesus explains that he might have lost the cross. "[W]ithout that," he declares,

> The fierce future world would never knee down to slake
>   its lusts at my fountain. Only a crucified
> God can fill the wolf bowels of Rome: only a torture
>   high up in the air, and crossed beams, hang
>   sovereign

When the blond savages exalt their kings; when
    the north moves, and the hairy-breasted
    north in unbound,
And Caesar a mouse under the hooves of the horses . . . .
    Alas poor dreamer,
Dreaming wildly because you must die. I know
    certainly the cross will conquer; but Rome
    to go down,
Or nations be born to colonize with new powers
    and peoples, and my gaunt pain erected in
    counterfeit,
The coasts of undreamed of oceans, is delirium.[7]

Thus, Jesus explains why Judas must betray him, unlike at all the received reason. Both orthodoxy and
Jeffers agree that the crucifixion was indeed to subdue
the lusts of the world. They differ on the precise purpose for it. Orthodoxy holds that it is for ultimate
spiritual transformation; Jeffers holds that it was for
the destruction of such an illusion. Orthodoxy claims
that what one does as a human determines spiritual success. Jeffers declares that the very human itself is
the chief obstacle to transformation. In the one case
man is glorified in spirituality; in the other, man is
repudiated, the flesh denigrated to a far greater extent than anything indulged by the Christian flagellants
and other mortifiers. Inhumanism completely denies
sense experience, proclaiming the ideal of a merger with
the universal vastness as an indistiguishable part of it,
no more sentient than a stone.

What was intended by Jesus' mission, therefore, has
been perverted by religion, a palliative which Jeffers
sees as designed to preserve the very aspect of life
which the crucifixion was to destroy. Jesus declares
that

Religion is the most tyrannous, worming its way
    through the ears and eyes to the cup of the
    spirit, overgrowing
The life in its pool with alien and stronger life,
    drugging the water at the well-head: so I pos-
    sess them from inward: no man shall live
As if *I* had not lived. The hawk of my love is not
    left hungry. I sacrifice to this end all the
    hopes
Of these good villagers who've come up from Galli-
    lee expecting kingdom; and the woman my moth-
    er; and my own
Flesh to be tortured; and my poor Judas, who'll do
    his office and break; and dreadful beyond

                    these, unnumberd,
          Multitudes of souls from wombs unborn yet; the
               wasted valor of ten thousand martyrs: Oh
               my people
          Perhaps will stab each other in a sacred madness,
               disputing some chance word that my mouth made
          While the mind slept. And men will imagine hells
               and go mad with terror, for so I have feather-
               ed the arrows
          Of persuasion with fire, and men will put out the
               eyes of their minds, lest faith
          Become impossible being looked at, and their souls
               perish.[8]

     It is not difficult to perceive what Jeffers' Je-
sus is deploring: the preservation of momentary expedience provoked by a specific problem of time and place
rigidified into cast iron dogma neither meant for, nor
applicable to, future conditions for which there is no
solution before the grave. Religion is an embalmer of
corpses which should have remained in their tombs, the
chief of which, of course, is that of Jesus.

     Crucifixion in inhumanist terms, then, is in no
sense a sacrifice or an injustice; it is the ultimate
route to blissful oblivion, to reunion with those millions of galaxies of the universe whence Jesus came.
Camus' Meursault came quite close to this concept at the
moment of his execution. That few men can accept the
principle, much less follow it, imparts to inhumanism a
kind of compelling aspect which, while nihilistic to the
extent of denying all meaning to human effort, proposes
a solution that only the towering in spiritual stature,
who have confronted human evil and wrestled vainly with
its invincible nature, need even contemplate beyond academic exercise.

     In The Loving Shepherdess, the companion piece to
Dear Judas, the other side of the stereotype of Jesus
is tackled. Here we have the meek and lowly preacher
of the Beatitudes, whose downfall is the desire to
save the people from their pain. The characterization
in ordinary terms is caricature; in inhumanist terms the
reaction is utter revulsion. Nowhere in modern serious
literature is misanthropy so intense. Nowhere is the
traditional view of the mission of Jesus so scathingly
contemned. The Christ figure is a young woman named
Clare fleeing up the rugged central California coast
from the unremitting menace of mankind. In twelve sections Jeffers explores Clare's compulsion for loving
those who despitefully use her. At best she is an un-

bearably bathetic saint; at worst, an incredible fool. We last see her in labor, having been impregnated by a boy whom she had politely seduced, hiding herself in a thicket, alone, without nine of her ten remaining sheep that she had fanatically protected during her flight.

The importance of this dreadful story is its vision of the uselessness of striving, the waste of humanity on humanity. Clara's saga spells the futility of kindness, compassion, tenderness, and care. Driven as by a demon Clare is first harrassed by children as she cares for her sheep which had originally numbered fifty--those helpless creatures which she loses, one by one, in spite of her desperate efforts. Dogs torment them. Men along the way alternately sleep with her and mistreat her. One old man, Onorio Vasquez, is kind to her. His is an ambiguous character. He thinks he has seen God in the mysterious man who was occupying the old house to which he has taken Clare. He searches, but fruitlessly for confirmation of that ultimate place of peace which Clare has found only in the womb. Birth is a crime; it is a punishment. For all of her efforts she has to show only an engorged belly from which to issue an indictment and a sentence, a nameless waif who in his own turn will continue the crime.

Thus, the power-deluded Jesus of Dear Judas and the pathetically compulsive Clare of The Good Shepherdess combine to project an inhumanist proposition of the received version of the Christian story. It boils down to a delusion and coughing sheep. Jeffers was human enough to want men to escape the terrible reality of a world for whose ills the Christians claim a yet unproduced panacea, but inhumanist enough to face the awful truth of their incurability. Relinquishing the hope for both made it possible for him to live without both, immersed in the unfeeling universal order into which death most surely releases all to return.

208

SAMUEL BECKETT: THE MEANING OF MEANINGLESSNESS

A sharp cleavage obtains between the nihilism of
Jeffers and that of Samuel Beckett, comprising the literary difference between the foolishness of man and his
absurdity. In the former, man's self-proclaimed importance is founded upon presumptuous arrogance. He has
dethroned the God of his own invention, announced his
demise, and deified himself. This is the "humanism"
which Jeffers so fervently rejected. With equal fervor
Beckett has also rejected humanism, but quite the opposite of Jeffers he has found no haven in the vast depths
of the universe. It is an endless sea of nothingness,
composed of insensate objects neither directed, controlled, nor purposeful. The prime distinction between the
nihilism of the absurd, therefore, and inhumanist nothingness is the absence of humanism in the one, and the
negation of humanism in the other.

The significant nihilist in British (and in this
case Irish) and American literature is rare. Several
reasons might be suggested: one, it is almost impossible
to be completely negative and yet feel compelled to
write; two, the capacity to react to nothingness is in
itself a strong positive; and three, British and American culture, in spite of cataclysmic encounter with war,
socio-political and economic revolutions around the
world, upheaval at home, and eclipse of traditional religious value, is too dynamic for the hopeless attitude
to become entrenched. This may spell part of the reason
why Beckett found the French atmosphere more conducive
than his native Ireland, or England. As every historian
reminds us, two major wars of this century were fought
in France. In little more than thirty years the country
was twice devastated, with huge numbers of its young men
slaughtered, a staggering loss of resources, and in the
second of those wars, humiliated by German occupation.
The haven of the lost generation of World War I became
the barren pasture of the nihilist after World War II.
Even here, however, nihilism has proved to be a tempor-
ary condition. The whole world is aware of the reconstruction and reassertion of the French national identity and character. Thus, when we speak of nihilism properly we speak of a period in twentieth-century literature, not a movement of some decisive long-range influ-

ence such as, for example, romanticism,

What distinguishes nihilism from all other literary
expressions is its total loss of a sense of human dignity. Even at his most pessimistic, Hemingway profoundly respected human worth. Camus, Sartre, and Malraux
representing aspects of existentialism were all principally concerned to reassert the individual right to be.
The absurd as delineated by Camus never lost track of
the human equation. Among the existentialists, the
loss of meaning, alienation, estrangement, and the absurd did not portend the repudiation of the human claim.
Even among the orthodox writers, those whose hatred of
the common masses of man reach paranoid proportions,
such as three of those in our study--Graham Greene,
Flannery O'Connor, and T.S. Eliot--man's lack of dignity
is a matter of grave concern. Nihilism has no concern.
The human creature is little more than a buffoon, a form
of life no one can take seriously. Awareness of his
plight is all he can expect.

To stage this version of futility Beckett developed
a dramaturgy radically opposed to Aristotelian principles. Rational concepts, obviously, are inadequate.
The theater of the absurd required a new approach. Incoherence, incongruity, purposelessness--these are the
stuff of absurd drama. In Chapter I we illustrated
Ionesco's techniques to achieve the effect sought.
Beckett's are comparable.

In Waiting for Godot the stage is practically bare.
The props consist of a tree and a country road. A story
line is non-existent. Dialogue is silly, non-logical,
and punctuated with non-sequiturs. The significance, as
opposed to meaning, of the play is discernible in paying
close attention to entrances, exits, the monologues, the
erratic nature of the dialogues, and the careful, detailed stage directions. Together they evoke an impression
of absolute abjection.

The play is divided into two acts, both almost iden-
tical. A day elapses between acts, The characters remain the same, the scene the same. Ruby Cohn records
Beckett's retort to a complaining reviewer: "One act
would have been too little, and three would have been
too much."9 Ms. Cohn, however, searches for the play's
depth in its comic elements. Taking seriously Beckett's
claim to have written a "tragicomedy," Ms. Cohn says
that the centrality of the comic will be more apparent
if the play is viewed as a tragedy. Nothing, of course,
could be more literally absurd, as we have already abun-

210

dantly shown. The comic element in the play is basically mockery of moral oughtness and settled value. The
two clown-like tramps, Gogo and Didi, originally played
by vaudeville comedians both in New York and Paris, are
Chaplinesque on stage; in some productions the clowns
studiously ape Chaplin's famous mannerisms. Ionesco
calls the characters of the play demystifiers, symbolizing anything the viewer wishes, from prototypes of modern man in a meaningless world to monstrous distortions
of what man is supposed to be. Ms. Cohn has forgotten
the fact that tragedy <u>must</u> have a God--fate. The whole
point of Beckett is the absence of a God. What, for example, is the dramatic significance of the stage directions on the hats?

> *Estragon takes Vladimir's hat. Vladimir adjusts
> Lucky's hat on his head. Estragon puts on Vladi-
> mir's hat in place of his own which he hands to
> Vladimir. Vladimir takes Estragon's hat. Estra-
> gon adjusts Vladimir's hat on his head. Vladimir
> puts Estragon's hat in place of Lucky's which he
> hands to Estragon. Estragon takes Lucky's hat.
> Vladimir adjusts Estragon's hat on his head. Es-
> tragon puts on Lucky's hat in place of Vladimir's
> which he hands to Vladimir. Vladimir takes his
> hat. Vladimir adjusts Lucky's hat on his head.
> Vladimir puts on his hat in place of Estragon's
> which he hands to Estragon. Estragon takes his
> hat. Vladimir adjusts his hat on his head. Es-
> tragon puts on his hat in place of Lucky's which
> he hands to Vladimir. Vladimir takes Lucky's hat.
> Estragon adjusts his hat on his head. Vladimir puts
> on Lucky's hat in place of his own which he hands to
> Estragon. Estragon takes Vladimir's hat. Vladimir
> adjusts Lucky's hat on his head. Estragon hands
> Vladimir's hat back to Estragon who takes it and
> hands it back to Vladimir who takes it and throws
> it down.*[10]

The hat ordinarily is an indicator of status and
station; here it can be a symbol of the absurdity of
status and station. Tragic implications? Slapstick is
the very opposite. Humor in Beckett is akin to satire,
whose purpose is to knock down because the thing de-
serves to be knocked down. Humor in tragicomedy elicits
sympathy and identification with the characters. It is
gentler, at best ruefully ironic. In Shaw, for example,
humor defends the moral oughtness of behavior, the best
that dignifies men. Absurd pretense would be Beckett's
pronouncement of a Shavian universe. Where we may not
hold Beckett to so strict a literary understanding of

of his tools, we feel free in pointing them out to others.

The play begins with Estragon trying to pull off his boot. He and Vladimir are waiting for Godot, unspecified, undescribed. Bawdy joking and affectionate clowning mix with commentary on the four gospel accounts of what happened to the two thieves who died with Christ. It is early established that the name "Godot" carries an implication of the Christian God,

The central question ponders the major theological dilemma of our time: to say that God <u>exist</u> or does <u>not</u> exist means precisely what?

In Chapter I we discussed Paul Tillich's answer to this question, pointing to the Latin root meaning of "exist" to mean "standing out of something." He held, of course, that such a representation could not characterize a God who is the "ground of being" participating in all that is, while infinitely transcending it. In such an instance, certainly, God <u>is</u> as long as man and universe <u>are</u>. However, to incarnate him <u>within</u> existence--here today, gone tomorrow--makes him a natural target for skepticism and disbelief. As we have further pointed out throughout our study, the whole history of humanism is the chronicle of gradual disbelief. It remained for the twentieth century to challenge the very idea of worth of any kind in the human condition, whose first major exponent of meaninglessness was Franz Kafka. K of <u>The Castle</u>, who never got to the castle, or ever saw Count West=west who had sent for him, is the prototype of the absurd man, appearing in 1926. That fine, but crucial, distinction must be made among writers for whom God is asleep or indifferent, such as Hemingway; for whom he is dead such as Nietzscheans like Shaw; and for whom he never came into being. The Hemingways and Shaws must believe in something; man is their only hope. The latter must believe in nothing; man is their greatest proof. Jeffers turned from man in total disgust; Beckett turned from him in clownish ridicule.

While Tillich made it impossible to deny God without denying oneself, Beckett, like Jeffers, accomplishes an adroit epistemological sidestep: there can be no God because there is no self. There is only pathos--not tragedy--in man's fruitless flailings. He has enough rationality to understand his plight, enough logic to make discourse intelligible, to know that he is nothing, with no future, no ties beyond himself. Or so Estragon and Vladimir, who call each other Gogo and

212

Didi, indicate. They have consciousness and little more, without the grace of manners, decorum, or sensitivity. Reduced to the most primitive of human dimensions, they act what they are, men without souls, and thus without meaning. This, then, is Beckett's meaning of meaninglessness.

Tethered at the end of Pozzo's rope, Lucky is a dramatic device for caricaturing the traditional concept of God's relationship with man. Estragon and Vladimir question Pozzo about his callous treatment of the yoked Lucky:

> Vladimir: You want to get rid of him?
>
> Pozzo: I do. But instead of driving him away as I might have done, I mean instead of simply kicking him out on his arse, in the goodness of my heart I am bringing him to the fair, where I hope to get a good price for him. The truth is you can't drive such creatures away. The best thing would be to kill them. *Lucky weeps.*
>
> Estragon: He's crying!
>
> Pozzo: Old dogs have more dignity. *(He proffers his handkerchief to Estragon.)* Comfort him, since you pity him. *(Estragon hesitates.)* Come on. *(Estragon takes the handkerchief.)* Wipe away his tears, he'll feel less forsaken.
>
> Vladimir: Here, give it to me, I'll do it. *(Estragon refuses to give the handkerchief. Childish gestures.)*[11]

To this point the cruelty of the Old Testament God is figured, the wagering God of Job who asserts his supremacy by making his faithful suffer. But Beckett reverses the suffering faithful's reaction in a striking revelation of intent:

> Pozzo: Make haste, before he stops. *(Estragon approaches Lucky and makes to wipe his eyes. Lucky kicks him violently in the shins. Estragon drops the handkerchief, recoils, staggers about the stage howling with pain.)*
>
> Estragon: Oh the swine! *(He pulls up the leg of his*

	trousers.) He's crippled me!.
Pozzo:	I told you he didn't like strangers.
Vladimir:	*(To Estragon.)* Show. *(Estragon shows his leg. To Pozzo angrily.)* He's bleeding!
Pozzo:	It's a good sign.
Estragon:	*(On one leg.)* I'll never walk again!
Vladimir:	*(Tenderly.)* I'll carry you. *(Pause.)* If necessary.
Pozzo:	He's stopped crying. *(To Estragon.)* You have replaced him as it were. *(Lyrically.)* The tears of the world are a constant quantity. For each one who begins to weep somewhere else another stops. *(He laughs.)* Let us not then speak ill of our generation, it is not any unhappier than its predecessors. *(Pause. Judiciously.)* It is true the population has increased.[12]

Implicit are the unpredictable viciousness of man
to his fellows, his distrust of others, whether he knows
them or not, and his undeserving nature. The creature
is no better than the God who bedevils him. Pozzo's
philosophizing, ludicrous in the circumstances, contains,
nevertheless, the stasis in human affairs which Beckett
sees. Causation leading to some determinable result
does not obtain. Coherent explanation of happenings is
impossible. Man and God are the figments of their de-
luded imaginations. Neither makes sense for the other.
Yet, the compulsion for each other remains, the most in-
explicable of all.

Later in the scene Pozzo jerks Lucky's rope and
several times commands him to think, to "Think, pig!"
Lucky begins a lengthy derisive comment on the nature
of the personal God, peppered with meaningless phrases,
coined words, and torturous logic all in one sentence
lasting three pages. Its intent is to put down the
Scholastic-like nature of Christian apologetics, philosophy, and theology. An example are the following lines:

Lucky:	Given the existence as uttered forth in the public works of Puncher and Wattman of a personal God quaquaquaqua with white bread quaquaquaqua outside time without extension who from the heights of divine

aphasia loves us dearly with some exceptions
for reasons unknown but time will tell and
suffers like the divine Miranda with those
who for reasons unknown but time will tell
are plunged in torment plunged in fire whose
fire flames if that continues and who can
doubt it will fire the firmament that is to
say blast hell to heaven blue still calm
with a calm which even though intermittent
is better than nothing . . . .[13]

Thus, the waiting itself for Godot is a profound
indictment of a religious situation in which the earthbound creature, confronted with the inevitability of
death, with little in between beyond the daily grubbing
for subsistence, is tricked by the religious huckster
into believing there is more, if not now, later, but
surely at the end. The greatest challenge to the nihilist of the everlastingly unkept promise is what to him
manifests as lies based upon the sheerest of fairy-tale
substance: magic conceptions, dead men rising to fly
among invisible angels, demons and spirits of all kinds,
wine and blood exchanging accidents. Science settled
these myths for Jeffers; the state of the world eliminated them for Beckett.

The precise determination of Waiting for Godot,
then, turns upon the disposition of time within the
structure of the play, upon who Godot is, and why. If
Pozzo and Lucky portend the master-slave relationship
between the Christian God and man, Godot becomes the
projection of an idea which is fundamentally a promise
never fulfilled. He is further a hope never realized.
He is the ultimate expectation without which the whole
enterprise collapses. His absence implies the lack of
telos, meaningful direction in the affairs of men. Yet
awareness of Gogo's and Didi's existence indicates his
is-ness sufficient to keep the clown-like men from utter
catatonic collapse, alive and mobile enough to perform
their antics which, without value pronouncement from Godot, can only be absurd. Thus, far from being a whimsi-
cal, comedic, nonsensical happening on stage, that "absurdity" is highly lucid in implication. Godot is that
illusion which Martin Luther referred to as Deus Abscon-
ditus, the God whom man is promised is, but whom he is
never privileged to know. The Deus Revelatus, the revealed God, is caricatured in Pozzo. If by inevitable
Beckett logic the degrading relationship between Pozzo
and Lucky, the latter named with masterful irony, symbolizes the Christian at the hands of the God he knows,
the hidden God can be little more than a clown in his

own right.

On these reflections, it is the existential impact of <u>Waiting for Godot</u> which reveals its enduring power. What it says about traditional Christian views has yet to be repudiated by contemporary writers seeking a way out of spiritual chaos and refusing the religious nostrums of the past. They do not wait with Gogo and Didi, but they are overwhelmed by the numbers of Gogos and Didis they daily see.

Given this ineluctable fact we can only conclude that the catalogue of Beckett's novels and plays is meant to shake us into an awareness of the frightening abyss created by the failure of religion to tailor itself to the needs of modern man, rather than fitting man to the tailor.

While men disintegrate and ordered society unravels everywhere, nihilism is closer than any other of the literary heresies to orthodoxy because it has reached the point at which further descent is impossible. It is in direct confrontation with its polar opposite to which, by the very nature of the religious phenomenon, it is tied. Consequently, traditional religion cannot remain the same; neither can nihilism remain unchanged. A new synthesis must result. While we have seen the literary reaction in the orthodox writer, we have further noted the far more significant development in the humanist writer. The current resurgence of the grim-faced Bible literalist need not concern us, as he is manifestly unliterary, but it is certain that Pozzo and Lucky must have a new relationship, one which will relieve the tension between the hidden God of traditional expectation and the revealed God of existence. While Gogo and Didi wait, the writer has begun to find his own.

NOTES: CHAPTER IV

[1]*The Double Axe & Other Poems Including Eleven Suppressed Poems* (New York: Liveright, 1977), p. xxi.

[2]See generally Mercedes C. Monjian, *Robinson Jeffers: A Study in Inhumanism* (University of Pittsburgh Press, 1958); William Everson, "Foreword," and Bill Hotchkiss, "Afterword," in *The Double Axe*, pp. vii-xix, and pp. 177-94.

[3]"Robinson Jeffers," in *Literary Opinion in America: Essays Illustrating the Status, Methods, and Problems of Criticism in the United States in the Twentieth Century*, ed. Morton D. Zabel (New York: Harper & Row, 1962), II, 442; rpt. in *Poetry: A Magazine of Verse*, xxxv (February 1930), 279-86.

[4]Robert J. Brophy, "Afterword," *Dear Judas and Other Poems by Robinson Jeffers* (New York: Liveright, 1977), pp. 132-33.

[5]Fully quoted by Bennett in *The Stone Mason of Tor House: The Life and Work of Robinson Jeffers* (n.p.: The Ward Ritchie Press, 1966), pp. 196-98.

[6]Liveright ed., p. 49.

[7]*Ibid.*, p. 37.

[8]*Ibid.*, pp. 37-38.

[9]*Samuel Beckett: The Comic Gamut* (New Brunswick: Rutgers University Press, 1962), p. 212, quoting Israel Shenker, "Moody Man of Letters," *New York Times*, 6 May 1956, Sec. 2, p. 1.

[10]Samuel Beckett, *Waiting for Godot: Tragicomedy in 2 Acts* (New York: Grove Press, 1954), [p. 46] Pagination in this edition is consecutive but only the verso pages are numbered. The recto pages are unpaginated, an "absurd" numbering system.

[11]*Ibid.*, [p. 21]

[12]*Ibid.*, [pp. 21-22]

[13]*Ibid.,* [p. 28]

THE ORTHODOX

CHAPTER V: ROMAN CATHOLIC ORTHODOXY

GRAHAM GREENE: BETWEEN THE ROCK AND A HARD PLACE

With Graham Greene we come full cycle, a writer in whom modern literary defection and reaffirmation of orthodoxy can find common ground. Were this Roman Catholic, converted at twenty-two, a singer of psalms and a mystical contemplator of the way of the Virgin to sanctification, we should find him of little moment in today's literary caldron. Instead, Greene is a writer who early felt the pangs of self-doubt, guilt, alienation, and a strong urge to suicide. At a time many of his contemporaries opted for the nihilistic route, he affirmed his wretchedness by seeking not refuge in, but propulsive strength from, the Roman faith.

Not able to withdraw from life, he plunged into reality in all of its sordidness and ugliness to pronounce upon it the judgment of sin and punishment, damnation and grace. He neither excuses nor apologizes for humanity. However much man may have been made in the image of God, he is the most foul, depraved, and unregenerate creature in the universe. Even as he does God's work, as the whiskey priest does in The Power and the Glory, he is steeped in sin. What saves Greene from Jeffers-like contempt is his stubborn belief in the ultimate right rule of a very much sovereign God who does not mitigate his law. While accepting the principle of grace, he does not seek it for those whose violation of God's law spells their own downfall--Pinkie Brown in Brighton Rock. Not completely misanthropic, he is no romantic. God is God; man is man. The gulf between them is absolute. The fragile bridge between them is crossable only at God's option. Therefore, man is doomed to eke out his existence in almost uniform dolor.

R.W.B. Lewis has attempted to discover the sources of Greene's anachronistic literary convictions in his background, travels, and personal experiences.[1] But it is beyond our scope to indulge extended discussion of the writer himself. Yet it is an intriguing question. Few writers significant in modern trends have been influenced by Greene's direction. Nevertheless an authentic artist, he has confirmed the conflict between his art and his faith. His most intense struggle is with the irreconcilable differences between dogma and exper-

ience. In a gruelling and mud-splashed Christic athleticism, Greene thrusts into muck and plucks out a sorry
specimen and finds in him the suggestion of Godly possibility. Lewis sees in Greene the "absorbed" Catholicism
of the convert, as opposed to the "applied" Catholicism
of one raised in the faith.[2] The distinction means accommodation and adaptation of the non-Catholic experience
to the beliefs and convictions of the faith assumed at
conversion. Thus, in spite of surface resemblance to
American Calvinist hostility to mankind, Greene's fiction maintains the paradox, as he puts it, of man's infinite rottenness, but his infinite importance to God.

Notwithstanding, the disturbing element in Greene's
unorthodox orthodoxy is his unwillingness to account
for man as _inherently_ worth saving. Humanism, then, is
no more an element of Greene's convictions than it is
of Eliot's. The sinner, convinced of his sinfulness,
wrestles with it, to lose inevitably, but in full awareness of God's judgment--Major Scobie in The Heart of the
Matter. This assessment of man in existence differs
from that of the nihilists only in the desperate will
to believe in the miracles of Romanism, but available
only to those privy by insistent will to believe.
Greene, therefore, is a dramatic example of the Roman
Catholic version of Kierkegaard's leap over the absurd
abyss.

What further distinguishes Greene from the mainstream of modern British and American literature is his
return to a simplistic early-church polarity of good
and evil. Any gradations between are ultimately insignificant and ineffective, such as Ida's earthy goodness
in Brighton Rock. Reduced to Greenian dogma, there are
only two concepts: unmitigated evil and absolute purity,
the one buried in the hearts of men, and the other symbolized in the Virgin Mother. Immaculacy is so essential to Greene's literary vision that he wrote an essay
in celebration of the announcement of the Assumption by
Pius XII in 1950.[3]

This elimination of middle ground, with no adequate
place for the purely human, is the chief problem of the
orthodox Roman Catholic writer. He is caught in a vise
that yields little ground to those outside of grace,
and is fiercely defended by a host of theological commentators following the official hierarchical line.
But Greene cannot be unaware of Joyce who could accept
immaculacy but could not deny it to the fleshly. Nor
can he easily deny Joyce's charge that literary art itself by which the writer functions is precluded by pro-

222

scription of the human. The very nature of the creative invites heresy; indeed, it cannot exist without entailing it. Greene's solution, therefore, is ambiguous, part incredible, and part fabulous. He is not the pure literary theoretician such as Hemingway, nor an out and out apologist like Thomas Merton. Lewis remarks that Brighton Rock, for example, is written on two levels of narrative techique, one reflecting a pessimistic estimate of man's chances on his own, and another animating Ida's appeal to the merely human.[4] At the same time, Greene reflects sympathy for the sinner who, like the whiskey priest of The Power and the Glory, can carry out his priestly function in the odor of his sexual exercise.

This mixed concept of man is primarily the result of the unresolved essence-existence dichotomy to which we have constantly adverted. Greene has compounded it. Having divided his novels into two groups, those written for "entertainment" and those for a "serious" purpose. he is sometimes unsure as to which category a given novel fits. He thought of Brighton Rock at first as entertainment focused on Ida's adventures and her determination to unmask the killer of Hale. But the characterization of Pinkie Brown changed all that. Pinkie descends to such a degree of sheer evil that he is almost unbelievable for a seventeen-year-old. Here, Greene loses control, compelled along a path of depravity for which he has laid no artistic foundation. Hell is quite real to Pinkie, but he is given only the vaguest concept of Heaven. Where his unsaved condition fits the demands of dogma it says little for Greene's artistic obligation, the difference between a tract and the writer's chief commitment.

Brighton Rock opens with Fred Hale running from racetrack hoodlums out to kill him in a mob-related act of revenge. He is unsuccessful in his flight. Ida Arnold attends his funeral and weeps at the most apocryphal eulogy in modern literature. However, it gives Greene a chance to reveal Ida's ground-level theology. A prostitute, she is unambiguously good-natured, churchless, and a menace to no one. We can easily recognize her:

> Death shocked her, life was so important. She
> wasn't religious. She didn't believe in heaven
> or hell, only in ghosts, ouija boards, tables
> that rapped and little inept voices speaking
> plaintively of flowers. Let Papists treat death
> with flippancy; life wasn't so important perhaps

223

to them as what came after; but to her death
was the end of everything. At one with the
One, it didn't mean a thing beside a glass of
Guinness on a sunny day.[5]

Since it is Ida who tracks down the actual murder-
er, Pinkie, her moral stance becomes significant. Fortified with Guinness stout, she tries to warn Rose
against Pinkie's ruthlessness:

> "He doesn't care for you," Ida said. "lis-
> ten, I'm human. You can take my word I've loved
> a boy òr two in my time. Why, it's natural.
> It's like breathing. Only you don't want to get
> all worked up about it. There's not one who's
> worth it--leave alone *him*. He's wicked. I'm
> not a Puritan, mind. I've done a thing or two in
> my time--that's *natural*. Why," she said, extend-
> ing towards the child her plump patronizing paw,
> "it's in my hand: the girdle of Venus. But I've
> always been on the side of Right. You're young.
> You'll have plenty of fun--if you don't let them
> get a grip on you, It's natural. Like breathing.
> Don't take away the notion I'm against Love. I
> should say not. Me. Ida Arnold. They'd laugh."[6]

Both Pinkie and Rose are teenage virgins. Sex, if
not distasteful to Pinkie, is not very high on his list
of priorities. He cannot even find Rose's mouth when
she expects him to kiss her. In contrast to his otherwise unrelieved depravity, his approach to sex is close
to puritannical. Rose is little better. They both
consider even the state of marriage as living in "mortal
sin." On their wedding night, after a cold, indifferent civil ceremony, they feel like being "shut out from
an Eden of ignorance." They spend their first night together in Pinkie's room at Billy's, where "everything
was familiar; nothing strange there," and where "it
shared his bitter virginity."

The wedding night itself requires no comment beyond
Greene's incomparable description:

> He had an odd sense of triumph: he had grad-
> uated in the last human shame--it wasn't so diffi-
> cult after all. He had exposed himself and nobody
> had laughed. He didn't need Mr. Drewitt or Spicer,
> only--a faint feeling of tenderness woke for his
> partner in the act. He put out a hand and pinched
> the lobe of her ear.[7]

But the gesture means little:

> The ugly bell clattered, the long wire humming
> in the hall, and the bare globe burnt above the
> bed--the girl, the washstand, the sooty window,
> the blank shape of a chimney, a voice whispered:
> "I love you, Pinkie." This was hell then; it
> wasn't anything to worry about: it was just his
> own familiar room.[8]

Alternately in four separate contexts Pinkie and
Rose consider sex as mortal sin, their tightly circumscribed bare-bulbed room a hell. Pinkie "glanced with
furious disgust at the made bed as if he contemplated
a repetition of the act there . . . . 'There's only
one thing worse,' he said."

Such puerile shame is utterly separated from Pinkie's crimes: two murders, attempted murder of Rose,
his unwanted wife, by a deceitful suicide pact; and his
criminal activities with the hoodlums. In these he is
proud. Having dispatched Hale without detection, he
would further show the world what a seventeen-year-old
can do: "He trailed the clouds of his own glory after
him: hell lay about him in his infancy. He was ready
for more deaths,"

In an essay entitled "The Vision of Graham Greene,"
Raymond Chapman transfers responsibility for Pinkie's
youthful crimes to the age in which he lived:

> Like the great Romantic Outsider, the Byronic
> rebel, he walks alone in the wilderness. Yet
> even his crime and violence are petty and ul-
> timately self-destructive, for he lives in an
> age that lacks scope not only for the great hero
> but also for the great rebel. The Satanic roar
> of defiance is now a whimper on Brighton Pier.[9]

However the monstrous character of Pinkie can be described, it is anything but "Romantic," and "petty."
Romantics and Byronic rebels are neither puritannical
about sexuality, nor do they find it disgusting. There
is not a romantic or Byronic bone in Pinkie's spare, un-
developed body. He has neither mystique nor social conscience. Nor is murder "petty." He is inherently cor-
rupt, with no saving grace whatsoever. He rejects sex
because it destroys his innocence, not his morality, a
sense of which he is wholly lacking. He has no capacity for love, and therefore, no compunctions about de-
stroying those who have. He has no place for people

like Rose who think that love is the universal principle
of mercy, compassion, and forgiveness. Sexuality men-
aces his defenses against Rose. She compromises his removal from sentiment and his calculated ascendance over
her. Other than in matters of personal expedience, he
is as coldly indifferent to Ida-like right and wrong as
he is to the emotional needs of others. This sharp
cleavage in Pinkie's personality permits Greene to pursue an authorial commitment to exposure of endemic depravity without having to accommodate pedestrian expectations about normal sexuality.[10]

Thus, Pinkie can be freed from Rose only by her
death. Ostensibly, her gradual complete knowledge of
his murder of Hale is the motivation for tricking her
into the suicide pact. His real enemy is Ida who is
systematically leading the police to him.

Throughout the novel Pinkie mutters "Dona nobis pacem. With Rose earlier, he sings "Agnus dei qui tollis
peccata mundi, dona nobis pacem," and snatches of other
religious music. Sharply denying that he goes to Mass,
he protests belief nonetheless.

> "What else could there be." he went on scornfully.
> "Why," he said, "it's the only thing that fits.
> These atheists, they don't know nothing. Of course
> there's Hell. Flames and damnation," he said with
> his eyes on the dark shifting water and the light-
> ning and the lamps going out above the black struts
> of the Palace Pier, "torments."
>
> "And Heaven too," Rose said with anxiety, while
> the rain fell interminably on.
>
> "Oh, maybe," the boy said, "maybe."[11]

Hell is quite real because he has lived his entire
life in its earthly precincts. Knowing quite well that
what he does leads to Hell, he is quite at home with it.
He has no corresponding awakening to Heaven, no sense
of regret resulting from knowledge of the opposite of
what he knows. Since he cannot respond even were Heaven revealed to him, he can only sing of what must be,
although never for him. Near the end of the novel he
contemplates the inevitable. Ida will have her evidence
against him, even though he succeeds in ridding himself
of Rose. That he is irrevocably lost becomes even more
grimly final as he realizes it himself:

> He thought: there'll be time enough in the

years ahead--sixty years--to repent of this.
Go to a priest. Say: Father, I've committed
murder twice. And there was a girl--she killed herself . . . . It didn't matter anyway.
. . . he wasnt made for peace, he couldn't believe in it. Heaven was a word; Hell was something he could trust. A brain was capable only
of what it could conceive, and it couldn't conceive what it had never experienced; his cells
were formed of the cement schoolground, the
dead fire and the dying man in the St. Pancras
writing room, his bed at Billy's and his parents' bed. An awful resentment stirred in him--
why shouldn't he have had his chance like all
the rest, seen his glimpse of Heaven if it was
only a crack between the Brighton walls?[12]

Now those, like Chapman, who insist upon reading
into Pinkie's yearning for "his glimpse of Heaven" a
cry for deeper religious experience should recall the
incredibly vast distance that separates Pinkie's natural depravity from his cognition. He is a crystalline
product of Greene's thesis that salvation is God-initi-
ated. "Repent and ye shall be saved" is not the doctrine by which Greene writes. Pinkie knows that he cannot save himself because he knows equally well that he
cannot change himself. Thus, change is not the key;
the inscrutable will of God is. That God has not willed
Pinkie's salvation is perfectly obvious to him. It is,
as he laments, a bit unfair.

The relentlessness of this theology makes Brighton
Rock one of the most depressing in the Greene corpus.
At each crisis or decisive moment Pinkie is carried
back to his childhood places. He re-lives intensely the
terrible hell they spell for him. Each time his accursed
state is more indelibly stamped upon him. Ida achieves
her goal of exposing him, and he dies in a splash of
self-blinding vitriol meant for the policeman closing
in, and a leap over a cliff. The middle morality tri-
umphs, but the evil remains untouched, the great mystery of God's sovereign justice barely hinted at. Beyond the human retribution there is starkness, the bleak
commentary on the most disconcerting vision of modern
man that orthodoxy has yet produced in the novel.

However, in the whiskey priest of The Power and
the Glory the confrontation of saintliness and evil is
in striking contrast. Father Montez would qualify as
a paradigm of what Lewis calls "the picaresque saint."
His story makes more compelling logic, has more perva-

sive impact, and strives for more spiritual beauty than
any other of Greene's novels. It strikes at the center
of the existential sickness of the spirit, while not
pandering to the other-worldly ascetic ideal. Where
Pinkie is damned man at his worst, Father Montez is
sinful man at his best. Although alcoholism today is
regarded both by the Roman Church and psychiatric medi-
cine as a disease rather than a wilful moral condition,
Greene treats it as a manifestation of undifferentiated
evil. But deliberate sinning does not affect the efficacy of Father Montez' priestly functions. The novel,
therefore, achieves a synthesis of Godliness and creatureliness in the whiskey priest. While saturated in
brandy he ponders his critical dilemma: with every
church destroyed and every priest but himself shot by
the government of Tabasco, Mexico, should he remain underground and perform his duties, or should he escape
to safety? He is not only alone, but stripped of all
intellectual support, books, and spiritual stimulation.
He remembers that the Church has taught that a man's
first duty is to save his own soul. Knowing that he
is no example of moral rectitude, he yet worries about
the people:

> If he left them, they would be safe; and
> they would be free from his example: he was the
> only priest the children could remember. It was
> from him they would take their ideas of the
> faith. But it was from him too they took their
> God--in their mouths. When he was gone it would
> be as if God in all this space between the sea
> and the mountains ceased to exist. Wasn't it his
> duty to stay, even if they despised him, even if
> they murdered for his sake, even if they were
> corrupted by his example? He was shaken with the
> enormity of the problem: he lay with his hands
> over his eyes; nowhere, in all the wide flat marshy
> land, was there a single person he could consult.
> He raised the brandy bottle to his mouth.[13]

Lewis suggests the Christic analogue for Father
Montez, who in addition to being persecuted dies by
betrayal.[14] Here once again the old problem is patent:
the insistent effort to convert every novel with a religious theme into a specific religious symbolism. To
be valid in any artistic sense a point-by-point similar-
ity should obtain in the major areas of comparison.
And as Tillich reminded us, a symbol must point to, and
participate in that which is symbolized. Lewis has forgotten Greene's estimate of man. Unlike Father Montez,
to begin with, Jesus was not picaresque, nor did he fa-

ther a child to our knowledge. Father Montez has one that Greene tells us of. Where Jesus seems to have enjoyed wine, no evidence has been adduced that he was a drunk. By concept, he was absolutely sinless--without which orthodoxy would collapse, particularly Greene's. Of greater importance to the artistic economy of the novel, the attempt at Christic analogue robs Montez of his humanity, and thus the power of his characterization. Where Jesus was a predetermined martyr, living out the stages of his martyrdom according to plan, Montez must extemporize from day to day without consultation with God or anybody else. Making a martyr of the priest also deprives him of spiritual struggle which, rarely encountered among modern protagonists, takes him close to classically heroic stature. As we have insistently seen, the hero is pre-eminently human with inherent faults and weaknesses. But he is God-driven, usually suffering ill or dying in the job fated. But here, Montez adds the Christian feature. He is not tragic; his life is a triumph. When he dies by betrayal his death is a confirmation of victory. Christian death is never tragic--there awaits the life to come. The classical hero awaits nothing beyond the grave; at best he can leave the people purged, the national wrong righted. Father Montez's death purges nothing, nor rights any wrong. It simply testifies to the beauty of spirit emanating from the corrupted body, and the strength of one man overcoming his own weaknesses to remain faithful to his chosen mission. No greater triumph can be imagined. And the mission goes on: another priest secretly slips in to take Montez' place. In this result one can hardly make a case for Montez as an "alter Christus." But he can marvel and participate in the priest's humanity.

Our reading of Greene's intent is doubly fortified by the characterization of Father José. As morally liable as Montez, he lacks the spiritual qualities which bring Montez close to besmudged sainthood--though far from Christhood: contrition and commitment. While Montez worries about the people José worries about himself. Perhaps the most fatuous self-condemnation in all Greenian characterizations is José's. He hears his wife calling him:

> "José. Come to bed." He shivered: he knew
> that he was a buffoon. An old man who married
> was grotesque enough, but an old priest. . . . He
> stood outside himself and wondered whether he was
> even fit for hell. He was just a fat old impotent
> man mocked and taunted between the sheets. But

then he remembered the gift he had been given
which nobody could take away. That was what
made him worthy of damnation--the power he still
had of turning the wafer into the flesh and
blood of God. He was a sacrilege. Wherever
he went, whatever he did, he defiled God. Some
mad renegade Catholic, puffed up with the Gover-
nor's policies, had once broken into a church
(in the days when there were still churches) and
seized the Host. He had spat on it, trampled it,
and then the people had got him and hanged him
as they did the stuffed Judas on Holy Thursday
from the belfry. He wasn't a bad man, Padre José
thought--he would be forgiven, he was just a poli-
tician, but he himself, he was worse than that--he
was like an obscene picture hung every day to cor-
rupt children with.[15]

A joke to himself and everybody throughout the
book, this caricature of a priest jars the reader into
an awareness of the extent to which the grotesque
spinelessness of men can go. His combination of priestly efficacy and human impotence, the diametrically opposite of Montez', reinforces Greene's conviction of the
endemic nature of depravity. Where Montez is within a
state of grace however flawed, José is only able to
contemplate his sterility. Having capitulated to the
rabidly anti-clerical government he is without duties
having lived "for two years now in a continuous state
of mortal sin with no one to hear his confession!"[16]

His crowning achievement is refusal to attend Montez at his execution, even at the urging of the police
lieutenant who captured him. Marie-Beatrice Mesnet sees
the novel as pitting two religions against each other,
the religion of Montez' God and that of Communism represented by the police lieutenant. The latter believes
that men can be changed by changing society, particularly by ridding it of the church. His method is murder of those who disagree. The religion of God, as
even José knows, works through the worst in men because
it knows that men cannot be changed.[17]

When that religion, however, works to man's destruction, as in the case of Major Scobie in The Heart
of the Matter, the third of the religious novels sometimes loosely referred to as a trilogy, we see even
more startlingly Greene's obsession with the mysterious
abyss between the implausible ways of God and the imper-
atives of the human heart. This time the block to God
is the cold unyielding granite of the Church itself in

the heart of one man. A devout Roman Catholic, Scobie nevertheless displays a genius for botching up his life. He is compelled against himself by career disappointments, his wife's dissatisfactions, his affair with an attractive widow, and his involvement in industrial diamond smuggling. His ultimate solution is suicide, which he hopes to make look like natural death caused by illness. His chief problem is his affair with Mrs. Rolt, the war widow. He can neither give her up nor abide by the rules of the Church. To protect his adultery from his wife he agrees to take communion with her. For a man of Scobie's temperament this act amounts to self-damnation. His sense of guilt is too much to bear. Few suspect the truth, that he deliberately took an over dose of evipan. His wife is among the few. In discussing the matter with Father Rank, she says "He was a bad Catholic." Father Rank scoffs and calls it "the silliest phrase in common use." When she insists, Rank exclaims "For Goodness sake, Mrs. Scobie, don't imagine you--or I--know a thing about God's mercy." He then makes the oft-quoted comment: "I know the Church says," interrupting Mrs. Scobie, "The Church knows all the rules. But it doesn't know what goes on in a single human heart."

Roman Catholic commentators have not been uniform in interpreting this comment. Few deny the clear implication, in any event, of the ineradicable nature of sin. Whether one takes Father Rank's comment to mean the Church's unsympathetic stance on human frailty, or its ignorance of the needs of the human heart, Scobie is a consistent creature of Greene's vision. Little different in this respect from Pinkie Brown and José, Scobie is convinced in his own damnation. He is not worthy of God, nor can he ever be. It is the inescapable principle of existence. When, as in Montez' instance, grace saves him, it is wholly at the caprice of God. When damnation results in ineluctable destruction without grace, as with Pinkie and Scobie, it is not without awareness and warning; it is never unexpected or undeserved. This is why José is under no illusions.

The message of orthodoxy in Greene is unique. It combines the pessimism of nihilistic existentialism with a postulate of Godly concurrence in that dim estimate of man's chances. Greene does not reject human struggle itself, because of his basic hope implicit in his fiction that God will ultimately explain his justice, that it will be based on the same kind of sympathy that Greene shows for his fellow strivers' predica-

231

ment.

FLANNERY O'CONNOR: THE SAINTLY GROTESQUE

During the past decade few writers have acquired more scholarly interest than Flannery O'Connor, whose short life produced only a modest corpus consisting of two novels, several volumes of short stories, and other assorted prose. Her commitment to Roman Catholic orthodoxy, nevertheless, was as complete as that of many of her contemporaries was opposed. For our study her major significance lies in her direct confrontation of secular humanism, particularly in her first novel, Wise Blood.

We have gone to some lengths to establish the various forms of humanism, tracing their development from Petrarch to Beckett. The ultimate result, as we have noted, is self-deification, man's self-embrace in lieu of divine embrace, a solipsistic obsession producing the theories of supermen on the one hand and abject self-rejecting reaction on the other.

To the orthodox such a development is little short of blasphemy. Greene, we have seen, is himself too personally involved in the grotesque to extricate himself. His quarrel is not with humanism as an involvement in humanity, but with man himself whose heart is wicked because it cannot be otherwise. In Greene self-determinative choice is severely limited; concomitantly, ultimate responsibility is wrenched away from man. O'Connor, on the other hand, poses the opposite: the heart is good; wickedness is a deliberate turning from God. Evil is a removable condition. The hopeless state does not exist within the capacious folds of the Church. Ms. O'Connor came as close as Father Lynch can wish to the anagogical vision, excepting that she chose almost exclusively the demonic level.

Two interesting views about Ms. O'Connor and humanism are advanced by David Eggenschwiler and Henry A. Blackwell. The one finds O'Connor a Christian humanist; the other discerns her decidedly anti-humanist stance.

Eggenschwiler argues that O'Connor's Christian humanism was based on that of Romano Guardini, two of whose textbooks she read. Guardini speaks of life as a

233

whole rather than a truncated experience. It should be
approached as such instead of being sliced into areas
of independent study such as theology, psychology, and
philosophy. Stating that the early Christians had a
unified view of life, he sees no epistemological or ontological separations. This unity is restored, he asserts, through the Roman Catholic vision of the Incarnation and sacramentalism; the wholeness of life broken
by the fall is restored by grace. Thus, according to
Eggenschwiler, Ms. O'Connor approached the alienation
and estrangement of modern man through a vision of his
separation from the goodness around him which, if he
would but accept it, would restore him to oneness with
God. In this view existence is more than the miserable
state in which Greene identifies, which Jeffers rejects
outrightly. Divine presence is within it. Awareness
of this reality, then, keeps the Christian humanist
from jumping off the deep end.

Now Eggenschwiler attempts an adroit sleight of
hand, wedding Roman Catholic sacramentalism to a fundamentally Protestant ontological apprehension. Tillich,
the prime example, has grounded the concept of God in
being participating in all that is, while infinitely
transcending it, a spiritual insurance against nihilism,
despair, deterministic naturalism. Tillich urged the
in-spite-of principle in self-affirmation, and in turn
the affirmation of the power of love--itself a power,
not a sentiment--to hold the shattered pieces of the
world together in an unbreakable bond which regenerates
the pieces into a new whole.

However, Tillich would not support the sacramental
principle with which O'Connor infused her fiction, for
the Incarnation is an event whose symbolic power is far
more meaningful to Tillich than the literalism of Ms.
O'Connor. The existential element in Tillich is considerably more determinative than the several-layered
anagoge of O'Connor. In Jeffers Tillich would have
found strong evidence of the activity of God; the very
vehemence of Jeffers' rejection of traditional Christianity would be the strongest evidence. Therefore,
Eggenschwiler's yoking together the literalism of Roman
sacramentalism and the symbolism of existentially liber-
ated ontology is by violence and does not rest easy.

On the other hand, Eggenschwiler resorts to Augustinian Neo-Platonism, which is especially unfortunate.
It perpetuates the impasse of dualism.[18] We are once
more confronted by the bedeviling problem: how to evalu-
ate in literary significance a modern author who denies

234

man a worth outside a closed Christian epistemological position. Trapped in his dualistic prison Greene can only rub dung from his nostrils, hoping to smell, however faintly, the altar incense. O'Connor, as we are about to see, can only recover the Holy by creating a pantheon of freaks and monstrosities, the likes of whom MacLeish would put in a circus tent and blow the top off, leaving "nothing, nothing, nothing--nothing at all." The insistent notion that epistemological dualism maintains the vigor of the faith rather than enervates it is the most stubborn bar to rapprochement with the existential vision. O'Connor presumes as a matter of unquestionable fact that Heaven and Hell are absolutely separated places, that the prime mission of Christianity is to maintain that separation. The grotesque, the perverse, the monstrous which people O'Connor's pages are perpetrated upon us to do just that.

But not acceptably to Henry A. Blackwell. In a brilliant doctoral dissertation he makes a sharp distinction between O'Connor's orthodoxy and humanism. He mistakes neither for the other.[19] With specific reference to Wise Blood he writes:

> Because it thrives upon the material and centers in the "self," humanism in Wise Blood is in diametric opposition to Christianity, which, belonging with original sin and ending with the notion of everlasting life achieved through being "born again" through Christ, denies the self and is heedless of the material. The conflict is portrayed as virulent because humanism is not merely self-righteous, but chauvinistic. The novel implies that the Humane and the Normal have silently intruded upon the dominions of the Holy, leaving in their wake a net set of orthodoxies and an exhausted sensibility that has lost its capacities for outrage and wonder.[20]

Blackwell seems alone among O'Connor students to have realized that her Christianity is anti-human, intent upon imposing upon the artistic conscience the ancient dualistic dissociation of the Holy from the human enterprise. She has invalidated modern experience as an authentic reflection of her closed reality fabricated of Christian myth. She is concerned to return to Augustinian Neo-Platonism, to erase almost sixteen centuries of Western man's march toward himself, even with its attendant dangers, and to revivify Gnostic-based eternal battles between light and darkness. As she proceeds with her mission in Wise Blood, Blackwell notes that she levels

> a devastating attack upon the customary ways
> that Godless men have come to apprehend, or-
> ganize, and think about reality, and devotes
> its entire armada of forces against humanism
> to the production of a single effect--alien-
> ation.[21]

Thus, O'Connor's own expression, "the grotesque intensified," imports considerably more than what the grotesque usually does. Instead of a means of exposing
the ridiculous, or of attacking the pretensions of men,
the grotesque in O'Connor is a lethal weapon against
men themselves. In Wise Blood few characters resemble
people.

Hazel Motes from Mrs. Wally Bee Hitchcock's point
of view:

> He has a nose like a shrike's bill and a long ver-
> tical crease on either side of his mouth; his hair
> looked as if it had been permanently flattened un-
> der the heavy hat . . . his eyes were . . . like
> passages leading somewhere. . . . (Ch. 1; p. 10).[22]

Haze's grandfather from Haze's point of view:

> [He] had been a circuit preacher, a waspish old
> man who had ridden over three counties with Je-
> sus hidden in his head like a stinger. (Ch. 1;
> p. 15).

Asa Hawks from the narrator's point of view:

> He was a tall cadaverous man with a black suit
> and a black hat on. He had on dark glasses and
> his cheeks were streaked with lines that looked
> as if they had been painted on and had faded.
> They gave him the expression of a grinning man-
> drill. (Ch. 3; p. 25).

The woman at the swimming pool whom Enoch looked
upon with pleasure:

> First her face appeared long and cadaverous, with
> a bandage-like bathing cap coming down almost to
> her eyes, and sharp teeth protruding from her
> mouth. Then she rose on her hands until a large
> foot and leg came up from behind her and another
> on the other side and she was out, squatting

236

there, panting. (Ch. 5; p. 49).

The woman behind the soda counter, upbraiding Haze for keeping company with Enoch:

> "What you come in here with a son of a bitch
> like that for?" she shouted. "A nice quiet boy
> like you to come in here with a son of a bitch.
> You ought to mind the company you keep." Her
> name was Maud and she drank whiskey all day
> from a fruit jar under the counter. "Jesus,"
> she said, wiping her hand under her nose. (Ch.
> 5; p. 52).

At the zoo:

> Two black bears sat in the first one [steel cage],
> facing each other like two matrons having tea,
> their faces polite and self-absorbed. (Ch. 5,
> p. 54).

Hoover Shoates, known professionally as Omnie Jay Holy:

> The man was plumpish, and he had curly blond
> hair that was cut with showy sideburns. . . .
> He looked like an ex-preacher turned cowboy,
> or an ex-cowboy turned mortician. He was not
> handsome but under his smile, there was an hon-
> est look that fitted into his face like a set
> of false teeth. (Ch. 9, p. 80).

What Blackwell calls the "dehumanization" of the grotesque is O'Connor's means of denying the reality of the phenomenal world, seeing only an underlying distortion of the human spirit by the absence of the Roman concept of God. With a cast as described above, the scenario of Wise Blood is as follows:

Back from a stint in the Army, Hazel Motes is on a train leaving his abandoned hometown, Eastrod, Tennessee. He had grown up believing that he would be a preacher. But cauterized by his grandfather's hellfire-and-damnation evangelizing, he believes he has no religion. In any event, "the way to avoid Jesus was to avoid sin." (Cp. 1; p. 16). But once in the city his first act is to begin a liaison with the prostitute, Leora Watts. In spite of his disavowal he is obsessed with Jesus. Enoch Emery, a young-mannish caricature of humanistic mysticism, attaches himself to Haze. Haze also meets Asa Hawks, the fake blind preacher, and his fifteen-

237

year-old daughter, Sabbath Lily. Haze begins his mission by denouncing Hawk's message of salvation and preaching his own:

> "Sweet Jesus Christ crucified," he said, "I
> want to tell you people something. Maybe
> you think you're not clean because you don't
> believe. Well you are clean, let me tell
> you that. Every one of you people are clean
> and let me tell you why if you think it's be-
> cause of Jesus Christ crucified you're wrong.
> I don't say he wasn't crucified but I say it
> wasn't for you. Listen here, I'm a preacher
> myself and I preach the truth." Ch. 3; p. 34).

Haze launches his new "Church without Christ," calling for a new "jesus (sic) . . . one that can't waste his blood redeeming people with it, because he's all man and ain't got any God in him." (Ch. 7; p. 68). Enoch heeds Haze's call. Living in the world of caged animals, guarding them at the zoo, Enoch envies their seemingly comfortable lives. But Enoch looks for the "mystery" of things, finding it to his fascination in a shrunken mummy case enclosed in glass at the museum. He attributes his perceptivity and sensitivity to the "wise blood" which he has inherited from his father. Everything he does, then, is a parody of religious rit- ual, more grotesque as his narrator describes it. His ultimate reward from the new "jesus" without blood--his mummy--is to become one of the beasts he admires in the cages. Dressed in a gorilla suit and seeking to be friendly, he terrifies a necking couple.

Haze discovers what frauds Hawks and his daughter are. Hawks not only is not blind, but has fathered Sabbath Lily illegitimately. She overwhelms Haze's in- tention of seducing her with her own lecherous designs on him. Taking up residence in his bed, Sabbath Lily presents Haze a new mockery. Standing in the doorway holding the new-jesus mummy given her by Enoch, she is a grotesque parody of the Virgin and Child. In a fit Haze throws the mummy against the wall and pitches what is left out the door into the rain. He begins to wonder about his vaunted ability to see things as they are.

Hoover Shoats sets up a rival Holy Church without Christ and hires Solace Layfield as prophet, a Haze look-alike, even to blue suit and hat. Solace, though, seems to believe in Jesus in spite of disclaimer. The implication is that Haze does also. Haze must, there-

fore, must rid himself of the "conscience" image, and
proceeds to do so in as brutally efficient a way as
pre-meditated murder can devise, running over Solace
with his car, and then thumping the last breath out of
him as the blood flows.

Having decided to leave Talkinham to preach elsewhere, Haze is stopped in his ramshackle car by a policeman. He is discovered without a driver's license.
The policeman decides that an unlicensed driver needs
no car; therefore, he pushes it over an embankment.
It is totally wrecked. Haze sits gazing helplessly into space. He had placed great faith in the jalopy to
take him anywhere. Like Enoch in his gorilla suit,
Haze is reduced to nothing. The utter ridiculousness
of Enoch is the absolute failure of Haze. He can see
no better than the blind man whom Hawks pretended to be.
He buys lime--as Hawks had to deceive people--to blind
himself. His actions become truly irrational, as O'Connor beclouds his motives with her own monolithic, equally irrational intent. Now that there really seems to
be a Jesus who has indeed damned him, he can no longer
proclaim himself clean. His metamorphosis is compete.

Literally blind now, Haze is also blind to the
world about him. He boards with Mrs. Flood, mortifying
himself by putting gravel and pebbles in his shoes, and
sleeping with three strands of barbed wire around his
chest. Mrs. Flood wants his pension checks. An initial
decision to marry him changes into an intent to put him
in an insane asylum. Accepting neither alternative, he
departs with no place to go. Two days later two policemen find him semi-conscious in a drainage ditch. In the
kind of mind-chilling, senseless cruelty at which O'Connor is more than adept, one of the policemen strikes
Haze over the head with his club. They bring him back
dead.

Now it may be argued that O'Connor has achieved a
justification of her religion, her Roman Catholic conviction of the sacramental and incarnated anagoge.
What she has also accomplished is a calculated attack
on her era's artistic direction, and has given a literary boost to the current Fundamentalist hysterical cry
of "Godless humanism!" Whether this unbridled hostility to modern man is worthy of the scholarly attention
bestowed upon it depends upon the vantage of the reader.
Where Blackwell notes that "The novel aspires to juxta-
pose human inadequacy and Christian sufficiency,"23
Isaac Rosenfeld, writing in The New Republic, leaves
the carefully proper academic prose of Blackwell to put

the case more bluntly:

> It is clear what Miss O'Connor means to say
> . . . there is no escaping Christ. But the
> author's style, in my opinion, is inconsis-
> tent with this statement. Everything she
> says through image and metaphor has the mean-
> ing only of degeneration, and she writes of
> an insane world, peopled by monsters and sub-
> men.[24]

To describe the novel as a tragicomedy is again to
misread and misapply literary labels. Ms. O'Connor's
humor is a vehicle of attack, not identification; of
misanthropy, not understanding. She is naturalistic
in style and content, but theological in intent. These
incompatible elements clash fatally in the characterization of Haze. He is a white Southerner, obviously a
Southern Protestant of the twentieth century. O'Connor
injects into his character and personality a medieval
Roman Catholic psychic response to religious stimuli,
as incredible for his heritage and culture as a Baptist
convert in a revival tent muttering Hail Marys.

Dorothy T. McFarland apologizes for O'Connor's artistic flaws by claiming that O'Connor wanted "to
arouse in the reader a visceral as well as an intellectual awareness of the unpleasantly harrowing and un-
heroic and unromantic nature of man's journey to
God. . . ."[25]

In any event, O'Connor's theology is at war with
her art. The artistic potential of her theology, particularly in relationship to its nearest estimate of
humanity, nihilism, shows considerable distance from
the modern artistic demand for autonomous integrity
and freedom from didactic subjugation. James Joyce had
sought to win that battle.

[1]"Graham Greene: The Religious Affair," in *The Picaresque Saint*, pp. 220-39.

[2]*Ibid.*, pp. 225.

[3]In 1952 Greene published in Dublin "The Glory of Mary: Written in Homage" in which he stated that the protection of the divinity of Christ lay in the protection of the divinity of his mother. See John Athens, *Graham Greene* (London: John Calder, 1957), p. 205.

[4]*The Picaresque Saint*, p. 244.

[5]*Brighton Rock* (New York: Viking Press, 1962), p. 46.

[6]*Ibid.*, p. 174.

[7]*Ibid.*, p. 264.

[8]*Ibid.*

[9]*Forms of Extremity in the Modern Novel*, p. 80.

[10]For remoteness from contemporary literary trends *cf.* T.S. Eliot's *Murder in the Cathedral, infra*, pp. 247-49.

[11]*Brighton Rock*, p. 72.

[12]*Ibid.*, p. 331.

[13]*The Power and the Glory* (New York: The Viking Press, 1946), p. 89.

[14]*The Picaresque Saint*, p. 257.

[15]*The Power and the Glory*, p. 39.

[16]*Ibid.*, p. 111.

241

[17]"Graham Greene," *The Politics of the Twentieth-Century Novel*, ed. George A. Panichas (New York: Hawthorn Books Inc., 1971), pp. 109-10.

[18]*The Christian Humanism of Flannery O'Connor* (Detroit: Wayne State University Press, 1972), pp. 9=30.

[19]"Technique and the Pressure of Belief in the Fiction of Flannery O'Connor," Diss. University of Chicago, 1976, p. 131.

[20]*Ibid.*, p. 131.

[21]*Ibid.*, pp. 131-32.

[22]*Three: Wise Blood, A Good Man Is Hard to Find, The Violent Bear It Away* (New York: Signet-New American Library, 1960). All further references to this work appear in the text.

[23]Diss., p. 147.

[24]Quoted by Dorothy Tuck McFarland, *Flannery O'Connor* (New York: Frederick Ungar Publishing Co., 1976), p. 88.

[25]*Ibid.*, p. 88.

CHAPTER VI: ANGLICAN ORTHODOXY

THOMAS STEARNS ELIOT: THE HIPPOPOTAMUS
AND THE CATHEDRAL

The two images which mark the two major phases of
T.S. Eliot's religious experience are those of the
hippopotamus and the cathedral, the one of his earlier
disaffection, and the other of his conversion. His remarkable change of heart came at a time artistic estrangement was nearly uniform, circa 1927. Perhaps
the most decisive poet of the modern era, Eliot was
born in 1888 in St. Louis when all of the conditions
which conflated the catastrophes of the twentieth
century were beginning to gather. Having rejected the
Unitarianism into which he was born, and travelled the
alienated road with his now equally famous contemporaries, he would die in the arms of the Church of England.

To express in poetry the shattering experiences
of his age of disillusion required a vast new poetic
theory and prosodic ingenuity. His major artistic aim
was to avoid romanticism. In order to avert excessive
self-identification in his poetry, and to prevent confusion of the poet with his poem, Eliot reflected much
of the New Critics whom we distinguished in Chapter I.
He wrote, for example, "The Love Song of J. Alfred Prufrock," the lament of aging impotence, at Harvard when
he was twenty-one. Similarly, Tiresias of The Waste
Land, another impotent old man, was written in first
person without poetic implication of the poet. The
sensation which Eliot wished to evoke within the structure and imagerial relationships of a poem was that of
the world which produced it. He made use of four major
technical devices:

1. The disjunctive experience.

To evoke a sense of the break-down of settled value, meaning, and expectability, Eliot paired an image
whose normal associations suggested a specific pattern
of response with another suggesting the opposite. He
piled these contradictory images upon each other with
little apparent progression or natural relatedness. He
added esoteric allusions which few readers can understand, and expressions in foreign languages which per-
vade the whole. The total effect--if more than bewil-

derment--is illumination or startled awareness. Sometimes shock is results. "Prufrock" is a good example:

The title of this celebrated poem is composed of two diametrically opposed images, "love song" and the rather forbidding or stuffy name, "J. Alfred Prufrock." Natural associations of so formal a name conjure up anything but the qualities of "love song." Rather, one imagines a prim old celibate, a stiffly cold businessman, perhaps even an undertaker. Together, the two images jar the reader.

The epigraph, taken from the "Inferno" of Dante's Divina Commedia, is even more intensely grim for a "love song":

> *S'io credesse che mia riposta fosse*
> *A persona che mai tornasse al mondo,*
> *Questa fiamma staria senza piu scosse.*
> *Ma perciocche giammai di questo fondo*
> *Non torno vivo alcun, s'odo il vero,*
> *Senza tema d'infamia ti rispondo.*[1]

The average English-speaking reader cannot be expected to know Italian and Eliot was aware of this. His purpose is accomplished, however, by the strange quotation following a title which has established the unexpected, the paradoxical. For the reader who insists upon discovering what the Italian translates into, the disjunctive sense is intensified:

> If I believe my answer were being made
> to one who could ever return to the world,
> this flame would glean [*i.e.*, this spirit
> would speak] no more; but since, if what
> I hear is true, never from this abyss did
> living man return, I answer thee without
> fear of infmany.

The suggestion is of ultimate divine judgment, of reward for the faithful, and punishment for the wicked. The Divina Commedia depicts a thirteenth-century Christian conception of Heaven, Hell, and Purgatory, and why who goes to each place. The "Inferno" (Hell) is a strange place for "love." The reader is aware now, for certain, that irony inheres, that impotence, sterility, abjection are what the poem is about.

Eliot frequently quoted lines from famous poems, but in radically different contexts of his own. For example, in "Ash Wednesday" he borrowed "Desiring this man's art and that man's scope" from Shakespeare's Sonnet 29, not to proclaim ultimately singular good fortune amid many adversities, but to reinforce penitential rejection of flesh in favor of spirit.

2.   The device of repetition.

As with most modern poets of alienation and loss of meaning, repetition is frequently Eliot's means of suggesting the endless, monotonous cycle, the sense of going nowhere. The suggestion contains the incantations of religious ritual, the sing-songy mumblings of the priest at Mass, the mechanical drone of meaningless rote prayers. Repetition can also suggest the sheerest of irony, of absurdity, such as the following lines repeated abruptly throughout "Prufrock": "In the room the women come and go / Talking of Michelangelo"--women discussing perhaps the most masculine of paintings in Western history of the most awesome events in Christian mythology. We read in "The Hollow Men" the lines "We are the hollow men / We are the stuffed men," which end with the ring of the child's ditty, "Here we go round the mulberry bush":

> This is the way the world ends
> This is the way the world ends
> This is the way the world ends
> Not with a bang but a whimper.[2]

3.   The diction of realism.

Eliot's poetry abounds in slang, argot, and the vernacular. In "A Game of Chess" of The Waste Land we find "I think we are in rats' alley / Where the dead men lost their bones." In "The Fire Sermon" we read "Twit twit twit / Jug jug jug jug jug jug / So rudely forc'd," which in street-level Elizabethan English had to do with an ugly woman, a mistress, or a woman for the night. Further, the third of the "Preludes" is a prime illustration of realistic diction used to evoke the experience of the waste and sordid backwash of night life:

> You tossed a blanket from the bed,
> You lay upon your back and waited;
> You dozed, and watched the night revealing
> The thousand sordid images
> Of which your soul was constituted;
> They flickered against the ceiling.
> And when all the world came back
> And the light crept up between the shutters

And you heard the sparrows in the gutters,
You had such a vision of the street
As the street hardly understands;
Sitting along the bed's edge, where
You curled the papers from your hair,
Or clasped the yellow soles of feet
In the palms of both hands.[3]

4.   The form-content synthesis.

The dichotomy of form and content has always been
a perplexing matter both metaphysically and poetically.
The neo-classical poets thought primarily of form in
terms of their construct of a hierarchically formulated
universe. Content was determined by the function of
form. It reduced in practice to not so much what one
said, but how one said it. The romantic revolt went to
the other extreme. What was said became more important
than form, particularly when the personal, the mystical,
the uniquely individual demanded means to fit the feel-
ings expressed.

With deep respect for classical structure, and
none for the excessively personal, Eliot sought to
achieve a synthesis of content and form. In prosody
form is calculated to equal content in tone, sense,
mood. Rhyme, meter, feet, and stanzas are integrally
devised to enhance the evocation sought for the whole.

All four of these devices are used in "The Hippopotamus" to evoke derision of the church as Eliot saw
it in 1917. "The True Church" is figured in that huge
wallowing beast. But even when ridiculing the church
Eliot prefigured his retreat into religious conserva-
tism which, to some like Stephen Spender, smacked a
little of the Fascism which tarnished Eliot's great
teacher, Ezra Pound.[4] The epigraph of the poem is as
follows:

*Similiter et omnes revereantur Diaconos,
ut mandatus Jesus Christi; et Episcopum, ut Je-
sum Christum, existentem filium Patris; Presby-
teros autem, ut concilium Dei et conjunctionem
Apostolorum. Sine his Ecclesia non vocatur; de
quibus suadeo vos sic habeo.*
                S. Ignatii ad Traillanos.

And when this epistle is read among you, cause
that it be read also in the church of the Lao-
diceans.[5]

Once more we note Eliot's technique of dazzling,

246

or befuddling, his reader with obscure references. But
his purpose here is to set up an example from the early
church as authority for his accusation against the
church of his time. The Latin epigraph is taken from
St. Ignatius' advice to the Trallians. Translated, it
reads:

> In like manner, let all reverence the Dea-
> cons as Jesus Christ, and the Bishop as the fa-
> ther, and the Presbyteries as the council of God,
> and the assembly of the Apostles. Without these
> there is no Church. Concerning all which I am
> persuaded that ye think after the same manner.6

The actually "true" church then is composed of
those in the Apostolic Succession. The English lines
of the epigraph are taken from Paul's letter to the
Colossians, 4:16. The Laodicean Church had earlier been
known for its zeal in the faith but had become especially torpid in self-sufficiency. John of Patmos became
so incensed by its indifference that he denounced it at
Revelation 3:14-18. "The Hippopotamus" characterizes
the true church of Eliot's experience as latter-day Lao-
diceans:

> The broad-backed hippopotamus
> Rests on his belly in the mud;
> Although he seems firm to us
> He is merely flesh and blood.

This huge ugly creature which looks so powerful is
yet "weak and frail" and is "susceptible to nervous
shock." In dry contempt the poet adds "While the True
Church can never fail / For it is based upon a rock."
Mocking contrasts continue. The fat, squat animal cannot reach the mango tree, but "the True Church" eats
imported fruit--the revenue from the congregations.
The crudeness of the hippopotamus' mating call is contrasted to the apocryphal rejoicing of the Church's
"being one with God." The jungle denizen must sleep and
hunt alternately, while the Church may do both at once,
"For God works in a mysterious way."

Having peeled off the skin of the contemporary
church, Eliot dons the robe of Patmos John to reverse
the Divine's vision. The last three stanzas have the
tone of an apocalypse, perhaps the most sardonic in
modern poetry:

> I saw the 'potamus take wing
> Ascending from the damp savannas,

247

And quiring angels round him sing
The praise of God, in loud hosannas.

Blood of the Lamb shall wash him clean
And him shall heavenly arms enfold,
Among the saints he shall be seen
Performing on a harp of gold.

He shall be washed as white as snow,
By all the martyr'd virgins kist,
While the True Church remains below
Wrapt in the old miasmal mist.[7]

One can, of course, carry Eliot's satirical irony to the length of double derision, both of the "True Church" and the beast. The very thought of so ungainly a creature taking flight evokes either incredulous laughter or a sneer. In either case, Eliot's estimate of mankind is little short of open revulsion. His conversion did not improve his anthropology. But beginning with his Ariel poems, the first of which is "Ash Wednesday," he chronicles his spiritual rise from the depth of despair to hope in the promises of God. His rejection of humanism is as total as that of Greene and O'Connor, relegating all varieties both mystical and secular to the freaks and criminals, the ash cans and rats of their disgust with mankind.

In a penetrating study of Eliot's essay <u>Christianity and Culture</u>,[8] S.S. Hoskot discerns the wide gap between Eliot's misanthropic religious position and that of a more spiritual type.[9] In another essay, "Religion and Culture," Eliot pointedly rejects secularism which, from his point of view, is tantamount to humanism:

What I do wish to affirm is that the whole of modern literature is corrupted by what I call Secularism, that it is simply unaware of, simply cannot understand the meaning of, the primacy of the supernatural over the natural life: of something which I assume to be our primary concern.[10]

His essay, "The Humanism of Irving Babbitt," further denies any concept of humanity outside his own notion of the Christian society:

Humanism is either an alternative to religion or is ancillary to it. To my mind, it always flourishes most when religion has been strong; and if you find examples of humanism

248

which are anti-religious, or at least in opposition to the religious faith of the place
and time, such humanism is purely destructive,
for it has never found anything to replace
what it destroyed.[11]

His distrust of ordinary men extends to democracy:

There is a fallacy in democracy, for instance,
in assuming that a majority of natural and unregenerate men is likely to want the right
things; there may be also a fallacy in dicta-
torship in so far as it represents a willingness
of a majority to surrender responsibility.[12]

In the remainder of the passage Eliot opens himself to
the charge of anti-Semitism, as his vague racial admo-
nitions have been construed to imply the Jews:

In nations so self-contained as to be able to ignore each other, culture and perhaps even blood
would become too inbred; but if the races of the
world mixed until racial strains and local cultures disappeared, the result might still be more
disastrous.[13]

But one need not be restricted to Jews in the quoted passage, however much Eliot's mentor, Pound, ranted
against the Jewish bankers whom he claimed controlled
the American war effort during World War II.[14] It is
broad enough to encompass the human race.

Such iconoclasm nevertheless produced perhaps the
modern era's finest poetic expression of the now widely
repudiated ancient Christian claim of superiority over
the state. In the dramatic poem, <u>Murder in the Cathe-
dral</u>, we have the symbol of Eliot's later phase.

The play is modelled on Ancient Greek tragedy, a
series of episodes held together by stasima (choral
odes). The episodes correspond to the acts of modern
plays. The stasima reveal Eliot's essential motif.
The episodes merely illumine them. As a result, the
play is mainly commentary rather than action. The
Greek form also permitted Eliot to include the audience.
The chorus, he said, "mediates between the action and
the audience; it intensifies the action by projecting
its emotional consequence, so that we as the audience
see it doubly, by seeing its effect on other people."[15]
Less elegantly put, the play's primary intent is didactic. Eliot wants to teach us a lesson.

249

The subject is Thomas Becket's sacrifice of his life in service of God over the state. Six versions of the play have been published. Three consecutive revisions followed the original, with a film version in 1952 containing significant new material. All of the versions, however, maintain a clear separation between the church and the world. The original play was written expressly on commission for the Canterbury Festival of June 1935, and meant for an avowedly Christian audience. Most reviewers comment on it in connection with The Rock, a preceding play written for The Forty-Five Churches Fund of the Diocese of London.

In Part I Becket returns to England after seven years of exile, and is confronted by four tempters offering bribes for his service: past pleasures, his former chancellorship, coalition with the barons against the king, and the truth of selfishness in his intent on martyrdom. Certainly, Becket stands firm. In the closing lines of Part I he utters the heart of the Christian denunciation of the world, the theory of vicarious liability:

> I know
> What yet remains to show you of my history
> Will seem to most of you at best a futility
> Senseless self-slaughter of a lunatic,
> Arrogant passion of a fanatic.
> I know that history at all times draws
> The strangest consequence from remotest cause.
> But for every evil, every sacrilege,
> Crime, wrong, oppression and the axe's edge,
> Indifference, exploitation, you, and you,
> And you, must all be punished. So must you.
> I shall no longer act or suffer, to the sword's end.
> Now my good Angel, whom God appoints
> To be my guardian, hover over the swords' point.[16]

During the Interlude Becket delivers a sermon on the true glory of martyrdom. In Part II the four knights come to do the foul deed. They charge Becket with revolt against the king, reminding him of his past misdeeds. They demand that he remove the anathema on those who crowned the king's son against the wishes of the Church, and that he declare the coronation legal. Becket begs off, blaming the pope. He says that he has returned from exile only because his people need him. In the eyes of the knights he is still a traitor. The chorus senses his true martyrdom and asks forgiveness for doubting him. He is warned to go to the Cathedral vespers for safety. He refuses. The chorus warns of

250

impending death. Fortified by drink, the knights demand
abject surrender of every principle, and utter obeisance
to the king. Standing resolute, Becket is assassinated.

While the knights justify their act by patriotism,
the priests thank God for Becket's defense of the
Church. <u>Murder in the Cathedral</u>, therefore, is pristine
medieval orthodoxy, a step as far back into the past as
any modern writer has taken. One wonders whether Eliot's
cause justifies his omission of historical fact. King
Henry II, Becket's erstwhile friend, was engaged in a
power struggle with the Roman Catholic Church, feudal
barons, and sundry other recalcitrants. The issue was
simply who would run England, a matter which took some
bloody centuries to decide. Becket decided against his
king. For that he paid with his life, although Henry
would much regret it. So great was Becket's popular
appeal that Henry was compelled to do penance. Becket
was canonized in 1173 by Pope Alexander III. It remained, however, for Henry VIII, some three centuries
later, to re-establish the primary issue. He reduced
Becket to nothing more than a traitor, had his bones
exhumed and burned, and his name erased from all of the
service books.

Between the caricature of the church and its beati-
fication we find the strange Thomas Stearns Eliot as
dissociated from his age as he said the poetry after
John Donne and Andrew Marvell was dissociated from sensibility. He could exhibit in his essays unbridled
snobbery, and at the same time probe to the frustrated
heart of an era. He could sneer at the religious sterility of an age and reach toward divine forgiveness for
the most wretched. Yet with his unparallelled stature
his religious views are out of date. The religiously
significant literature of our times is passing him by.

W. H. AUDEN: THE KIERKEGAARDIAN LEAP

It is easy for the reader acquainted with W.H. Auden's work to recognize the influence of T.S. Eliot. As Auden matured, both as a man and as a poetic theorist, he reflected increasingly the didactic purpose. Yet, no two poets could have viewed man, the creature, more differently. When both embraced the same Christian communion their differences became only more sharply etched. Although Auden divided his life roughly into three major periods--with others dividing it into four--his religious development is analogous to Eliot's in there being an early Auden up to about 1940, and a later Auden from that year on. The early years were a period of reaction to the same disillusion expressed in Eliot's The Waste Land. However, Auden was involved in idealism, liberal schemes, and Marxist zeal to restore moral and spiritual health to England. The main product of these years came in 1932 with The Orators: An English Study. The later period, particularly during World War II, was marked by reversion to Christianity for solutions to problems for which his earlier convictions were no match. His New Year Letter is the poem of this period, suggesting his new turn of faith. Between these two events lies a complex poet whose regious significance can be appreciated only through a review of his attitude toward himself and mankind.

John C. Blair describes his early poems as "frontal assaults on the reader." The Orators aimed at the decadence of English society. Much of the book is obscure and in poetic code. Its claim to modernity lies in its baffling erratic nature, disjointed fragmentation, and plethora of images and fanciful metaphors bearing little decipherable relation to each other. Yet this pastiche helped establish Auden in the thirties as a poet to be reckoned with. By 1945, however, he was ready to withdraw the book and to excuse his having written it at all. In the context of his newly embraced faith, of course, the book was embarrassingly puerile. He ultimately accepted it, and in the Preface of the 1966 edition dedicated to his friend and collaborator Stephen Spender, he wrote

As a rule, when I re-read something I wrote

> when I was younger, I can think myself back
> into the frame of mind in which I wrote it.
> *The Orators*, though, defeats me. My name on
> the title-page seems a pseudonym for someone
> else, someone talented but nearer the border
> of sanity, who might well, in a year or two,
> become a Nazi.[17]

He placed blame upon that "dangerous figure," D.H.
Lawrence, "the ideologue" who wrote "those sinister
novels <u>Kangaroo</u> and <u>The Plumed Serpent</u>," and loomed
like a shadow over him. In these novels Lawrence dealt
with the dark gods of passion whom he found as necessary as the gods of light. Auden states, nonetheless,
that the central theme of <u>The Orators</u> is hero worship.
Whatever the book means to us today, it echoes the sen-
timents of the lost generation, the disenchanted. Its
abrupt, staccato style, its suspensions and terseness
led John Hayward of <u>The Criterion</u> to call it the suc-
cessor to Eliot's <u>The Waste Land</u>.[18]

Hayward is either naive, or has deliberately ignored the sharp differences between Eliot and Auden at
this stage of their development. For example, the persistent allusions to homosexuality in Auden have no sub-
stantial counterpart in Eliot. In <u>The Waste Land</u> sexuality is ugly, spent heterosexuality--the liaison of
whores, "carbuncular" young men, impotent old men, and
lecherous soldiers, at worst the loss of sexual identity in sterile androgynous waste. Eliot's Tiresias is
not Auden's homosexual Uncle Henry of <u>The Orators</u>. Nor
can the young airman of Book II of <u>The Orators</u>, himself
struggling with homosexuality--not as a disease as it
would be in Eliot--be thought an Auden version of Prufrock worrying about whether to eat a peach.

The point, certainly, is Auden's attitude toward
the human condition. Unlike Eliot, he is an active,
dynamic participant always, even in religious conversion.
He has a MacLeish-like commitment to the human race, exhibiting in no sense the misanthropy of the staid ex-
St. Louis aesthete clerking behind a bank teller's cage
in England. We do not imply that the homosexual element
so native to Auden determines or detracts from the authenticity of his approach to experience, but to identify what critics sometimes tread much too lightly over
in reaching their sometimes glib conclusions, and to
shed some light on the motivations of a poet whose later
religious emphases did not contradict his earlier lusti-
ness.

One critic, though, has bitten the bullet. Noting how reluctant critics are to commit themselves about Auden, Monroe K. Spears resolutely proffers an interpretation of The Orators. The book, he states, poses the English public school system as a microcosm of English society, related from the point of view of the adolescent boy whose ambivalent fantasies of revolt against the schoolmaster, of heroes and heroic sacrifices, reflect what Auden found wrong with the adult world.[19]

The title suggests that the speakers are but "orators" and little more, verbalizing fancies which the poet uses to symbolize a wider malaise. The book prefigures Auden's poetic life in which all styles, views, anthropologies, and religiosities merge into a conglomerate hash. In "The Prologue" the boy is reminded of his mother by the landscape, suggesting maternal domination which emasculates him. She ultimately upbraids him because he is unable to move from "worshipping" girls to "Lying" with them.

In Section I, "Address of a Prize-Day," of Book I which is entitled "The Initiates," Auden writes as though addressing a boys' classroom, using Dante's distinctions among self-love, defective love, and perverted love to draw fatuous analogies with the pupils. Self-lovers fall in love with the voices of foreign broadcasters whom they can never see. Defective lovers wear soiled linen and do not change the cotton in their ears. Perverted lovers are somewhat prone to influenza.

In Section II, "Argument" of Book I, the boyish dreams of a deliverer are explored in breathless lines, with a prayer at the end of every two, three, or four lines to some mythological hero:

O Four Just Men, spare us.

. . . .

O Dixon Hawke, deliver us

. . . .

O Sexton Blake, deliver us.

. . . .

O Bulldog Drummond, deliver us.

And the ridiculous list goes on, satirizing the English.

Section III, "Statement," purports to be a factual report of those deserving praise. The tone is one of mocking irony, as those singled out are miscreants, idiots, stupes, and the inept:

> One makes leather instruments of torture for
> titled masochists.
>
> . . . .
>
> One is clumsy but amazes by his knowledge of
> timetables.
>
> . . . .
>
> One slips on crag, is buried by guides.
>
> . . . .
>
> One is arrested for indecent exposure.
>
> . . . .
>
> One is saved from drowning by a submerged stake.

In the final part of the section Auden recounts things which spell out the dull continuity of life, meaningless things, the routine, mechanical operations of an adult society which underscore sterility and lack of purpose:

> The muscular shall lounge in bars; the puny
> shall keep diaries in classical Greek. The
> soldier shall say "It is a fine day for hurt-
> ing": the doctor shall speak of death as a
> favourite dog.

Section IV, "Letter to a Wound," is subject to various interpretations. It is written as though a love letter with an overtone which, in an Auden context, makes any guess as good as the next. But it seems consistent with Auden's poetic code to suggest that the wound is some thorn in the flesh, some defect or deficiency as much of character as of physiology that must be born throughout life. Ineradicable, it becomes a friend:

> Do you realise we have been together now for
> almost a year? Eighteen months ago, if any-
> one had foretold this to me I should have ask-
> ed him to leave the house.

. . . .

"Who'll ever guess what that is? Once when a
whore accosted me, I bowed, "I deeply regret
it, Madam, but I have a friend."

. . . .

Nothing will ever part us. Good-night and God
bless you, my dear.

Better burn this.[20]

Joseph Warren Beach footnotes James G. Southwork's
conclusion that the wound is "the psychic illness of the
Urning,"[21] or simply put, homosexuality. This interpretation suggests, therefore, a dessication of spirit
and condition which characterizes the early Eliot. It
is not likely, however, that Auden so viewed a sexual
proclivity so intricately a part of his psyche and that
of many of his friends and fellow artists. The code
here seems to suggest, rather, what is today termed as
"closetry," the hidden but not repudiated sexual urge
by which all value-making and personal adaptation must
ultimately pass. Implicitly throughout Auden homosexuality is affirmed as a reality, although seldom is
there in the canon an outright positive affirmation.
Underground printings of his erotic poetry which is
blatantly and unequivocally homosexual circulate freely.

Book II, "Journal of an Airman," seems to confirm
this interpretation. It appears to be the poignant account of a homosexual airman unable to deal with his
problem, not, it seems further, because he believes
homosexuality—and attendant masturbation because of a
lack of sexual partners—is naturally evil, but because
his society will not accept it, and will repudiate everything he has worked for. The ambiguous problem with his
hands is paradigmatically illustrative. Kleptomania
may also be implied. It certainly is not an either/or
proposition. There is further the ambivalent Uncle Sam,
a person in an intimate relationship with the airman,
and also the personification of the country for which
he fights. "Uncle Sam, is he one too?" the airman asks.
"He has the same backward-bending thumb I have." One
what?

And the "wound." The poet hopes it is healing
"without such very painful memories," which can be that
gash of aberrant sexuality beyond any immediate connection with the war.

257

However, the wound does not heal; the airman faces blank frustration. His only out is suicide. Whatever his hands have done, he pleads, it was not compulsive, but deliberate, "to force a hearing." With love and gratitude for his uncle, he capitulates. He dives his plane to his death: "His hands in perfect order."

Edward Mendelson has just published an energetic study of Auden's early poetry and its sources, from 1927 to 1939. While critical reception so far has been mixed,[22] he not only flatly labels the airman and his uncle as homosexuals, but candidly alludes to Auden's own homosexual activities throughout his life. While interpreting the airman's problem with his hands in this context, Mendelson sees it mainly as kleptomania, although suggesting metaphorical implication.[23]

There is nevertheless a Byronesque quality about the airman's vaguely identified, but poignant malady. One senses that the Journal is a muted cry for understanding. Mendelson argues that the airman and his uncle are "sexual outlaws," and that the airman's ultimate quest is to achieve "authentic love" instead of the conventional sexuality which he initially sought.[24] This may account for the lack of a sense of guilt; the airman does not appear to be apologizing. His aloneness does not appear to result from society's repudiation; he loves his country symbolized in his uncle. A further implication is thus carried of affirmation of his uncle's sexual legacy. Our conclusion, then, is that the airman's suicide is self-immolation for the sake of an unrealizable ideal.

The final book of The Orators consists of five expostulatory odes with much the same tenor as MacLeish's "Man!" Auden never lost the juvenile air which hangs over this book, even at his most serious, forever the mischievous schoolboy scribbling impudent notes about the master.

In whatever interpretive pose one assumes, he is consistently impressed with Auden's vigor and conviction. If the poet could jar, shock, lampoon the world out of its post-World War I sickness, he would achieve his poetic mission. At this early stage he required no religious help. The political left touted him as one of its own, until World War II. Hitler radically changed his mind. Reversing Eliot's pattern, Auden fell in love with the United States and was granted citizenship.[25] Convinced that his own dream of a world in

258

love, like that of his airman, could never be realized
without divine input, Auden took the Kierkegaardian leap
into a faith which promised sufficient spiritual compen-
sation for the loss. Yet, religious reversion did not
dilute Auden's commitment to humanity. Unlike Eliot's
Anglicanism, Auden's took root in existence. Where Eliot retreated within the arcane folds of the past, Auden
repudiated Platonic and Neo-Platonic dualisms, and rejected Rousseauistic rationalism. Neither could meet
the awful challenge of the is-ness of the world. In
New Year Letter January 1, 1940, Section III, we read

> The flood of tyranny and force
> Arises at a double source
> In Plato's lie of intellect
> That all are weak but the Elect
> Philosophers who must be strong,
> For, knowing Good, they will no Wrong,
> United in the abstract Word
> Above the low anarchic herd;
> Or Rousseau's falsehood of the flesh
> That stimulates our pride afresh
> To think all men identical
> And strong in the Irrational.
> And yet, although the social lie
> Looks double to the dreamer's eye
> The rain to fill the mountain's streams
> That water the opposing dreams
> By turns in favor with the crowd
> Is scattered from one common cloud.

At best, therefore, men are weak, their most exalted thought impotent in the face of monstrous evil such
as Nazism then engulfing Europe. By 1946 in his Phi
Beta Kappa poem at Harvard, "Under Which Lyre," Auden
was again the impish schoolboy poking out his tongue,
this time from under his spiritual umbrella. The last
two stanzas advise that

> Thou shalt not be on friendly terms
> With guys in advertising firms,
>   Nor read with such
> As read the Bible for its prose,
> Nor above all, make love to those
>   Who wash too much.
>
> Thou shalt not live within thy means
> Nor on plain water and raw greens
>   If you must choose
> Between the chances, choose the odd;
> Read *The New Yorker*, trust in God

And take short views.

Auden, of course, is the closest of the four orthodox writers in our study to man as he is, without writing off the human enterprise. But there is little evidence that his resolution of life, poetry, and God reflects the major direction of modern literature. He is, however, more nearly pointed toward it than his religious compeers.

[1]*Collected Poems 1909-1962* (New York: Harcourt, Brace & World, Inc., 1963), p. 3.

[2]*Ibid.*, p. 14.

[3]*Ibid.*, p. 82.

[4]*T.S. Eliot: A Selected Critique*, ed. Leonard Unger (New York: Rinehart & Co., 1948), pp. 285-86.

[5]*Ibid.*, p. 41.

[6]Trans. George Williamson in his *A Reader's Guide to T.S. Eliot: A Poem by Poem Analysis* (New York: Farrar, Straus & Cudahy, 1953), p. 92.

[7]*Collected Poems*, pp. 41-42.

[8]See in the context of *The Idea of a Christian Culture and Notes towards the Definition of Culture* (New York: Harcourt, Brace and World Inc., 1949).

[9]*T.S. Eliot: His Mind and Personality* (Bombay: University of Bombay, 1971), pp. 178-270.

[10]*Essays Ancient and Modern* (New York: Harcourt, Brace and Co., 1936), p. 118.

[11]*Ibid.*, p. 82.

[12]*Ibid.*, "Catholicism and International Order," p. 141.

[13]*Ibid.*

[14]For a summary of Ezra Pound's activities considered treasonous by the United States government, see *New Encyclopaedia Britannica: Macropaedia*, 1974 ed.

[15]"The Need for Poetic Drama," *The Listener*, 25 November 1936, 994-95, as quoted by David E. Jones, *The Plays of T.S. Eliot* (London: Routledge & Kegan Paul, 1962), p. 52.

[16]See in *Twenty-five Modern Plays*, ed. S. Marion Tucker, 3rd ed. by Alan S. Downer (New York: Harper & Brothers, 1953), pp. 892-93.

[17](London: Faber and Faber, 1966), p. 7.

[18]As quoted by John Fuller, *A Reader's Guide of W.H. Auden* (New York: Farrar, Straus and Giroux, 1970), p. 51.

[19]*The Poetry of W.H. Auden: The Disenchanted Island* (New York: Oxford University Press, 1963), p. 46.

[20]All selections of *The Orators: An English Study* are from the Faber and Faber edition, London, 1966. All other selections of Auden's poetry are from *Collected Poems*, ed. Edward Mendelson (New York: Random House, 1976).

[21]*The Making of the Auden Canon* (New York: Russell & Russell, 1971), p. 17.

[22]For example, Denis Donoghue reviews Mendelson's book, *Early Auden*, in the "Book Review" section of *The New York Times*, August 9, 1981, and charges Mendelson with having written "an odd book," roundly chiding both Mendelson's scholarship and factual accuracy. Donoghue seems unhappy because Mendelson appears to deprecate the "Early" poetry in favor of the "later" Auden which is the subject matter of his prospective sequel. See pp. 8-9 & 27 and the note below.

[23]*Early Auden* (New York: The Viking Press, 1981), p. 110; according to Mendelson on p. 8, secret kleptomania stands between the airman and "E" in the poem whom the airman loves. The compulsion to steal is the airman's attempt to find a replacement for his desire to love. While Donoghue seems to favor the "perpetual adolescent" theory of interpretation, the matter is certainly not an either/or proposition.

[24]*Ibid.*, p. 24.

[25]Donoghue cites the opinion of some of Auden's compatriots in England that his infatuation with America was its freedom from "war and bombs." See p. 8.

CONCLUSION

The most remarkable aspect of modern literature is
its concern for spiritual values, those human realities
for which no satisfactory definition has ever been coined. Called various names by writers struggling to isolate and define them--essence by by Aristotle, soul by
Plato and the Christians, noumenon by Kant, élan vital
by Bergson--these realities are never ignored. They
are either affirmed in some way, merely acknowledged in
another, or specifically denied. Their very nature defies all attempts to ignore them.

With the decline of orthodoxy in literature, what
has been bantered about, particularly in the fifties and
sixties, as our "post-Christian" world is in no sense a
post-religious world. Indeed, we are in the midst of a
religious resurgence, not a theological return, in artistic consciousness. The former is a cover term for
spiritual awareness and ultimate concern; the latter is
a systematized rationale for specific beliefs about the
religious. Where the writer has been concerned to affirm theological values he has been decidedly isolated
from the mainstream of literary development. The orthodox writers, therefore, while including some of the most
influential and innovative craftsmen of the era, find no
large market for their position. If the literary conscious is also the conscience of its time, the orthodox
writer represents little of it.

With the vogue of theological criticism of literature arising after World War II, the cry was for prophecy, for the voice crying out in the wilderness. With
no Jeremiahs or Ezekiels in the modern era, the man of
integrity was sought, someone who would sell no ersatz,
huckster no instant nostrums, but would peel off the
layers of indifference to reveal to the struggling soul
its true condition and deepest need. No one fitted the
requirements better than the artist, the writer in particular. He struggled with his own soul, gifted with
the genius to project his own heightened awareness to
the world. Any cheap compromise with Mammon would be
easily detectable. The true writer would not sell his
soul for pottage.

Thus, when Eliot cried forth from the waste land,

and his compatriots of the twenties revealed the sterility of the post-World War I generation--the Fitzgeralds, O'Neills, the Hemingways--some orthodox critics found in these revelations little more than a lamentable loss of faith. Hence they spent much energy in spelling out how the greatest writers of our era were object lessons in what happened to those wilfully outside the pale.

However, these critics misread the prophecy they sought so eagerly. Certainly, Eliot, Auden, Greene, and O'Connor poured their talents into reaffirmation of orthodox faith, cutting into the human pie with a literary scalpel meant more to excise than to repair. O'Connor found the human being so grotesque that she built her artistry around the freak. Her literary import is as unacceptable as her presumption of theological inerrancy, as her implicit denial of beauty in the human being transcending her ascriptions of damnation, as her granting nothing inherently good in man, and as her notion that the Holy is a complete negation of the human. Greene in no less a manner yet approaches man as though a reptile slithering around on his moral belly because he is an inveterate cripple without the spiritual crutches of the Virgin Mother. Eliot added a unique class and religious snobbery of his own, reducing salvation to a property of the Anglo-Saxons, and seeking to turn the religious clock back to the Middle Ages. Auden alone among the orthodox of our study evinced a belief and participation in man the creature. Conversion saved him from despair, not from his fellow man. But what the orthodox held in common was perfervid anti-romanticism, the unmistakable Calvinist outlook on the prospects of man without divine intervention. They preach no bootstraps salvation, no moral or spiritual evolution. For them nineteenth-century optimism died in the trenches of the Argonne.

The main trend of literary development remained submerged in despair for a much longer time. It reached its nadir in Jeffers who was determined to escape himself and all men wholly. His disgust, expressed in his inhumanism, was so profound that he could only parody in the most shocking of ways orthodox distortion of Jesus with whom he was obsessed perhaps more than any other writer in our study. He demonstrates brilliantly what perceptive critics have frequently noted: the impossibility of escape from Christian culture. Its effect is the surest sign of its permeation, artistically more enduring in a page of grim doubt and fierce wrestling than in a volume of presumptively damning ideation of the human enterprise. Thus in Jeffers, the polarities

264

conjoin where they are most alike. If prophecy is
sought in the modern writer it is found sans exemple in
Jeffers, the atheist and believer cemented in a common
revulsion of man the unsaved. But since both are the
extremes of human experience they can appeal only to
extremes. The center can tolerate neither. As a literary proposition Jeffers' effort was foredoomed the
moment he embarked upon it.

   In Beckett the revolt was more against the pretensions of men than against the idea of an ultimate directive God. One need only reflect upon the clowns Gogo and Didi to grasp the central idea that the human
experiment of such absurd dimensions cannot command the
majestic God of theological myth. They get what they
deserve, a God who is not there, whose absent dimensions
fit those who wait for him. Those commentators who see
in the dramatized antics the underlying call for men to
reclaim their linear historicity through a return to
orthodoxy miss the point entirely. To return would be
even more absurd than waiting for a procrastinating em-
blem of theological futility. Depiction of the absent
God is not a denial of his being extant, but a put-down
of claim for his presence.

   In contrast are the writers who form the major aspect of twentieth-century development, the mystical and
social humanists. Equally obsessed with the Christ figure, many seek in ways compatible with their experience
to appropriate him to modern needs. No one tried more
poetically than Yeats who never forgave orthodoxy for
failing to fulfill its promise of a Christ mighty in
deed along side the bleeding heart and pierced side.
Dylan Thomas, whose prose sometimes defies the most dil-
igent effort to decipher it, written--who knows--under
such conditions that the poet himself most likely did
not know what he was writing, struggled in his own in-
imitably esoteric way to claim in poetry a Jesus united
to his own experience. In like manner, D.H. Lawrence
wrenched his Christ out of the docetic crypt and depos-
ited him in the sexual sweat of mortal man. No other
twentieth-century writer of any significance has dared
to take the concept of Jesus so far out of tradition.
Where Lawrence purported dead seriousness, Jeffers made
his sexual Christ a parody, a girl at that, fully mortal.

   On the other hand, the problems of Joyce and
O'Neill were those peculiarly of Roman Catholics for
whom no other faith can exist. Loss of faith for them
is tantamount to extirpation of meaning by its roots no
matter how heroically they try to develop compensatory

myth. In Joyce sexuality never quite loses its origin in sin, its ultimately obscene nature. Adolescent adoration of the female form can constitute an epiphany so long as it does not reduce to Lawrence's noisy humping. Nor could O'Neill find release from his own suffering reflected in the agonies of his characters. The overwhelming Christ figure for him was diverted into Nina's cry in <u>Strange Interlude</u> for a female God in whom sexuality was concomitant with motherhood and wifeliness to obviate the cold mechanistic docetism of the male Christ. These, the myth-makers, were unwilling to cut themselves off from any power beyond themselves. But we are not likely to see more Yeatses and Thomases desperately animating new symbols to express a radically new experience of the holy in terms both essentialistic and secularistic The social humanists comprise the strain which seems most likely to prevail. They have turned away from the ancient notion of essence outside existence. Faulkner perhaps put it best in his Nobel Prize acceptance speech: "I believe that man will not merely endure; he will prevail."

Now this declaration represents a complete revolution in literary consciousness over the past fifty years. The pessimism, anarchy, the misanthropy and depravity have all had their literary day, sometimes eloquently and superbly artfully, and sometimes almost unintelligibly. Together they have brought the literary enterprise almost to the brink of extinction. Most apparently, they have almost killed the novel as the dominant literary form of the twentieth century. The writer now seems to be opting for a new genre consisting of fictionalized actuality as opposed to Aristotelian mimesis, for a mixture of fact and fiction determined by what is, rather than by what ought to be, in an artistic setting of merged imagination and reality. The world of the novel and the world of the reader are one. This is strikingly evident in Anthony Burgess' most recent novel, <u>Man of Nazareth</u>, where Jesus not only retains his mythic divinity, but is as sexually lustful as any mere mortal. Unlike Lawrence and Jeffers, Burgess has no real quarrel with orthodoxy. Jesus simply likes women, marries, and mourns the death of his wife in a fully human and normal way. Except for the incidents of historical period and custom, the novel could have taken place in modern suburbia.[1] Religious significance, therefore, takes place in a Tillichian universe in which culture itself contains the religious impulse. In such a recognition it may no longer theoretically be useful to speak of religious significance; significance itself will mean religious in the sense that ultimate concern and God will manifest as the quest for self as it reflects and meets in others who form the world of experience. This would mean, of course, development consistent with the course of literary movement since Western man began to turn inward, rather than upward, for religious directive.

Along the dominant path, the superman of Shaw, however, has become little more than the irreverent impertinence of a supremely witty and entertaining writer. The dogged hopelessness of a Hemingway symbolically ended with his death. The humanism of MacLeish endures in a less pessimistic way.

But Bellow's Herzog seems most to pre-figure the future of the Anglo-American novel, not because it was first in the trend, but because to date it is the best. In it man is not depraved, and without capacity on his own to be equally good; salvation of the soul cannot be accomplished without salvation of the body, not later, but now, here on this earth in this existence; purposiveness in the universe is no less obvious than claims for its absence; man is self-determining to no less an extent than his potential permits, both spiritually and materially: by his own struggle he creates his own destiny. Life is no more a dark misery than a giddy flight into ecstatic fancy; its polar elements of good and evil are inextricably intertwined, balanceable to the extent that reason, hope, spirit, and acceptance can balance them.

These conclusions were reached by a character born a Jew who suffered both religious and existential alienation. Through his trials of the body, spirit, and intellect he managed to free himself of the diseases of the grotesque (O'Connor), the depraved (Greene), the hopeless (Hemingway, and the inhumanistic (Jeffers), together with the pessimistic (MacLeish), the need for new myth (Yeats), and the socially acceptable (Eliot).

Into this world the reader is increasingly invited to bring his own, to produce from initial solipsistic groping and unfamiliarity a new consciousness of religion and art as one in a literature of man and God, not hostile, indifferent, or distant, but in a tandem of mutual reality.

[1] (New York: MacGraw-Hill Book Co, 1979).

WORKS CITED

Adams, Henry. *The Education of . . .* Introd. James Truslow Adams. New York: The Modern Library, 1931.

Adams, Richard P. "The American Renaissance: An Epistemological Problem." In *Essays on Ethos and Perception in the Age of Emerson, Melville, Whitman and Poe.* Ed. Kenneth Walter Cameron. Hartford: Conn.: Transcendental Books, 1977, pp. 2-7.

Allt, Peter, and Russell K. Alspach, eds. *The Variorum Edition of the Poems of W.B. Yeats.* New York: The MacMillan Co., 1957.

Athens, John. *Graham Greene.* London: John Calder, 1957.

Auden, W.H. *The Collected Poems of . . .* Ed. Edward Mendelson. New York: Random House, 1976.

----------. *The Orators: An English Study.* London: Faber and Faber, 1966.

Beckett, Samuel. *Waiting for Godot: Tragicomedy in 2 Acts.* New York: Avon Books, 1976.

Bellow, Saul. *The Adventures of Augie March.* New York: Modern Library, 1965.

----------. *Henderson the Rain King.* New York: Avon Books, 1976.

----------. *Herzog.* New York: The Viking Press, 1964.

Bennett, Melba. *The Stone Mason of Tor House: The Life and Work of Robinson Jeffers.* n.p.: The Ward Ritchie Press, 1966.

Bentley, Eric. *The Playwright as a Thinker: A Study of Drama in Modern Times.* New York: Meridian Books, Inc., 1958.

----------. *Bernard Shaw.* London: Methuen & Co., 1967.

Bible, The Holy. Revised Standard Version, 1952.

Blackwell, Henry A. "Technique and the Pressure of Belief in the Fiction of Flannery O'Connor." Diss. University of Chicago, 1976.

Blair, John C. *The Poetic Art of W.H. Auden.* Princeton: Princeton University Press, 1965.

Bogard, Travis. *Contours in Time: The Plays of Eugene O'Neill*. New York: Oxford University Press, 1972.

Bonaparte, Marie. *The Life and Works of Edgar Allan Poe: A Psychoanalytical Interpretation*. Foreword Sigmund Freud. Trans. John Rodker. London: Image Publishing Co., 1949.

Booth, Wayne C. *The Rhetoric of Fiction*. Chicago: University of Chicago Press, 1961.

Bradstreet, Ann. *The Works of . . . : In Prose and Verse*. Ed. John Howard Ellis. Gloucester, Mass.: Peter Smith, 1962.

Brinnin, John Malcolm. *Dylan Thomas in America: An Intimate Journal*. Boston: Little, Brown & Co., 1955.

Brooks, Cleanth. *Modern Poetry and the Tradition*. New York: Galaxy-Oxford University Press, 1965.

Brophy, Robert J. "Afterword," *Dear Judas and Other Poems*. By Robinson Jeffers. New York: Liveright, 1977.

Brown, Norman O. *Life against Death: The Psychoanalytic Meaning of Death*. Middletown, Conn.: Wesleyan University Press, 1959.

Burgess, Anthony. *Man of Nazareth*. New York: McGraw-Hill, 1979.

Burke, Kenneth. *A Grammar of Motives and a Rhetoric of Motives*. Cleveland: Meridian-The World Book Co., 1962.

Camus, Albert. *The Myth of Sisyphus and Other Essays*. Trans. Justin O'Brien. New York: Vintage-Random House, 1961.

----------. *The Stranger*. Trans. Gilbert Stuart. New York: Vintage-Random House, 1946.

Carter, Everett. *Howells and the Age of Reason*. Philadelphia: J. B. Lippincott Co., 1954.

Casserly, Langmead J.V. "Gabriel Marcel." In *Christianity and the Existentialists*. Ed. Carl Michalson. New York: Charles Scribner's Sons, 1956, pp. 74-96.

Chabrowe, Leonard. *Ritual and Pathos--The Theater of O'Neill*. Lewisburg, Pa.,: Bucknell University Press, 1976.

Chapman, Raymond. "The Vision of Graham Greene." In *Forms of Extremity in the Modern Novel*. Ed. Nathan A. Scott, Jr. Richmond, Va.: John Knox Press, 1965.

Ciardi, John. "The Poetry of Archibald MacLeish." *The Atlantic Monthly*, May 1953, pp. 67-68.

Cohn, Ruby. *Samuel Beckett: The Comic Gamut*. New Brunswick: Rutgers University Press, 1962.

Coustillas, Pierre. *George Gissing: Essays and Fiction*. Baltimore: The Johns Hopkins University Press, 1970.

Cowley, Malcolm, ed. *The Portable Faulkner*. New York: The Viking Press, 1966.

Cox, Roger L. *Bewteen Earth and Heaven: Shakespeare, Dostoevsky, and the Meaning of Christian Tragedy*. New York: Holt, Rinehart and Winston, 1969.

Crane, Stephen. *Maggie, A Girl of the Streets*. Gainesville, Fla.: Scholars' Facsimiles & Reprints, 1966.

----------. *The Poems of . . . : A Critical Edition*. Ed. Joseph Katz. New York: Cooper Square Publishers, 1966.

----------. *The Red Badge of Courage: An Episode in the Civil War*. New York: Modern Library, 1951.

Draper, Ronald P. *D.H. Lawrence*. New York: Twayne Publishers, 1964.

Dreiser, Theodore. *Sister carrie*. New York: Bantam Books, 1963.

----------. *An American Tragedy*. Cleveland: The World Publishing Co., 1948.

Dunleavy, Janet E. *George Moore: The Artist's Vision, the Storyteller's Art*. Lewisburg, Pa.: Bucknell University Press, 1975.

Durant, Will. *The Renaissance: A History of Civilization in Italy from 1304-1576 A.D.* Part V of *The Story of Civilization*. New York: Simon and Schuster, 1953.

Durkheim, Emile. *The Elementary Forms of Religious Life: A study in Religious Sociology*. Trans. John Ward Swain. London: George Allen and Unwin Ltd., n.d.

Eggenschwiler, David. *The Christian Humanism of Flannery O'Connor*. Detroit: Wayne State University Press, 1972.

Eliade, Mircea. *Myth of the Eternal Return*. Trans. William R. Trask. London: Routledge and Kegan Paul, Ltd., 1955.

271

----------. *The Sacred and the Profane: The Nature of Religion*. Trans. William R. Trask. New York: Harcourt, Brace and Co., 1954.

Eliot. T.S. *Collected Poems 1909-1962*. New York: Harcourt, Brace & World, Inc., 1970.

----------. *Essays Ancient and Modern*. New York: Harcourt, Brace and Co., 1936.

----------. *The Idea of a Christian Society and Notes toward the Definition of Culture*. New York: Harcourt, Brace & World, Inc., 1949.

----------. *On Poetry and Poets*. New York: Farrar, Straus & Cudahy, 1961.

Elmann, Richard. *The Identity of Yeats*. London: Macmillan & Co., 1954.

Falk, Doris. *O'Neill and the Tragic Tension: An Interpretive Study of the Plays*. New Brunswick: Rutgers University Press, 1958.

Falk, Signi Lenea. *Archibald MacLeish*. New York: Twayne, 1965.

Faulkner, William. *A Fable*. New York: Random House, 1954.

----------. *The Bear*. In *The Portable Faulkner*. Ed. Malcolm Cowley. New York: The Viking Press, 1966, pp. 197-320.

Ferguson, Walter D. *The Influence of Flaubert on George Moore*. Philadelphia: n.p., 1934.

Fiedler, Leslie. "The Latest Dylan Thomas." *Western Review*, XI, No. 2 (1947), 103-06.

Finkelstein, Sidney. *Existentialism and Alienation in America Literature*. Chicago: University of Chicago Press, 1966.

Fitzgibbon, Constantine. *The Life of Dylan Thomas*. London: J.M. Dent & Sons, 1965.

Freud, Sigmund. *The Basic Writings of* . . . Trans. A.A. Brill. New York: The Modern Library, 1938.

Fuller, John. *A Reader's Guide to W.H. Auden*. New York: Farrar, Straus and Giroux, 1970.

Fuller, Edmund. *Books with Men behind Them*. New York: Random House, 1962.

----------. *Man in Modern Fiction: Some Minority Opinions on Contemporary American Writing*. New York: Random House, 1958.

Gardner, Helen. *Religion and Literature*. New York: Oxford University Press, 1976.

Gissing, George. *New Grub Street*. London: Oxford University Press, 1958.

Glicksberg, Charles I. *The Ironic Vision in Modern Literature*. The Hague: Martinus Nijhoff, 1969.

----------. *Literature and Religion: A Study in Conflict*. Dallas: Southern Methodist University Press, 1963.

----------. *Modern Literature and the Death of God*. The Hague: Martinus Nijhoff, 1966.

----------. *The Self in Modern Literature*. University Park, Pa.: The Pennsylvania State University Press, 1963.

----------. *The Sexual Revolution in Modern American Literature*. The Hague: Martinus Nijhoff, 1971.

----------. *The Tragic Vision in Twentieth-Century Literature*. Carbondale: Southern Illinois University Press, 1963

Goldberg, Michael. *Carlyle and Dickens*. Athens: University of Chicago Press, 1972.

Goodheart, Eugene. *The Failure of Criticism*. Cambridge: Harvard University Press, 1978.

Goodspeed, Edgar J. *An Introduction to the New Testament*. Chicago: University of Chicago Press, 1937.

Greene, Graham. *Brighton Rock*. New York: The Viking Press, 1962.

----------. *The End of the Affair*. New York: The Viking Press, 1951.

----------. *The Power and the Glory*. New York: The Viking Press, 1946.

Haller, William. *The Rise of Puritanism, Or, the Way to the New Jerusalem as Set Forth in Pulpit and Press from Thomas Cartwright to John Milton, 1570-1643*. Philadelphia: University of Pennsylvania Press, 1972.

----------. *Liberty and Reformation in the Puritan Revolution*. New York: Columbia University Press, 1967.

273

Hanna, Thomas L. "A Question: What Does One Mean by 'Religious Literature?'" In *Mansions of the Spirit: Essays in Literature and Religion*. Ed. George A. Panichas. New York: Hawthorn, 1967., pp. 74-86.

Hawthorne, Nathaniel. *The Scarlet Letter*. New York: Random House, 1952.

Hemingway, Ernest. *A Farewell to Arms*. New York: Scribner's, 1957.

----------. *The Old Man and the Sea*. New York: Scribner's, 1952.

----------. *The Sun Also Rises*. New York: Scribner's, 1954.

Henderson, Archibald. *Bernard Shaw: Playboy and Prophet*. New York: D. Appleton and Co., 1932.

Hesla, David H. *The Shape of Chaos: An Interpretation of the Art of Samuel Beckett*. Minneapolis: University of Minnesota Press, 1971.

Hoffman, Frederick J. *The Modern Novel in America: 1900-1950*. Chicago: Henry Regnery Co., 1951.

Holroyd, Stuart. *Emergence from Chaos*. London: Victor Gollancz, 1957.

Hoskot, S.S. *T.S. Eliot: His Mind and Personality*. Bombay: University og Bombay, 1961.

Hough, Graham. *The Dark Sun: A Study of D.H. Lawrence*. New York: The Macmillan Co., 1957.

Howe, Irving. *William Faulkner: A Critical Study*. New York: Vintage-Random House, 1951.

Howells, William Dean. *Criticism and Fiction and Other Essays*. Eds. Clara Marburg Kirk and Rudolph Kirk. New York: University Press, 1959.

----------. *The Shadow of a Dream* and *An Imperative Duty*. Ed. Edwin H. Cady. New Haven: College and University Press, 1962.

Husserl, Edmund. *Ideas: General Introduction to Pure Phenomenology*. Trans. W.R. Boyce Gibson. New York: Collier Books, 1962.

Ionesco, Eugene. *Four Plays: The Bald Soprano, The Lesson, Jack; or The Submission, The Chairs*. Trans. Donald M. Allen. New York: Grove Press, 1958.

James, Henry. *Art of the Novel: Critical Prefaces*. Introd. Richard P. Blackmur. New York: Charles Scribner's Sons, 1937.

Jarrett-Kerr, Martin. *D.H. Lawrence and Human Existence*. New York: Booksellers & Publishers, 1971.

Jeffares, A. Norman and A.S. Knowland. *A Commentary on the Collected Poems of W.B. Yeats*. Stanford: Stanford University Press, 1968.

Jeffers, Robinson. *Dear Judas & Other Poems*. New York: Liveright, 1977.

----------. *The Double Axe & Other Poems Including Eleven Suppressed Poems*. Liveright, 1977.

Jones, David E. *The Plays of T.S. Eliot*. London: Routledge & Kegan Paul, Ltd., 1962.

Joyce, James. *A Portrait of the Artist as a Young Man: Text, Criticism, and Notes*. Ed. Chester G. Anderson. New York: The Viking Press, 1968.

Kazin, Alfred. *On Native Grounds: An Interpretation of Modern American Prose Literature*. New York: Reynal and Hitchcock, 1942.

Kierkegaard, Soren. *Fear and Trembling and Sickness Unto Death*. Trans. and Introd. Walter Lowrie. Garden City: Doubleday Anchor Books, 1954.

Killinger, John. "Hemingway and Our 'Essential Worldliness.'" In *Forms of Extremity in the Modern Novel*. Ed. Nathan A. Scott, Jr. Richmond, Va.: John Knox Press, 1965.

Kirk, Russell. *Eliot and His Age: T.S. Eliot's Moral Imagination in the Twentieth Century*. New York: Random House, 1971.

Kleinman, H.H. *The Religious Sonnets of Dylan Thomas: A Study in Imagery and Meaning*. Berkeley: University of California Press, 1963.

Krutch, Joseph Wood, introd. *Nine Plays by Eugene O'Neill*. New York: The Modern Library, 1932.

Lang, Andrew. *Modern Theology*. London: Longmans, Green, and Co., 1897.

Latourette, Kenneth S. *A History of Christianity*. New York: Harper & Brothers, 1953.

Lawrence, D.H. *Apocalypse*. Introd. Richard Aldington. New York:

The Viking Press, 1932.

----------. *The Man Who Died*. New York: Vintage-Random House, 1953.

----------. *Phoenix: The Posthumous Papers of* . . . Ed. Edward D. McDonald. New York: The Viking Press, 1936.

----------. *Phoenix II: Uncollected, Unpublished, and Other Prose Works by* . . . Eds. Warren Roberts and Harry T. Moore. New York: The Viking Press, 1968.

Levin, Harry. *The Gates of Horn: A Study of Five French Realists*. New Tork: Oxford University Press, 1963.

Lewis, R.W.B. *The Picaresque Saint: Representative Figures in Contemporary Fiction*. Philadelphia: J.B. Lippincott Co., 1959.

Lovejoy, Arthur. *The Great Chain of Being: A Study of the History of an Idea*. New York: Torchbooks-Harper & Row, 1960.

Lowell, Robert. "Thomas, Bishop, and Williams." *Sewanee Review*, LV, No. 3 (1947), 493-96.

Lynch, William F. *Christ and Apollo: The Dimension of the Literary Imagination*. New York: New American Library, 1963.

----------. "Theology and Imagination II." *Thought: The Fordham University Quarterly*, (Spring 1954). Rpt. Divinity School, University of Chicago, 1960.

MacLeish, Archibald. *The Book of Job*. Farmington, Conn.: First Church of Christ [Congregational]: 1652], 1955.

----------. *The Collected Poems of* . . . Sentry ed. Boston: Houghton Mifflin Co., 1962.

----------. *J.B., A Play in Verse*. Boston: Houghton Mifflin Co., 1958.

----------. *Poetry and Experience*. Boston: Houghton Mifflin Co., 1954.

----------. *Yeats and the Belief in Life*. University of New Hampshire, 1958.

Malinowski, Bronislaw. *Magic, Science and Religion and Other Essays*. Garden City: Doubleday and Co., 1955.

Marcel, Gabriel. "An Outline of a Concrete Philosophy from Creative Fidelity." In *The Existentialist Tradition: Selected*

Writings. Ed. Nino Languilli. Garden City: Anchor-Doubleday, 1971.

Maxwell, Charles H. *The Adventures of the White Girl in Her Search for God*. Milwaukee: Morehouse Publishing Co., 1933.

McFarland, Dorothy Tuck. *Flannery O'Connor*. New York: Frederick Ungar Publishing Co., 1976.

Mendelson, Edward. *Early Auden*. New York: The Viking Press, 1981.

Mercanton, Jacques. "The Hours of James Joyce, Part II." Trans. Lloyd C. Parks. *The Kenyon Review*, XXV, No. 1 (1963), 93-117.

Merlan, Philip. *From Platonism to Neoplatonism*. 2nd. ed. Rev. The Hague: Martinus Nijhoff, 1960.

Mesnet, Marie-Béatrice. "Graham Greene." In *The Politics of the Twentieth-Century Novel*. Ed. George A. Panichas. New York: Hawthorn Books, 1971, pp. 100-23.

Miller, Madeleine S. and J. Lane Miller. *Harper Bible Dictionary*. New York: Harper & Brothers, 1956.

Miller, Perry. *The New England Mind of the Seventeenth Century*. New York: The Macmillan Co., 1939.

Milton, John. *The Complete English Poetry of . . . , Excluding His Translation of Psalms, 80-88*. Ed. John T. Shawcross. Garden City: Doubleday & Co., 1963.

Monjian, Mercedes C. *Robinson Jeffers: A Study in Inhumanism*. Pittsburgh: University of Pittsburgh Press, 1958.

Montgomery, Marion. "On First Looking into MacLeish's Play in Verse, *J.B.*" In *Modern Drama*, 2, No. 3 (1959) 231-42.

Moore, George. *Esther Waters, an English Story*. New York: Liveright, 1932.

----------. *A Mummer's Wife*. New York: Brentano's, 1917.

Moeller, Charles. "Religion and Literature: An Essay on Ways of Reading." Trans. Melvin Zimmerman. In *Mansions of the Spirit: Essays in Literature and Religion*. Ed. George A. Panichas. New York: Hawthorn Books, 1967, pp. 59-73.

Mueller, William R. and Josephine Jacobey. "Samuel Beckett's Long Saturday: To Wait or Not to Wait." In *Man in the Modern Theatre*. Ed. Nathan A. Scott, Jr. Richmond: John Knox Press, 1965, pp. 76-97.

Mueller, William R. *The Prophetic Voice in Modern Fiction*. New York: Haddam-House Association Press, 1959.

Nathan, Leonard A. *The Tragic Drama of William Butler Yeats: Figures in a Dance*. New York: Columbia University Press, 1965.

Neve, J.L. *A History of Christian Thought*. 2 vols. Philadelphia: The Muhlenberg Press, 1946.

Niebuhr, Reinhold. *Essays on the Christian Interpretation of History*. New York: Chales Scribner's Sons, 1937.

Noon, William T. *Poetry and Prayer*. New Brunswick: Rutgers University Press, 1967.

----------. *"A Portrait"*: After Fifty Years." In *James Joyce Today: Essays on the Major Works*. Ed. Thomas F. Staley. Bloomington: Indiana University Press, 1966.

Norris, Frank. *McTeague: A Story of San Francisco*. New York: New American Library, 1964.

O'Connor, Flannery. *Three: Wiseblood, A Good Man Is Hard to Find, The Violent Bear It Away*. New York: New American Library, 1962.

O'Donnell, Geroge M. "Faulkner's Mythology." In *Faulkner: A Collection of Critical Essays*. Englewood Cliffs: Prentice Hall, 1960, pp. 23-33.

Olson, Elder. *The Poetry of Dylan Thomas*. Chicago: University of Chicago Press, 1954.

O'Neill, Eugene. *The Plays of* . . . New York: Random House, 1947.

Otto, Rudolph. *Das Heilage (The Idea of the Holy: An Inquiry into the Non-Rational Factor in the Idea of the Divine and Its Relation to the Rational)*. 2nd ed. London: Geoffrey Cumberledge-Oxford University Press, 1952.

Pfeiffer, Robert H. *The Books of the Old Testament*. New York: Harper & Brothers, 1948.

Piddington, Ralph. "Malinowski's Theory of Needs." In *Man and Culture: An Evaluation of the Work of Bronislaw Malinowski*. Ed. Raymond Firth. London: Routledge and Kegan Paul, Ltd., 1957, pp. 33-51.

Pizer, Donald. *Realism and Naturalism in Nineteenth-Century American Literature*. Carbondale: Southern Illinois University Press, 1967.

Pope, Alexander. *Essay on Man*. In *The Poetry of Pope: A selection*. Ed. M. H. Abrams. New York: Appleton-Crofts, Inc., 1954.

Powers, Lyall H. *Henry James and the Naturalist Movement*. East Lansing: Michigan State University Press, 1971.

Richards, Audrey I. "The Concept of Culture in Malinowski's Work." In *Man and Culture: An Evaluation of the Work of Bronislaw Malinowski*. Ed. Raymond Firth. London: Routledge & Kegan Paul, Ltd., 1957, pp. 15-31.

Sagar, Keith. *The Art of D.H. Lawrence*. Cambridge: Cambridge University Press, 1975.

Sartre, Jean Paul. [*L'Être et le néant*] *Being and Nothingness: An Essay on Phenomenological Ontology*. Trans. and introd. Hazel E. Barnes. New York: Philosophical Library, 1956.

----------. [*La Nausée*] *Nausea*. Trans. Lloyd Alexander. New York: Hayden Carruth, 1964.

----------. [*Huis Clos*] *No Exit*. Eds. Jacques Hardré and George B. Daniel. Englewood Cliffs: Prentice-Hall, 1962.

Schorer, Mark. "The Humiliation of Emma Woodhouse." In *Jane Austen: A collection of Critical Essays*. Ed. Ian Watt. Englewood Cliffs: Prentice-Hall, 1963, pp. 98-111.

Scott, Nathan A. *Modern Literature and the Religious Frontier*. New York: Harper & Brothers, 1958.

----------. Ed. and Introd. "Theology and the Literary Imagination." In *Adversity and Grace: Studies in Recent American Literature*. Chicago: University of Chicago Press, 1968, pp. 1-25.

Seiden, Morton I. *William Butler Yeats: The Poet as Myth Maker*. n.p.: Michigan State University Press, 1962.

Shakespeare, William. *Hamlet*. In *The Complete Works of . . . The Cambridge Edition Text*. Ed. William Aldis Wright. New York: Garden City Books, 1936, pp. 733-79.

Shaw, Bernard. *The Adventures of the Black Girl in Her Search for God*. London: Constable & Co., 1932.

----------. *Man and Superman: A Comedy and a Philosophy*. London: Society of Authors, 1978.

----------. *Platform and Pulpit*. Ed. Dan H. Laurence. New York: Hill and Wang, 1961.

----------. *Prefaces*. London: Constable & Co., 1934.

Shulenberger, Arvid. *Cooper's Theory of Fiction: His Prefaces and Their Relation to His Novels*. University of Kansas Publications Humanistic Studies, No. 32. New York: Octagon-Farrar, Straus and Giroux, 1972.

Sidney, Sir Philip. *Defence of Poesy*. English Literature Series. Ed. Dorothy M. Maccardle, 1919, rpt. London: Macmillan Co., 1963.

Singh, Ram Sewak. *Absurd Drama, 1945-1965*. Delhi, India: Hariyama Prahashan, 1973.

Spears, Monroe, K. *The Poetry of W.H. Auden: The Disenchanted Island*. New York: Oxford University Press, 1963.

Spencer, Hazelton, *et. al.* Eds. *British Literature 1800 to the Present*. 3rd ed. Lexington, Mass.: D.C. Heath and Co., 1974. Vol. II.

Stallman, Robert W. *Stephen Crane: A Biography*. New York: George Braziller, 1973.

Starkie, Enid. "George Moore and French Naturalism." In *The Man of Wax: Critical Essays on George Moore*. Ed. and introd. Douglas A. Hughes. New York: Alfred Knopf, 1930.

Steiner, George. *The Death of Tragedy*. New York: Hill and Wang, 1961.

Sullivan, Kevin. *Joyce Among the Jesuits*. New York: Columbia University Press, 1967.

Swiggart, Peter. *The Art of Faulkner's Novels*. Austin: University of Texas Press, 1946.

Tate, Allen. *Reactionary Essays on Poetry and Ideas*. Charles Scribner's Sons, 1936.

Tedlock, E.W. Jr. *D.H. Lawrence: Artist and Rebel: A Study of Lawrence's Fiction*. Albuquerque: University of New Mexico Press, 1963.

Thomas, Dylan. *Collected Poems, 1934-1952*. London: J.M. Dent & Sons, Ltd., 1964.

----------. *Selected Letters of . . .* Ed. Constantine Fitzgibbon. London: J.M. Dent & Sons, Ltd., 1966.

Thompson, Lawrance. *Melville's Quarrel with God*. Princeton:

Princeton University Press, 1952.

Tillich, Paul. *The Courage to Be*. New Haven: Yale University Press, 1954.

----------. *Systematic Theology*. 3 vols. Chicago: University of Chicago Press, 1951-1963.

----------. *Theology of Culture*. Ed. Robert C. Kimball. New York: Oxford University Press, 1959.

Tillyard, E.M.W. *The Elizabethan World Picture*. 1943; rpt. New York: Vantage-Random Books, n.d.

Tindall, William Y. *A Reader's Guide to Dylan Thomas*. New York: Farrar, Straus and Cudahy, 1962.

Troeltsch, Ernst. *Protestatantism and Progress: A Historical Study of the Relation of Protestantism to the Modern World*. Trans. W. Montgomery. Boston: Beacon Press, 1966.

Tucker, S. and Alan S. Downer, eds. *Twenty-five Modern Plays*. 3rd ed. New York: Harper & Brothers, 1953.

Twain, Mark [Samuel S. Clemens]. *The Adventures of Huckleberry Finn*. In *The American Tradition in Literature*. 3rd ed. Eds. Sculley Bradley *et al*. New York: W.W. Norton & Co., 1967. Vol. II, pp. 266-487.

----------. "Fenimore Cooper's Literary Offenses." In *Selected Shorter Writings of* . . . Ed. Walter Blair. Boston: Houghton Mifflin Co., 1962.

Unger, Leonard, ed. *T.S. Eliot: A Selected Critique*. New York: Rinehart & Co., 1948.

Unterecker, John. *A Reader's Guide to William Butler Yeats*. New York: Farrar, Straus and Cudahy, 1962.

Untermeyer, Louis. *Lives of the Poets: The Story of One Thousand Years of English and American Poetry*. New York: Simon & Schuster, 1963.

Vahanian, Gabriel. *The Death of God: The Culture of Our Past Christian Era*. New York: George Braziller, 1961.

Van der Leeuw, G. *Religion in Essence and Manifestation*. Trans. J.E. Turner. 2nd ed. New York: Harper & Row, 1963.

Van Ghent, Dorothy. *The English Novel: Form and Function*. New York: Harper, 1953.

Vendler, Helen H. *Yeats' "Vision" and the Later Plays*. Cambridge: Harvard University Press, 1963.

Vickery, Olga W. *The Novels of William Faulkner: A Critical Interpretation*. n.p. : Louisiana State University Press, 1964.

Wach, Joachim. *Comparative Study of Religions*. ed. J.M. Kitagawa. New York: Columbia University Press, 1958.

----------. *Sociology of Religion*. Chicago: University of Chicago Press, 1958.

Waggoner, Hyatt H. *William Faulkner: From Jefferson to the World*. Lexington: University of Kentucky Press, 1966.

Weber, Max. *The Protestant Ethic and the Spirit of Capitalism*. Trans. Talcott Parson. New York: Charles Scribner's Sons, 1958.

Whittaker, Thomas. *The Neo-Platonists*. 4th ed. Hildesheim: Georg Olms: Verlagsbuchhandlung, 1961.

Wilder, Amos. *The Spiritual Aspects of the New Poetry*. New York: Harper & Brothers, 1940.

Williams, Ioan. *The Realist Novel in England: A Study in Development*. London: The Macmillan Press, Ltd., 1974.

Williamson, George. *A REader's Guide to T.S. Eliot: A Poem by Poem Analysis*. New York: Farrar, Straus and Cudahy, 1953.

Wilson, Colin. *Religion and the Rebel*. Westport, Conn.: Greenwood Press, 1957.

Wilson, F.A.C. *W.B. Yeats and Tradition*. London: Methuen, 1968.

Wimsatt, W.K., Jr. *The Verbal Icon: Studies in the Meaning of Poetry*. New York: The Noonday Press, 1958.

Wineberg, Helen. *The New Novel in America: The Kafkan Mode in Contemporary Fiction*. Ithaca: Cornell University Press, 1970.

Winters, Yvor. "Robinson Jeffers." In *Literary Opinions in America: Essays Illustrating the Status, Methods, and Problems of Criticism in the United States in the Twentieth Century*. Ed. Morton Zabel. New York: Torchbook-Harper & Row, 1962. Vol. II, pp. 449-43.

Winther, Sophus K. *Eugene O'Neill: A Critical Study*. New York: Random House, 1936.

Yeats, W.B. *Autobiography: Consisting of Reveries over Childhood and Youth: Trembling of the Veil and Dramatis Personnae.* New York: The Macmillan Co., 1953.

----------. *The Collected Plays.* New ed. with 5 additional plays. New York: The Macmillan Co., 1953.

----------. *The Collected Poems.* See Allt, Peter, and Russell K. Alspach, eds.

----------. *Essays and Introductions.* New York: The Macmillan Co., 1961.

----------. *A Vision'' A Reissue with the Author's Final Revisions.* New York: The Macmillan Co., 1966.

INDEX

Whittaker, Thomas, 48n
Whitfield, J.H., 52n
Wilder, Amos, 162
Williams, Ioan, 17
Wilson, Colin, 144
Wilson, F.A.C., 65
Wimsatt, W.K. Jr., 60n
Winters, Yvor, 201
Winther, Sophus, K., 109
Wise Blood, 235-39
Women in Love, 100
Wordsworth, William -
   Wordsworthian, 14-15,
   181, 200
World War I, 2, 28, 45, 181,
   209, , 258, 264
World War II, 2, 30, 32, 46n,
   165, 182, 190, 209, 258,
   263

Yahweh, 189
Yeats, William Butler, 39,
   65-82, 83, 100, 116, 117,
   121, 122, 129, 140n, 156,
   158, 168, 202, 265, 267

Zarathustra, 117
Zola, Emile, 46n

ABOUT THE AUTHOR

James L. Lucas was born in Canton, Ohio. Beginning his career in law, he changed his major interest to literature and religion, and embarked upon a new career of study and learning. He holds five degrees: the A.B. from Boston University, the LL.B. from the Cornell University Law School, two M.A.'s from the University of Chicago--one in English Language and Literature; the other in Theology and Literature--and the Ph.D. from Northern Illinois University, in which his work is combined.

He teaches in the Chicago City Colleges, particularly at the Wright Campus, and at Harper College of Palatine, Illinois. He has previously taught at the Chicago Circle Campus of the University of Illinois. He is well known in the area, especially for his televised courses in American literature.

He has previously published manuals geared to his televised courses in American literature, and earlier research in American Constitutional law.

Dr. Lucas makes his home in Chicago, Illinois.